Building Bridges with Multicultural Picture Books

For Children 3–5

Janice J. Beaty

Professor Emerita
Elmira College

Merrill, an imprint of
Prentice Hall

Upper Saddle River, New Jersey
Columbus, Ohio

Library of Congress Cataloging-in-Publication Data

Beaty, Janice J.
  Building bridges with multicultural picture books: for children 3–5/Janice J.
Beaty.
    p. cm.
  Includes bibliographical references and index.
  ISBN 0-13-400102-8
    1. Multicultural education. 2. Picture books. 3. Education, Preschool.   I. Title.
  LC1099.B43 1997
  370.19'6—dc20

96-6854
CIP

All photos were taken at Columbia Head Start, Columbia, Missouri, by Janice J. Beaty

Cover photo: © American Stock Photography, Inc.
Editor: Ann Castel Davis
Production Editor: Julie Anderson Peters
Design Coordinator: Julia Zonneveld Van Hook
Text Designer: Kip Shaw
Cover Designer: Tammy Johnson
Production Manager: Patricia A. Tonneman
Electronic Text Management: Marilyn Wilson Phelps, Matthew Williams, Karen L.
  Bretz, Tracey Ward

This book was set in Bookman ITC by Prentice Hall and was printed and bound by
R. R. Donnelley and Sons, Inc. The cover was printed by Phoenix Color Corp.

 © 1997 by Prentice-Hall, Inc.
Simon & Schuster/A Viacom Company
Upper Saddle River, New Jersey 07458

Printed in the United States of America

10 9 8 7 6 5 4 3 2 1

ISBN: 0-13-400102-8

Prentice-Hall International (UK) Limited, *London*
Prentice-Hall of Australia Pty. Limited, *Sydney*
Prentice-Hall of Canada, Inc., *Toronto*
Prentice-Hall Hispanoamericana, S. A., *Mexico*
Prentice-Hall of India Private Limited, *New Delhi*
Prentice-Hall of Japan, Inc., *Tokyo*
Simon & Schuster Asia Pte. Ltd., *Singapore*
Editora Prentice-Hall do Brasil, Ltda., *Rio de Janeiro*

To Winona Elliott Sample,
American Indian,
Early Childhood Advocate,
Indian Education Specialist,
and Friend

About the Author

Janice J. Beaty, Professor Emerita, Elmira College in Elmira, New York, is presently a fulltime writer of early childhood college textbooks from her new location in Gulf Breeze, Florida, near Pensacola. Dr. Beaty continues her long career of preparing teachers and caregivers to work with young children in this country and abroad. Her writing includes children's books *Nufu and the Turkeyfish*, *Plants in His Pack*, and *Seeker of Seaways*. College textbooks she has written include *Building Bridges with Multicultural Picture Books*; *Skills for Preschool Teachers*, Fifth Edition; *Observing Development of the Young Child*, Third Edition (all published by Merrill/Prentice Hall); *Preschool Appropriate Practices*; *Picture Book Storytelling*; and *Converting Conflicts in Preschool*. Dr. Beaty also participates as a guest speaker in a distance-learning television project, Early Childhood Professional Development Network, broadcasting to Head Start programs across the United States, the Caribbean, and the Pacific Islands.

Preface

Building Bridges with Multicultural Picture Books: For Children 3–5 addresses one of the important early childhood topics to emerge in the 1990s: multicultural education. Preschool and kindergarten teachers and students preparing to be teachers will learn how to engage their children in becoming acquainted with a world of fascinating multicultural book characters, thus helping them to relate to and accept the real multicultural people they meet.

The text focuses on the common bonds of all children everywhere while honoring their differences. Chapters describe books featuring multicultural family members, as well as children characters developing self-esteem, getting along with others, achieving physical expression, speaking other languages, eating fine foods, accomplishing arts and crafts, making music and dance, and caring about the earth.

Teachers and student teachers learn how to choose appropriate picture books, how to lead children into book extension activities featuring multicultural characters, and how to develop an entire multicultural curriculum with these books. A topical book list from *Adoption* and *Animals* to *Weather* and *Writing* helps teachers choose from among the 300 books described in this text. Making plans for children with curriculum webs and using *Accomplishment Cards* to evaluate individual gains give teachers powerful new tools to integrate multicultural education into every curriculum area.

Best of all, the children themselves relish the wonderful new book friends they meet, such as Asian-American Suki, who worries about whether her mother will remember to pick her up at the day care center in *Will You Come Back for Me?*; the Caribbean boy in *Hue Boy* who tries desperately to grow big and tall but can't seem to do it until his father returns; or the Caucasian girl, Anna, and her Navajo friend, Juanita, who build the biggest bridge in preschool when they finally put their blocks together in *Building a Bridge*.

Teachers and student teachers learn to use puppets, dolls, character cutouts, chopsticks, unit blocks, drums, tape recorders, magnifying glasses, role-plays, and story reenactments to bring these book characters to life. Children take it from there, converting their adventures with these multicultural characters into positive attitudes about all kinds of people that will last a lifetime.

ACKNOWLEDGMENTS

My heartfelt thanks go to Bonny Helm for her reading and critiquing of the manuscript in its early form; to Dr. Linda Pratt, Director of the Graduate Reading Program at Elmira College, Elmira, New York, for her valuable insights and comments; to Winona Sample and Mary Maples for sharing their knowledge during our visits to Native American Head Starts in New Mexico; to Carolyn Dorrell and the Early Childhood Professional Development Network in Columbia, South Carolina, for their continued support; to Gussie Worstell, Teacher/Director of Columbia Head Start in Columbia, Missouri, along with the children and their parents for allowing me to photograph their exciting involvement in this fine program; to Debbie Hagler, owner of My Bookstore in Pensacola, Florida, for her help in securing many of the picture books reviewed here; to the International Children's Book Fair in Bologna, Italy; to the insightful articles, books, and presentations of Patricia Ramsey; to the Elmira College Gannett Tripp Library for assisting my research activities; to my editor Ann Davis for her valuable support and ideas; and to the following reviewers of the manuscript: Barry Bussewitz, Solano Community College; Imelda D'Agostino, formerly of Mount St. Mary's College; Sue Grossman, Eastern Michigan University; Beverly Gulley, Southern Illinois University; Jeanne Morris, Illinois State University; Karen Paciorek, Eastern Michigan University; and Colleen Randel, University of Texas at Tyler.

Contents

3 Developing Self-Esteem   37

4 Relating to Family Members   61

7 *Speaking Other Languages* 133

8 *Eating Fine Foods* 155

9 *Creating Arts and Crafts* 175

12 *Creating a Multicultural Curriculum* 239

Building Bridges with Multicultural Picture Books

For Children 3–5

Discovering Common Bonds

1

We want our children, the children of our friends and neighbors, all children to grow up rejecting prejudice, fear and hatred, and instead be open to the fascinating qualities people of every color and culture have to offer. Let's make this our legacy. (Hopson & Hopson, 1993)

A NEW PEOPLE-PERSPECTIVE

We are each different from one another. From our fingerprints to our voices, from our toenails to our eyelashes, each of us is unique. But we are also alike. We eat. We sleep. We work. We play. We are born as babies, grow as children, and develop into mature human beings, the grand inheritors of Planet Earth. But what kind of world do we want for ourselves and for our children to inherit? Not a world of fear and fighting. We are tired of people hurting one another. Why should they? There is room on this planet for all of us. Can't we find a way to get along?

The time has come to make a change. Societies around the world are crying out for change. We know there must be a way for people to learn to appreciate one another. But it calls for a major shift in our thinking . . . a new people-perspective, if you will. What we must do is *focus on our likenesses and celebrate our differences.* It is as simple—and as difficult—as that. People who appreciate their common bonds come to celebrate their differences with pride.

This textbook, *Building Bridges with Multicultural Picture Books,* is intended as a step in that new direction, and you are invited to come along. You realize, of course, that to change the world we must start with the children. Teachers and caregivers of young children ages 3 to 5 understand that it is these youngsters, now on the first rungs of the learning ladder, who will shape the world to come. What today's preschool children learn about themselves and others in our classrooms and centers will make a difference in the world of tomorrow. What will they learn? That may well be up to you.

THE ROUTE TO APPRECIATING DIVERSITY

All children have the opportunity to learn about themselves and others simply by the way you treat them and their peers. If you show respect for their worth as human beings and encourage them to respect one another, they will begin the long process of learning to celebrate human differences. But this process is a subtle one. Like racial prejudice, the appreciation of diversity evolves along an indirect path. Nonverbal cues and body language are a part of its foundation. Role-modeling by the adults in the classroom add subtle touches. Most important of all, the development of children's appreciation of diversity in others must be worked on by you and by the children *every day.* It must be an integral part of the early childhood curriculum of every classroom and child care center. This does not mean that you should teach a unit on Asians or Africans or Hispanics every day . . . or any day. It does not mean you should point out differences in the way the children look or dress or speak. Teepees, tomahawks, and piñatas have little to do with developing children's appreciation of one another. What counts most of all is:

1. a deep *belief* in the worth of every child
2. an accepting *attitude* toward each of the children as a unique individual
3. unqualified *support* for each child's development of emotional, social, physical, cognitive, language, and creative skills on a daily basis.

But this is what I already do, you may reply. How does this speak to the cultural diversity in the children? How do beliefs and attitudes on the teacher's part help Lori to understand why Rosalba speaks so differently? And how do they stop Jamal from making fun of the clothes Quang wears to school?

The answer is not always obvious. Subtle attitude cues from teachers and caregivers help because the children look to the adults in charge to learn how to respond to daily situations. They want to know whether the teacher really likes Rosalba's "strange" speaking and Quang's "unusual" clothes. They look to see out how the teacher responds to their own behaviors toward these different peers.

A MULTICULTURAL CURRICULUM

In addition to your beliefs, attitudes, and support, you must address the curriculum itself as a supporter of diversity. Does your program follow a formal curriculum of any kind? Many preschool curricula are developed around themes such as the family, seasons, weather, holidays, animals, and community helpers. Making such programs multicultural has often meant inserting a Chinese New Year celebration or a Mexican party with a piñata. Although these activities may be fun for the children, they have little to do with the immediate interpersonal concerns of Lori, Rosalba, Jamal, or Quang and their peers.

Although such programs may seem to be teaching children to appreciate other cultures, more often than not they teach separateness instead. By focusing on a culture's differences from mainstream America, children from other cultures may come to feel different and somehow lesser. As Boutte and McCormick (1992) point out:

> *Multicultural ideas are "caught" rather than "taught"; that is, multicultural attitudes are developed through everyday experiences rather than formal lessons. Multicultural ideas and activities, therefore, should be thoroughly integrated throughout all activities every day—not only in fragmented units.* (p. 140)

How can this integration be done? It is easy to talk about integrating multicultural activities daily, but is it really possible or feasible in an early childhood curriculum? Given their already hectic schedule, how can teachers and caregivers add information about different cultures on a daily basis to every activity?

It can be done. But first of all, early childhood educators need to reconsider the concept of "curriculum." They need to think about a curriculum as a *process* of helping young children to grow and learn, rather than a *product* of knowledge that children must acquire.

CURRICULUM AREAS

Teachers must be sure that the physical setting of the classroom supports this process-oriented approach. In real terms, this means that the early childhood classroom should be set up in curriculum areas or learning centers that promote children's growth and learning in each of the areas of child development: physical, cognitive, language, social, emotional, and creative. The foundation for the curriculum in young children's programs is, in fact, the physical arrangement of the classroom. Well-organized and well-equipped curriculum areas make it possible for children to learn a great deal on their own through playful interaction with materials, while teachers give attention to individuals or small groups. A child development room arrangement should contain curriculum centers such as:

Block area	Book area
Dramatic play area	Art area
Manipulative/math area	Music area
Science area	Writing area
Large motor area	Computer area

A well-designed room arrangement is shown in Figure 1.1.

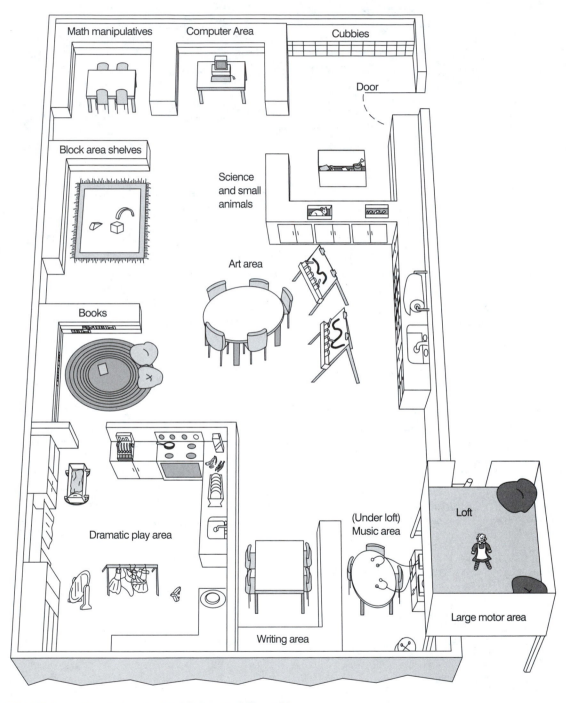

Math manipulatives   Computer Area   Cubbies

Door

Block area shelves

Science
and small
animals

Art area

Books

Dramatic play area

(Under loft)
Music area

Loft

Writing area

Large motor area

FIGURE 1.1   Example of a Well-Designed Floor Plan

But what about the various cultures themselves? How can they be integrated into the curriculum areas so that children can become familiar with multicultural attitudes on a daily basis? This is where the greatest paradox occurs: if we focus on children's likenesses—their common bonds—then they will be able to celebrate their differences with pride. The curriculum that follows is designed to involve children in multicultural activities in each of the curriculum areas on a daily basis.

CONSTRUCTING A COMMON BONDS CURRICULUM

An early childhood curriculum should be fashioned around the common bonds of all of us. What do most young children have in common? Make a list of the specifics. Although there may be some exceptions, does your list include any of the items in Figure 1.2?

From such a list you can begin constructing a curriculum that speaks to the common bonds of all young children. The cultural diversity of all children can be celebrated within such a common bonds curriculum.

FIGURE 1.2   Common Bonds of Young Children Throughout the World

They live in a family.

They live in a neighborhood.

They live in a natural environment.

One or both of their parents usually works for a living.

They eat the food their family provides.

They speak the language their family speaks.

They play with toys.

They play games.

They like to have fun.

They like to pretend.

They like to run, jump, and move.

They like to draw, dance and make music.

They want to have friends and get along well with others.

They want to be accepted and appreciated.

They want to feel good about themselves.

They want to succeed.

The chapters in this text contain topics that children have in common which can be included in such a curriculum. The chapters focus on children from many cultures as represented in the following common themes:

Self-esteem	Foods
Family	Arts and crafts
Other children	Music and dance
Physical expression	The Earth
Languages	

INCORPORATING CULTURAL DIVERSITY INTO A COMMON BONDS CURRICULUM

Once the common bonds are in place, the next step is to incorporate activities related to cultural diversity. New ideas become meaningful to young children when they relate directly to the children. What do youngsters of this age have the most intense interest in? First of all, themselves. Next on

Young children identify with picture book characters.

the list comes other children. Thus, if information about other cultures is to make a difference in the lives of children ages 3 to 5, it should relate directly to the youngsters and their peers. It should involve the children in learning firsthand about youngsters like themselves from different cultures. In fact, one of the most effective approaches to integrating cultural diversity into an early childhood curriculum is to *help children identify with and bond with children like themselves from other cultures.*

PICTURE-BOOK CHARACTERS AS MULTICULTURAL MODELS

Where can an early childhood teacher or caregiver find these other children . . . and on a daily basis? They have always been available if you knew where to look. Today there are more of them around than ever before: in children's multicultural picture books. They are the real or imagined African Americans, Asians, Hispanics, Native Americans, Caucasians, Middle Easterners, and the rainbow of other children whose lives are depicted in illustrated storybooks.

Your children can come to know these multicultural characters intimately by identifying with them, and, yes, even bonding with them, as you read stories about how children from different cultures play, work, and live; how they eat, dress, and go to preschool; how they feel, act, and even "act out." Introducing children to picture-book characters in the stories and activities you provide is an especially effective way for children to get to know youngsters from other cultures. The experience can be almost as real as having a new child from a different culture in the class.

As Barbara Z. Kiefer declares in her book *The Potential of Picturebooks: From Visual Literacy to Aesthetic Understanding* (1995):

> *I found that picturebooks inspired imaginative experiences for children. Their language in response to picture books allowed them to participate in the imaginary world created by the author and artist or to create their own images. Younger children often "chose" a character that they wanted to be as they read or looked through a book.* (pp. 29–30)

Even if the book characters are youngsters from a different culture, young children have no difficulty choosing them as models. Youngsters enjoy the characters in their story books, and if the story appeals to them, they want to hear it over and over. They come to love the characters in the stories they love. Such stories subtly let them know that multicultural children are accepted in our society because they appear in storybooks. Some educators actually call children's close identification with storybook protagonists "book-character bonding," or "book-bonding," for short (Pratt, 1994).

USING BOOK-BONDING TO INTEGRATE OTHER CULTURES INTO THE CURRICULUM

To celebrate the diversity of all children everywhere, this textbook takes the distinctive approach of using multicultural picture books as springboards to activities about children from a profusion of different cultures. In other words, by picking up a particular culture-based story and reading it to the children, a teacher can involve the youngsters vicariously in the lives of children from that culture. Afterwards, the youngsters can participate in activities provided in the various curriculum areas of the classroom which are similar to the activities experienced by the book characters. When children take on the roles of the characters in a book, they bond with the characters.

In her study of children and their use of picture books, Kiefer (1995) observed that: "Some children assumed the roles of characters and created dialogue as they viewed the illustrations" (p. 30). Kiefer's observation suggests a strategy for assisting children with specific problems. For example, if one of your preschool children is having a separation-anxiety problem at the beginning of the year, you might read to her and the others *Will You Come Back for Me?* (Tompert, 1988), a story about a little Asian American girl named Suki who is worried about going to day care for the first time. Afterwards, give each child the opportunity to discuss his or her own fears or feelings about coming to a new class. In this way, the youngster subtly gains new insights about how other children also have these same feelings—even children from another culture.

If the story interests them, you can provide follow-up activities that involve role playing, puppet plays, and songs. For instance, children can pretend to be Suki as a puppet or as a character in a role play. This helps them learn firsthand how a new child like Suki feels in a strange classroom.

Children who are having trouble accepting themselves may appreciate hearing you read *Kelly in the Mirror* (Vertreace, 1993), about an African American girl named Kelly who becomes upset when she looks in the mirror because she thinks she does not resemble anyone in her family. This experience can become even more meaningful when the children look in mirrors and think about their resemblance to members of their own families.

Youngsters can participate in large-muscle exercises to grow tall, just as Hue Boy, the Caribbean boy in the book of the same name, does (Mitchell, 1993). Or they can kick a soccer ball, as the Native American children do in *Northern Lights: Soccer Trails* (Kusugak, 1993). Your children can develop small-motor coordination by manipulating all kinds of cooking and eating implements, as the Hawaiian-Korean-Japanese girl does in *Dumpling Soup* (Rattigan, 1993). Counting and astronomy can be combined in your program just as they are by the African American boy who asks *How Many Stars in the Sky?* (Hort, 1991).

Your children can learn Spanish or improve their English along with Uncle Nacho after hearing *Uncle Nacho's Hat* (Rohmer, 1989). Or they can visit Russia and learn some Russian words along with little Rachel in *Rachel's Splendifilous Adventure* (Bansemer, 1991). They may want to write (or dictate) a birthday invitation like the African American boy Peter does in *A Letter to Amy* (Keats, 1968), or make Chinese word characters as Mei-Mei does in *I Hate English!* (Levine, 1989).

This textbook, then, provides opportunities and suggests activities for an array of multicultural experiences for children in an early childhood classroom based on multicultural picture books. Whether or not the culture being read about is present in the classroom makes no difference. All children can celebrate any culture on a daily basis simply by looking at or listening to a multicultural picture book and following up with cultural activities. Any child can relive vicariously a book character's predicaments and accomplishments and thereby bond with that character.

Remember your own favorite childhood books? Most were undoubtedly based on characters for whom you had a strong affinity. They were children you wanted to emulate and whose adventures you wanted to experience. Today they can be children from more cultures than ever before.

BOOK-BONDING AS A NEW APPROACH

Why hasn't such an approach to multicultural early childhood education been done before, you may wonder? One reason is that such books were scarce. It is only in the past few years that a large number of outstanding multicultural picture books have come on the market. Many of these books have gained attention because of the quality of their writing by new authors in the field. Many of these authors are themselves multicultural writers whose books come from their own background and experience.

In addition, new technology breakthroughs in reproducing book art have encouraged outstanding artists to enter the field of book illustration. Sumptuous art on double-page spreads fill many of the books described here. Because the artists share the background of the book characters, the realistic scenes they portray transport readers or listeners directly into the lives of the book characters. Such portrayals are of great importance in picture books, where illustrations carry more than the story line. We sometimes overlook the importance of visual representation in the lives of today's young children. Picture books provide an opportunity to use visual imagery in a positive manner. Children bond much more easily with characters they can see, just as they do with the so-called super-heroes on television. "To see them is to know them," seems to be the rule about children's TV heroes.

Multicultural children in picture books can actually become "super-characters" in our youngster's lives. We can now introduce our children to picture-book heroes from every culture, and then follow up with extension activities that bring about real bonding.

The importance of picture books in children's growing awareness of people from different cultures cannot be underestimated. Early childhood specialist Patricia G. Ramsey (1991) declares:

> *Children's books are a primary vehicle for this kind of teaching. By engaging children in stories, we enable our young readers and listeners to empathize with different experiences and points of view and experience a wide range of social dilemmas. . . . When children role play situations and characters in a book, they learn how to perceive situations from a variety of perspectives and literally be "in another person's shoes."* (pp. 168–169)

It is difficult to grow up prejudiced against someone of another race or culture when you have been in their shoes. Thus, the multicultural picture book experience gives our youngsters the opportunity to bond with and develop positive feelings toward all children everywhere.

USE OF PICTURE BOOKS IN THE CURRICULUM

A second important reason for teachers' lack of using multicultural picture books in their curriculum is the under-use of children's picture books in general. Traditionally, teachers have used books in two ways: they read the stories to their children and they put the books in the book center to be looked at or read by the children on their own. This is a serious under-use of a valuable asset in a preschool or early elementary curriculum. Each picture book is an extraordinary resource for activities that can be extended throughout the curriculum. Picture books can lead children into art and music activities, science projects, math and language learning, physical activities, and all sorts of dramatics, such as dancing, writing, and storytelling—not to mention prereading activities. In other words, picture books can and should be used as introductions or lead-ins to *all* of your curriculum activities, all year long.

The books themselves should be selected by teachers for such purposes. When planning curriculum activities, teachers need to consider using a book to introduce each experience. This is an especially meaningful way to get youngsters involved in the same sort of activities that the book character engages in (Beaty, 1994, pp. 20–21).

CURRICULUM WEBS

Teachers who look to curriculum areas as the structure of their program can plan the entire curriculum for several weeks at a time around multicultural books. A simple "curriculum web" like the one shown in Figure 1.3 can be constructed to help plan these learning area activities. Choose a theme you plan to follow, such as "alike and different," and then brainstorm the activities you want children to become involved with in each curriculum area. The reading of multicultural books in the centers can lead children into activities similar to those engaged in by the characters in the books.

INCORPORATING LEARNING ACTIVITIES

Keep these activities going in each of the curriculum areas until all of the children get a chance to try them and repeat them as many times as they want. We realize that young children learn best by repeating activities of their choice over and over. They also learn more from activities that are personal, that focus on themselves. Bonding with book characters helps this to

**FIGURE 1.3
Curriculum Web**

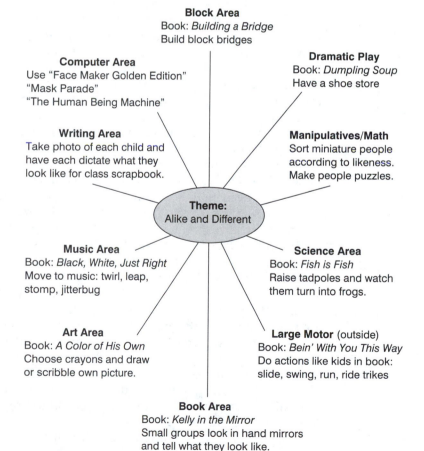

Block Area
Book: *Building a Bridge*
Build block bridges

Computer Area
Use "Face Maker Golden Edition"
"Mask Parade"
"The Human Being Machine"

Dramatic Play
Book: *Dumpling Soup*
Have a shoe store

Writing Area
Take photo of each child and
have each dictate what they
look like for class scrapbook.

Manipulatives/Math
Sort miniature people
according to likeness.
Make people puzzles.

**Theme:
Alike and Different**

Music Area
Book: *Black, White, Just Right*
Move to music: twirl, leap,
stomp, jitterbug

Science Area
Book: *Fish is Fish*
Raise tadpoles and watch
them turn into frogs.

Art Area
Book: *A Color of His Own*
Choose crayons and draw
or scribble own picture.

Large Motor (outside)
Book: *Bein' With You This Way*
Do actions like kids in book:
slide, swing, run, ride trikes

Book Area
Book: *Kelly in the Mirror*
Small groups look in hand mirrors
and tell what they look like.

happen. Then the curriculum area activities you provide give youngsters an opportunity to try out these new concepts for themselves.

Be sure to accept all the different ways children interpret the stories. For instance, after hearing each rap verse of *Bein' with You This Way* (Nikola-Lisa, 1994), your children can do movements on the playground any way they want, not only like the different ethnic children portrayed in the book. You may want to call them back after they perform each verse to see what happens next in the story. Then they can try out the next action for themselves. Have you ever read a book like this out on the playground? Break your old habits and try something new! The children will love it.

As young children explore the concept of alike and different through picture books, they will begin to see that all of us are alike yet different in a variety of ways. From *Bein' with You This Way*, children look at the curly hair and straight hair, big nose and little nose, brown eyes and blue eyes, thick arms and thin arms, long legs and short legs, and light skin and dark skin of the different children on the playground as they all slide, run, swing, ride trikes, and have fun together.

Don't forget the computer area. Appropriate children's software programs can add still another dimension to your multicultural activities. When children are examining their own likenesses and differences, have a program such as *The Human Being Machine* (Cooper, 1990) available. Children can put together the different parts of a face or body and print off the resulting picture. They use either the keyboard, TouchWindow, or a single switch to choose facial features. If you have an Echo speech synthesizer, directions are spoken aloud (Buckleitner, 1993, p. 92).

Other favorite computer programs include *Facemaker Golden Edition* (Queue, 1986), in which children build a funny face from various eyes, ears, noses, mouths, and hair, which then becomes animated. The youngest children may need help with this program unless they are experienced computer users. (Many are!) These faces can also be printed out.

Children have great fun playing around with noses and ears or mustaches and eyelashes to create weird and wonderful faces with eyes that wink and ears that wiggle on the computer screen. With *Mask Parade* (Queue, 1984), children design their own face masks and then print them out to be cut out and worn. Although this may not seem to be a multicultural activity as such, it does fit in with the alike and different theme, as well as with your children's exploration of facial features.

To get things going in the music area, read *Black, White, Just Right!* (Davol, 1993), in which a little girl narrator who has an African-American mother and Caucasian father tells what she likes to do with each of her parents: twirl and leap with her mom; rap, stomp, and jitterbug with her dad; and all of it is "just right." Play different kinds of music on different days to see what your children like best.

Animals are the same and different, just like people. Bring in tadpoles for the science area and be prepared to read the book *Fish is Fish* (Lionni,

1970), about a minnow and a tadpole who befriend one another until the tadpole turns into a frog and hops out of their pond. Can your children watch what happens to their own tadpoles and make up fantastic stories about them just like the minnow in the story does?

In *A Color of His Own* (Lionni, 1975), a little chameleon who changes color whenever his background changes wishes for a color all his own, but finds instead another chameleon . . . and they both change colors together! As a lead-in art activity, this book can encourage your children to find a color of their own and draw or scribble their own picture. As a lead-in science activity, you can read this story when the children have access to a live chameleon in their science area or on a field trip to a pet store or science museum.

In *All the Colors of the Earth* (Hamanaka, 1994), children from all over the world are compared with the colors of the animal world: the browns of bears and soaring eagles, the golds of lions and late summer grasses, the pinks of tiny sea shells, and the russets of fallen leaves. One line of text weaves its way in a rippling line across the double-page pictures, comparing hair to bouncy baby lambs or flowing water. Read this book to individuals or small groups and ask them to find a child they would like to be. The next time you read it, have children find a multicultural doll or puppet that looks like one of the children in the book. Ask them to have the dolls speak and tell who they are and what kinds of things they would want to do like their counterpart in the book.

Many picture books like this are excellent resources for dramatic play experiences in which children can pretend to be book characters. *Dumpling Soup*, mentioned previously, can also motivate the setting up of a shoe store like the Hawaiian, Japanese, Korean, and Caucasian cousins do when they visit their grandma's house for New Year's and find the front steps covered with slippers, sandals, thongs, and shoes. The custom of many Hawaiian families to remove their shoes before entering a house gives these cousins wonderful props for their pretend store. Be sure to have a large shoe collection on hand before reading this book.

Your block area can also feature multicultural building activities after you read *Building a Bridge* (Begaye & Tracy, 1993), in which a little Caucasian girl named Anna and a Native American girl named Juanita go to school for the first time on the Navajo reservation. Both girls are scared but excited about their first day of school, but Anna feels out of place being the only Caucasian child in the school. The Navajo teacher gives the girls a set of purple and green blocks to play with and says that they are magic. At first the girls build separate bridges exactly alike except that one is green and one is purple. But by the end of the day, the blocks have truly worked their magic: the girls have combined them to build a wonderful single bridge with the colors all mixed together. The girls have decided that it was okay that the blocks were different colors, that differences make things magical.

Differences can become magical in your classroom too, if you focus on common bonds and base your curriculum on books like these. *Building*

Bridges with Multicultural Picture Books can show you how. Other educators agree. In their excellent book *Raising the Rainbow Generation*, Hopson and Hopson (1993) ask—and answer—an important question about such books:

> *Why do we read stories to our children? . . . We choose stories that will entertain and inform. In a relaxing way, stories teach children about our own culture and the values we want to impart to them. . . . The second reason is that these stories provide a window through which your children, and maybe you, too, can gain an understanding of other cultures.* (p. 145)

It is an exciting thought. This textbook proposes to make it a reality by opening the book-bonding window for everyone.

 ## LEARNING ACTIVITIES

1. How do the children in your classroom or center deal with children from other cultures? Give a real example. Describe one activity you have used to help them deal in a positive manner.
2. Give an example of how you support a child in your classroom or center in each of the child development areas every day: emotional, social, physical, cognitive, language, creative. Be specific.
3. Which curriculum areas in your classroom support cultural diversity? Describe how.
4. Make a list of the common bonds that your particular children seem to have.
5. How can you incorporate your children's common bonds into a multicultural curriculum? Be specific.

 ## REFERENCES

Beaty, J. J. (1994). *Picture book storytelling*. Fort Worth, TX: Harcourt Brace.

Boutte, G. S., & McCormick, C. B. (1992). Authentic multicultural activities. *Childhood Education*, 68(3), 140–144.

Buckleitner, W. (1993). *High/Scope buyer's guide to children's software*. Ypsilanti, MI: High/Scope Press.

Hopson, D. P., & Hopson, D. S. (1993). *Raising the rainbow generation: Teaching your children to be successful in a multicultural society*. New York: Simon & Schuster.

Kiefer, B. Z. (1995). *The potential of picturebooks: From visual literacy to aesthetic understanding*. Upper Saddle River, NJ: Merrill/Prentice Hall.

Pratt, L. (1994). Personal interview.

Ramsey, P. G. (1991). *Making friends in school: Promoting peer relationships in early childhood*. New York: Teachers College Press.

ADDITIONAL READINGS

Clark, L., DeWolf, S., & Clark, C. (1992). Teaching teachers to avoid having culturally assaultive classrooms. *Young Children, 47*(5), 4–9.

Hendrick, J. (1986). *Total learning: Curriculum for the young child.* Upper Saddle River, NJ: Merrill/Prentice Hall.

King, E. W., Chipman, M., & Cruz-Janzen, M. (1994). *Educating young children in a diverse society.* Boston: Allyn and Bacon.

Ramsey, P. G., & Derman-Sparks, L. (1992). Multicultural education reaffirmed. *Young Children, 47*(2), 10-11.

Williams, L. R. (1992). Determining the multicultural curriculum. In E. B. Vold (Ed.), *Multicultural education in early childhood classrooms.* Washington, DC: National Education Association.

 ## CHILDREN'S BOOKS

Bansemer, R. (1991). *Rachel's splendifilous adventure.* Mt. Desert, ME: Windswept House. (American-Russian)

Begaye, L. S., & Tracy, L. (1993). *Building a bridge.* Flagstaff, AZ: Northland Publishing Co. (Caucasian-Native American)

Davol, M. W. (1993). *Black, white, just right!* Morton Grove, IL: Whitman. (African American)

Hamanaka, S. (1994). *All the colors of the Earth.* New York: Morrow.

Hort, L. (1991). *How many stars in the sky?* New York: Tambourine Books. (African-American)

Keats, E. J. (1968). *A letter to Amy.* New York: Harper & Row. (African-American)

Kusugak, M. A. (1993). *Northern lights: Soccer trails.* Toronto, Canada: Annick Press. (Inuit)

Levine, E. (1989). *I hate English!* New York: Scholastic. (Chinese-American)

Lionni, L. (1970). *Fish is fish.* New York: Pantheon Books. (Animal)

Lionni, L. (1975). *A color of his own.* New York: Knopf. (Animal)

Mitchell, R. P. (1993). *Hue Boy.* New York: Dial Books for Young Readers. (Caribbean)

Nikola-Lisa, W. (1994). *Bein' with you this way.* New York: Lee & Low Books. (Multicultural)

Rattigan, J. K. (1993). *Dumpling soup.* Boston: Little Brown. (Hawaiian-multicultural)

Rohmer, H. (1989). *Uncle Nacho's hat.* San Francisco: Children's Book Press. (Hispanic)

Tompert, A. (1988). *Will you come back for me?* Morton Grove, IL: Albert Whitman Co. (Asian-American)

Vertreace, M. M. (1993). *Kelly in the mirror.* Morton Grove, IL: Albert Whitman Co. (African American)

CHILDREN'S SOFTWARE PROGRAMS

R. J. Cooper & Associates
24843 Del Prado, Suite 283
Dana Point, CA 92629
The Human Being Machine (1990; Apple)

Queue, Inc.
338 Commerce Drive
Fairfield, CT 06434
Facemaker Golden Edition (1986; Apple, IBM)
Mask Parade (1984; Apple, IBM)

Choosing Appropriate Picture Books

2

Through multicultural literature, children who are members of racial or ethnic minority groups realize that they have a cultural heritage of which they can be proud, and that their culture has made important contributions to the United States and to the world. (Norton, 1995, p. 561)

ASSEMBLING A LIBRARY OF BOOKS SHOWING DIFFERENT FACETS OF EACH CULTURE

As you assemble a library of multicultural picture books, you need to pay particular attention to the range of people, places, ideas, and beliefs of each culture presented by the books. As Rudman (1984) points out in her valuable book *Children's Literature: An Issues Approach*: "Members of a particular group should be able to see themselves mirrored in literature with as many facets of their heritage as possible presented and developed" (p. 162). Although each of your picture books may feature only one particular facet, you should assemble enough books on the same culture to illustrate a well-rounded picture of the people. Otherwise, you run the risk of perpetuating cultural stereotypes.

Urban vs. Rural

Although a great many picture books are set in rural Africa, not every child in Africa lives in a tribal village. Books that feature contemporary African children should show them not only engaged in village life, as Osa is in *The Village of Round and Square Houses* (Grifalconi, 1986), and Yemi is in *It Takes a Village* (Cowen-Fletcher, 1994), and as Mcheshi is in *Mcheshi Goes to the Market* (Jacaranda Designs, 1991). Your collection should also include city children, such as Shepherd in *Not So Fast Songololo* (Daly, 1985), Nerinder and Leroy in *The Day of the Rainbow* (Craft, 1988), and Zolani, Sipho, and Noma in *At the Crossroads* (Isadora, 1991)

African village life is very different from anything most American children have experienced. Children wear different clothing, live in different houses, and engage in different customs than American children have encountered. Nevertheless, both teachers and children are attracted to such colorful books, as well they should be. Cultural differences can be celebrated when American youngsters see other children involved in the same kinds of dilemmas or situations that they experience.

The Village of Round and Square Houses, a book awarded a Caldecott Honor for its outstanding art, is a true first-person narrative by a little girl named Osa who grew up in the village of Tos in West Africa, with its neat woven thatch-and-mud dwellings. From the book's words and pictures, American children can see how respectfully the children treat their elders, how Osa helps prepare the *fou-fou* for supper, and how Grandma tells her the story of why men live in square houses and women live in round ones. The women and girls of the village are clothed in colorful wrap-around skirts and headdresses, amid an exotic and tropical backdrop of palm and banana trees.

It Takes a Village shows similar houses, but in this story Yemi must take care of her little brother Kokou, who somehow wanders away from her while Mama sells mangoes in the marketplace. In *Mcheshi Goes to the Market*, little Mcheshi visits all the stalls in the village market while her mother shops. Four Kenyan artists make this book a delectable feast of colorful wares, clothing, and food.

Nevertheless, if American children see only these three books, they may come away with some stereotyped ideas about Africans: that most African people go barefoot; that African women wear turbans and carry baskets on their heads; that most Africans sit on the ground; that everyone in Africa walks because no one has a car. Because these books feature only village life, they do not show a complete picture of modern Africans. It is important, therefore, to have on hand a number of other books that show African children who live in modern cities.

In *Not So Fast Songololo*, children will see little Shepherd accompany his granny on a shopping trip to the city where they ride a bus, cross the crowded streets, look in the store windows, and finally buy new red sneakers for Shepherd.

In *The Day of the Rainbow*, everyone seems to be losing things on the busy city street or in the crowded bus: little Nerinder, an East Indian girl, has lost her library book; the roller-skating boy, Leroy, has lost a present for his girlfriend, and Mrs. Poppodopolous has lost her precious recipe for raisin cake. Eventually a rainbow appears and brings them all back together. Even though this book is written for older children, preschoolers can enjoy the pictures, and teachers can tell what happens instead of reading every word.

In *At the Crossroads*, the children Sipho, Noma, and Zolani, and their friends live in the one of the formerly segregated townships outside a South African city. They dress much like American children, but live in gray dwellings of tin and boards on unpaved streets. The story focuses on a most exciting day and night in the children's lives: when their fathers finally come home from working far away in the mines. Books like these bring an added dimension to the perspective your children are developing about African people.

Picture books about African American children should also show a balanced view of characters from both urban and rural cultures. For instance, the wonderfully crafted stories by Ezra Jack Keats, about the African American children Peter, Archie, and their friends, take place in New York City. Children and teachers alike love *The Snowy Day* (1962), the Caldecott Medal winning book in which Peter makes angels on the snowy ground; *Whistle for Willie* (1964), in which Peter puts on his daddy's hat so he will feel grown up enough to whistle; *Goggles!* (1969), in which the big boys take Peter's glasses, but his dog, Willie, gets them back; and *Hi, Cat!* (1970), in which a black alley cat follows Archie home.

Many more recent books featuring African American children are also set in the cities, just as Keats' stories are. *The Leaving Morning* (Johnson, 1992) tells a realistic goodbye-story about two children who are moving away from their beloved city apartment. *Jonathan and His Mommy* (Smalls-Hector, 1992) shows a high-spirited mother and son who love to zigzag, criss-cross, and reggae down the city street on their daily afternoon walk. *Tar Beach* (Ringgold, 1991), another Caldecott Honor book, has the children stretched out on a blanket at a night picnic on the roof of their New York apartment building, their own "tar" beach.

To present a more complete picture of African American children, teachers should try to balance urban and rural stories by including books portraying these youngsters in the country or at a real beach. *Kinda Blue* (Grifalconi, 1993) shows little Sissy feeling lonely around her Georgia farm until Uncle Dan swoops her up and takes her out to visit his "corn children." *Knoxville, Tennessee* (Giovanni, 1994) is about a little girl who loves summer in the country, where she can eat fresh corn from daddy's garden, go barefoot, and be warm all the time. *Father and Son* (Lauture, 1992) shows a boy and his father flying kites, riding horses, rowing a boat, and walking on the beach together in the bright South Carolina sunlight.

Other books should include additional features of cultures, such as the different economic conditions of the people, different jobs people engage in, and different subgroups within a culture. Authentic, true-to-life stories are best for the youngest children. Try to include books that portray a balance of cultural aspects so that your children experience the variety of ways that children from a culture live.

Different Subgroups

Most cultures can be divided into subgroups that may be quite different from one another. Native Americans, for instance, are represented by tribal groups such as Pueblo, Navajo, Sioux, Cherokee, Inuit, Iroquois, Seminole, and many more. Black Africans can be Ashanti, Benin, Masai, Fulani, Wolof, Zulu, Ibo, and many others. Asian American children may come from Chinese, Japanese, Korean, Filipino, Vietnamese, Laotian, Hmong, or Cambodian backgrounds. Hispanic or Latino children may have backgrounds from Mexico, Cuba, Puerto Rico, Nicaragua, or many other Latin American countries. It is important that your picture books portraying children from these cultures show a balance of subgroups, especially if there are children from those cultural subgroups in your classroom. If you have children from Puerto Rico, for example, they may enjoy hearing *Abuelita's Paradise* (Nodar, 1992), about Marita and her grandma, who brings to life delightful stories about her own island girlhood. The boy Ramon makes a mask and becomes *Vejigante Masquerader* (Delacre, 1993) during the carnival celebration in Puerto Rico. Kindergarten children respond especially well to Ramon's excitement and then despair when his costume gets ripped apart by a rambunctious goat.

Your collection of multicultural books should be balanced in several other ways. Some guidelines are given in Figure 2.1.

A BALANCE OF BOOKS SHOWING PAST AND PRESENT

Children 3 to 5 years of age live almost exclusively in the present. Thus, the picture books they look at or have read to them take place in their present as far as they are concerned, no matter what the book's actual time frame may be. *Pedro and the Padre* (Aardema, 1991), for example, seems to be a realistic Mexican story about a lazy boy who goes to work for a village priest. Actually it is a wonderfully told and illustrated folktale that takes place in earlier times when villages had no electricity, transportation was by donkey or on foot, and everyone wore serapes and sombreros.

Be sure to balance your use of tales from the past with books showing modern Hispanic children, such as *A Christmas Surprise for Chabelita* (Palacios, 1993), about a little girl whose absent mother appears by surprise at Chabelita's school performance. In *Aunt Flossie's Hats (and Crab Cakes Later)* (Howard, 1991), an African American girl named Sarah and

FIGURE 2.1   Guidelines for Choosing Appropriate Multicultural Books

1. A balance of books showing different facets of each culture.
2. A balance of books showing past and present.
3. A balance of simple folktales and contemporary stories.
4. Books with detailed illustrations, not oversimplified stereotypes.
5. Books with language or dialect showing respect for the culture.
6. Books with characters that children can identify with.
7. Books with characters from different cultures in one story.

her sister visit their Aunt Flossie and try on her hats, each one of which reminds Aunt Flossie of a story from her past. The girls have fun acting out the stories themselves, which then lead them to the crab cakes for dinner.

The history of a people is important even for the youngest children to hear about, but they need to be able to relate it to their own world. In *Our People* (Medearis, 1994), a little girl narrator translates the simple stories her daddy tells her about the history of their African American people by acting out these roles in her own way. When daddy tells her their people built the pyramids of Egypt, the little girl wishes she could have been there and proceeds to build her own pyramids out of blocks on the living room floor. When he says they were once the kings and queens of Africa, she dresses up with a bright scarf and a cooking pan for a crown.

Historical stories can come alive more easily for your youngsters if they can identify with book characters like these and act out their roles. If they cannot, then the book may be too old for them or the concepts too complex.

A BALANCE OF SIMPLE FOLKTALES AND CONTEMPORARY STORIES

The flood of new multicultural books currently being published includes many folktales from cultures seldom written about before. Look them over carefully before using them with children aged 3 to 5. Although most of these books are well-written and beautifully illustrated, they may be too complex for the youngest children to understand. The ones you do decide to use must then be balanced in your curriculum by realistic modern stories about the same culture. Otherwise, your children may come to believe that modern children from other cultures look like folktale characters from the past.

Folktales about Native Americans are a good example. They often show Indians in traditional tribal outfits interacting with one another or with the animals of their region. For instance, young children enjoy hearing the simple Native American folktale *Baby Rattlesnake* (Ata & Moroney, 1989), about what happens if you get something before you're ready for it. Baby rattlesnake gets the rattle at the end of his tale before he is old enough to use it properly. He has a grand time scaring all of the desert animals, but when the chief's daughter comes along, instead of running away she crushes his rattle under her foot. The girl's outfit of buckskins and moccasins is appropriate for a folktale but not for a modern Indian story. Your children should also experience a modern story featuring contemporary Native Americans to balance their appearance as depicted in the folktale. *It Rained on the Desert Today* (Buchanan and Buchanan, 1994) shows animals of the Arizona desert as well as an Indian girl and her neighbors, all dressed in modern clothes, as they gather on the desert to lift up their faces and revel in the first rain of the summer.

Chester Bear, Where Are You? (Eyvindson, 1988) shows a modern Canadian Indian family with a little boy who has lost his teddy bear and can't seem to find him anywhere. In *Two Pairs of Shoes* (Sanderson, 1992), a contemporary Indian girl named Maggie receives two pairs of shoes for her birthday: a pair of black, patent leather shoes and a pair of hand-beaded moccasins.

The Funny Little Woman (Mosel, 1972), another Caldecott Medal winner, is a simple Japanese folktale of a funny little woman in a red and yellow kimono who likes to laugh and make dumplings out of rice. She is captured by the wicked *oni* monsters, who make her cook rice for them with a magic paddle. Eventually she tricks them and escapes back home with the magic paddle, where she makes and sells rice dumplings and becomes the richest woman in all Japan.

To build a bridge from a folktale into a contemporary setting, read the previously mentioned *Dumpling Soup* (Rattigan, 1993). It can help your children visualize modern Japanese-Hawaiian people cooking the same sort of rice dumplings as the funny little woman. Then you can all prepare this festive food together.

BOOKS WITH DETAILED ILLUSTRATIONS, NOT OVERSIMPLIFIED STEREOTYPES

Picture-book illustrations may be the most important aspect in helping your children develop a good feeling about children from other cultures. Detailed, realistic depictions are the best. However, many older ethnic stories, especially folktales, have oversimplified illustrations showing all the people looking alike and wearing similar, stereotypical clothing. If these are the only books children are exposed to about a particular culture, they may well develop racial stereotypes about the people depicted.

In *The Five Chinese Brothers* (Bishop, 1938), not only the brothers but all the characters have cartoon-like slant eyes, wear their hair in queues, and are dressed in skull caps and long gowns. The story is about the five brothers who look alike but have different, wonderful skills: one can swallow the sea, one has an iron neck, one can stretch his legs, one cannot be burned, and one can hold his breath indefinitely. Young children still respond so well to this simple but exciting folktale that the book has remained in print all these years.

Some day we will have so many books showing realistic Chinese characters that stories like *The Five Chinese Brothers* may be accepted as an old time folktale, just as *Hansel and Gretel* or *Little Red Riding Hood* are, rather than as a stereotyped depiction of all Chinese people. In the meantime, older children can be encouraged to look at Margaret Mahy's *The Seven Chinese Brothers* (1990), a longer version of this same tale but with lively, historically accurate depictions of the people and setting by Chinese artists Jean and Mou-sein Tseng.

Good source for softcover books on contemporary Indians:

Send for a catalog:

> Pemmican Publications, Inc.
> Unit #2- 1635 Burrows Ave.
> Winnipeg, Manitoba R2X 0T1
> Canada

As mentioned earlier, many books featuring Native Americans show them dressed in buckskin clothing and feathered headdresses. Although Native Americans today do wear traditional garb for ceremonial occasions, their everyday dress is the same as yours and mine. When the story is not a traditional folktale or does not depict a ceremonial event, it should show characters in modern dress. Although *Little Eagle Lots of Owls* (Edmiston, 1993) tells a delightful naming story, once again it perpetuates the idea that modern Native American children and grownups wear buckskin and feathers as everyday dress.

Be sure to use books depicting Native American children as they really are today. *A Salmon for Simon* (Waterton, 1980), for instance, shows little Simon dressed in blue jeans, a shirt, and rubber boots as he struggles to catch a salmon near his native village on the west coast of Canada. *Seya's Song* (Hirschi, 1992) tells another salmon story from the perspective of a S'Klallum girl who lives on the coastal shores of Washington State. The little girl rides a bike, wears a t-shirt, and builds sand castles on the beach, and also follows the baby salmon on their long swim to the sea.

In *The Shepherd Boy* (Franklin, 1994), a Navajo boy named Ben lives in a hogan, but wears jeans and a blue t-shirt as he and his dogs trek across the mesa searching for a lost lamb before the sun goes down. In *The Mystery of the Navajo Moon* (Green, 1991), a Navajo girl named Wilma has an exciting nighttime adventure. Wilma also lives in a hogan, but her bedroom, with its chest of drawers and stuffed teddy bear, could belong to any little girl. Wilma herself, in her pink nightgown and red-and-white knee socks, could also be any little girl—until she is visited by a silvery pony who carries her out across the desert, higher than the hawk owls dare to fly.

Books like these depict the lives of children from another culture in a non-stereotyped manner that all youngsters can understand. As Rudman (1984) points out:

> *Illustrations are very influential and particularly critical in the case of books on Native Americans. Physical features, dress, and environment should be depicted correctly. It is a hopeful sign that Native American illustrators as*

well as writers have been recognized in recent years and have been employed by publishers who care about presenting the Indian people's perspective. (p. 173)

BOOKS WITH LANGUAGE OR DIALECT
SHOWING RESPECT FOR THE CULTURE

In most multicultural picture books for young children, characters are portrayed as children who speak standard English. A few are bilingual, with the words of the story in a second language at the bottom or side of the page. Those that do have a dialect use it mainly for the purpose of distinguishing their characters, either as children whose use of English may not be up to adult standards, or perhaps who belong to a special subgroup of a culture.

In *She Come Bringing Me That Little Baby Girl* (Greenfield, 1974) the main character, an African-American boy named Kevin, is made more real to the readers by the realistic contrast of his language and his mother's. When she says, "You're a big brother now," Kevin's reply is typical of any boy his age: "I don't want to be a brother to no girl."

In *Kinda Blue* (Grifalconi, 1993), both Sissy and her Uncle Dan talk a Black English dialect. However, the language is used as poetry, painting a flowing word picture of Sissy, Uncle Dan, and the cornfield, much like the swirling colors of the illustrations. Of the corn, Uncle Dan says: "See them fling they leafy arms? They wavin' hello!" His words bend and sway like corn in the wind. A dialect used in this manner does not demean its users, but makes them more interesting and real. Your children may not speak English in this manner, but they come to appreciate characters who can paint pictures with their words in this way. As Sadker and Sadker (1977) remark about Black English in *Now Upon a Time: A Contemporary View of Children's Literature*: " . . . as a literary technique used to reflect the reality of black America it is appropriate and powerful" (p. 154).

In *Angel Child, Dragon Child* (Surat, 1983), a book more appropriate for children 6 years old and older, Ut, the new Vietnamese girl who is being teased by her classmate Raymond, speaks in broken English: "Raymond, not cry. I give you cookie." Her narrative, however, is in standard English: "Later, across the room, I heard a sniffle. Raymond's shoulders jiggled like little Quang's when he cried for Mother." In this case, Ut's use of broken English when she speaks aloud fits the story of a new immigrant struggling to learn a different language and new customs.

Today's multicultural picture books are more often written by authors from the culture being described. Their use of dialect tends to be minimal but appropriate, and in keeping with Rudman's (1984) opinion:

Literature should reflect the linguistic richness of a culture. Dialect should not be used as a differentiating mechanism with negative intent. (p. 163)

BOOKS WITH CHARACTERS WITH WHOM CHILDREN CAN IDENTIFY

All of the books discussed in this chapter have characters with whom your youngsters can identify. No matter how different looking the children are, no matter how far removed the setting is from mainstream America, the characters in these books have certain common bonds with their readers that children are able to understand. As early childhood specialist Ramsey (1987) notes:

> *Stories introduce children to unfamiliar people in a personalized and appealing fashion. By involving the children with characters and situations that they can identify with, books increase children's appreciation of other ways of life and help them see unfamiliar people as individuals.* (p. 69)

Is this the case with your youngsters? Can they really bond with a child from an African village, for instance? They can if they learn from the words and pictures that the character gets into similar situations and has similar feelings to their own—in other words, when the character has common bonds with them.

Children can tell from the pictures of Mcheshi in *Mcheshi Goes to the Market* (Jacaranda Designs, 1991) that she is a little girl 3 to 4 years old, wearing a red and white dress, white vest, red knee socks, and blue shoes: clothes not unlike their own. She invites the readers to come along with her

Good sources for multicultural books for young children:

Send for catalogs:

Gryphon House
Early Childhood Books
P.O. Box 275
Mt. Rainier. MD 20712

The Book Vine
Preschool Book Catalog
3980 Albany Street
McHenry, IL 60050

Redleaf Press
450 N. Syndicate, Suite 5
St. Paul, MN 55104

and her mother on a shopping trip to the village market. Although the market is an open-air one with booths and stalls rather than a supermarket, Mcheshi's adventures are not that different from your own children's when they go shopping with their mothers.

Mcheshi's mother warns her to stay with her, but the excited little girl runs ahead. While her mother talks with one of the vendors, Mcheshi hops into a big basket and hides. (Can your children find her?) Afterwards she wants her mother to buy her daddy the yellow men's shoes that catch her eye, and she slips her foot into one. When her mother is engaged in buying a chicken (a live one) for Grandma, Mcheshi opens a basket to get one, and the rest fly out. Then her mother warns her not to touch the fruit, but Mcheshi has already picked up an orange and then dropped it. She then gets permission to exchange her orange for a hard-boiled egg from a bicycle vendor. All in all, as Mcheshi and her mother prepare to board the bus and go home, it has been an exciting adventure for the little girl—just a normal day of shopping, as many of your own children can attest to.

What about boys from a different culture? Can your boys identify with anyone like Sipho or Zolani and their friends from a township in South Africa in *At the Crossroads* (Isadora, 1991)? The children pictured on the front cover immediately make common bonds possible with their broad smiles and waves at the reader. Inside, the strikingly realistic art brings township activities to life as the boys wash in an open tub, start off for

Cover illustrations help children identify with book characters.

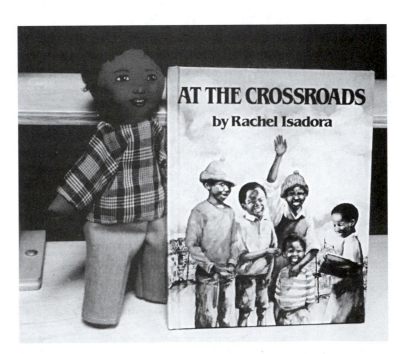

school, sing about their fathers' coming home from the mines, make musical instruments from a tin can and a stick in preparation for the great arrival, and finally wait all night at the crossroads until their fathers' truck pulls up at daybreak. The joyful and caring emotions expressed by the children against a background of poverty light up the lives of all who experience this uplifting story. Which of the six children featured would each of your listeners like to be?

BOOKS WITH CHARACTERS FROM DIFFERENT CULTURES IN ONE STORY

Most of the books discussed thus far contain characters from a single culture. Your classroom library should also include books showing child characters from more than one culture interacting in an equal manner. This means that all the principal characters should function from an equal position. One from a particular culture may be the lead character, but the others should not be dominated by a Caucasian protagonist, for instance. Neither should any characters be mere tokens of their race or ethnic group.

In *Three at Sea* (Bush, 1994), three little boys from three different cultures go tubing on the river, but somehow drift out to sea and have a fantastic ecological adventure. Dark-haired Alex, blond Joel, and African American Zachariah Jr. have equal roles in trying to persuade different sea creatures to help them, but it is Zachariah Jr. who knows more about endangered animals. He is able to tie Joel's red bandanna around the snout of a crocodile who is threatening them, and he is the one who finally takes charge of getting them back to shore. Wonderfully witty illustrations burst from double-page spreads as this rollicking escapade shakes up all three boys. Your boys especially should be able to identify with any or all of its characters. Ask them who they would like to be in the story.

In *Building a Bridge* (Begaye, 1993), the story opens with little Anna, a Caucasian girl, tying her shoes but being scared and excited about the first day of school on the Navajo Reservation. The next two pages show little Juanita, a Navajo girl, getting ready for school by herding the sheep out of their pen and carrying some fry bread to Grandmother on her way to the school bus. She is scared and excited too. The author uses the same inventive expression to describe each of the two girls' feelings: "a tummy full of

Good source for multicultural books:

Your public library. Visit it soon!

butterflies and bouncy rubber balls." As your children listeners hear these similar words and feelings but see the different pictures, they are able to build a bridge from one girl to the other even before the two girls do. In other words, your children are able to recognize the common bonds but celebrate the differences between two children from completely different cultures. The author, a Caucasian woman who is married to a Navajo husband, dedicates her book as follows:

> *To the people of the Navajo Nation, many of whom have gone out of their way not only to build a bridge but to walk with me across it. And to my husband—may we build many bridges together.*

This textbook extends this same book dedication to you, the teachers and teachers-to-be, who serve as behavior models for young children of every culture. May your use of children's picture books show them the way to bond with others, no matter how different they may seem to be.

 ## LEARNING ACTIVITIES

1. Which multicultural picture books do you presently possess? Which of the seven criteria in Figure 2.1 do they reflect?
2. What are the gaps in your book collection? Make a list of several books that you might obtain to fill these gaps. If you have no gaps, what books could you add to extend your collection?
3. Choose three books not discussed here and evaluate them according to the criteria in Figure 2.1.
4. Which cultural folktales do you or your children especially like? What makes them appealing? Which realistic stories can you use that would give children a balanced outlook about the cultures?
5. Which book illustrations are your or your children's favorites? Why? Are they in any way stereotyped? What characteristics cause illustrations to foster stereotypes about a culture? Give examples.

 ## REFERENCES

Norton, D. E. (1995). *Through the eyes of a child: An introduction to children's literature.* Upper Saddle River, NJ: Merrill/Prentice Hall.

Ramsey, P. G. (1987). *Teaching and learning in a diverse world: Multicultural education for young children.* New York: Teachers College Press.

Rudman, M. K. (1984). *Children's literature: An issues approach.* New York: Longman.

Sadker, M. P., & Sadker, D. M. (1977). *Now upon a time: A contemporary view of children's literature.* New York: Harper & Row.

ADDITIONAL READINGS

Boutte, G. S., LaPoint, S., & Davis, B. (1993). Racial issues in education: Real or imagined? *Young Children, 49*(1), 19–23.

Kiefer, B. Z. (1995). *The potential of picturebooks: From visual literacy to aesthetic understanding.* Upper Saddle River, NJ: Merrill/Prentice Hall.

Ramirez, G., & Ramirez, J. L. (1994). *Multiethnic children's literature.* Albany, NY: Delmar.

Walker-Dalhouse, D. (1993). Beginning reading and the African American child at risk. *Young Children, 49*(1), 24–27.

 ## CHILDREN'S BOOKS

Aardema, V. (1991). *Pedro and the padre.* New York: Dial.

Ata, T., & Moroney, L. (1989). *Baby rattlesnake.* San Francisco: Children's Book Press.

Begaye, L. S. (1993). *Building a bridge.* Flagstaff, AZ: Northland.

Bishop, C. H. (1938). *The five Chinese brothers.* New York: Coward-McCann.

Buchanan, K., & Buchanan, D. (1994). *It rained on the desert today.* Flagstaff, AZ: Northland.

Bush, T. (1994). *Three at sea.* New York: Crown.

Cowen-Fletcher, J. (1994). *It Takes a Village.* New York: Scholastic.

Craft, R. (1988). *The day of the rainbow.* New York: Viking Penguin.

Daly, N. (1985). *Not so fast Songololo.* New York: Viking Penguin.

Delacre, L. (1993). *Vejigante masquerader.* New York: Scholastic.

Edmiston, J. (1993). *Little eagle lots of owls.* Boston: Houghton Mifflin.

Eyvindson, P. (1988). *Chester Bear, Where are you?* Winnipeg, Canada: Pemmican Publications.

Franklin, K. L. (1994). *The shepherd boy.* New York: Maxwell/Macmillan.

Giovanni, N. (1994). *Knoxville, Tennessee.* New York: Scholastic.

Green, R. (1991). *Mystery of the Navajo moon.* Flagstaff, AZ: Northland.

Greenfield, E. (1974). *She come bringing me that little baby girl.* Philadelphia: Lippincott.

Grifalconi, A. (1986). *The village of round and square houses.* Boston: Little Brown.

Grifalconi, A. (1993). *Kinda blue.* Boston: Little Brown.

Hirschi, R. (1992). *Seya's song.* Seattle: Sasquatch Books.

Howard, E. F. (1991). *Aunt Flossie's hats (and crab cakes later).* New York: Clarion.

Isadora, R. (1991). *At the crossroads.* New York: Greenwillow.

Johnson, A. (1992). *The leaving morning.* New York: Orchard.

Keats, E. J. (1962). *The snowy day.* New York, Viking.

Keats, E. J. (1964). *Whistle for Willie.* New York, Viking.

Keats, E. J. (1969). *Goggles!* New York: Collier.

Keats, E. J. (1970). *Hi, cat!* New York: Collier.

Lauture, D. (1992). *Father and son.* New York: Philomel.

Mahy, M. (1990). *The seven Chinese brothers.* New York: Scholastic.

Mcheshi goes to the market. (1991). Nairobi, Kenya: Jacaranda Designs.

Medearis, A. S. (1994). *Our people.* New York: Atheneum.

Mosel, A. (1972). *The funny little woman.* New York: E. P. Dutton.

Nodar, C. S. (1992). *Abuelita's paradise.* Morton Grove, IL: Whitman.

Palacios, A. (1993). *A Christmas surprise for Chabelita.* New York: Troll Associates.

Rattigan, J. K. (1993). *Dumpling soup.* Boston: Little Brown.

Ringgold, F. (1991). *Tar beach.* New York: Crown Publishers.

Sanderson, E. (1992). *Two pairs of shoes.* Winnipeg, Canada: Pemmican Publications.

Smalls-Hector, R. (1992). *Jonathan and his mommy.* Boston: Little, Brown.

Surat, M. M. (1983). *Angel child, dragon child.* New York: Scholastic.

Waterton, B. (1980). *A salmon for Simon.* Toronto, Canada: Douglas & McIntyre.

Developing Self-Esteem 3

A fairly large body of books deals with constructing and
reinforcing a sense of pride and positive self-image for
children, while at the same time, helping the unin-
formed reader to develop awareness and appreciation
of others' qualities and contributions. Differences are
cherished rather than discouraged in the best of these
books. (Rudman, 1984, pp. 164–165)

THE IMPORTANCE OF ACCEPTANCE

We may accept the fact that each of us is a unique individual, different from anyone else on earth. This may make us feel good about ourselves . . . until we meet someone else. Often our first reaction is "How does this person feel about me?" It is the people around us, in fact, that become our principal yardsticks for measuring ourselves. How we are treated by our parents, our siblings, our teachers, our peers, tends to become the most important factor in determining how we feel about ourselves . . . our self-esteem.

Our differences or our likenesses to one another may partly influence the treatment we receive, but it is *the treatment* itself that is most significant. If we are accepted as one of the family, the neighborhood, or the class, then we feel good about ourselves. But if we are rejected, ignored, or ridiculed, then our self-esteem may plunge. Both children and adults feel the effects of acceptance or rejection, no matter how subtly communicated.

As teachers and caregivers of young children, we must make it our professional goal to accept each of the children in our class as a worthy human being, and show our acceptance by our actions. All of our children, no matter what their race, ethnicity, religion, social class, gender, economic situation, family background, physical or mental condition, deserve our full acceptance and respect. It is unethical for teachers to do otherwise.

The way we treat each child in our class or center affects not only that child's self-esteem, but also his or her treatment by peers. Children watch carefully how the teacher behaves toward the other youngsters. Does the teacher make a fuss over a pretty girl? Does he or she avoid a poorly dressed boy? Does he or she call on Hispanic children less frequently than

Caucasians, or seldom smile at African Americans? Or does the teacher beam at all the children and interact equally with each of them? The other children notice and take their cues from the teacher's actions, and behave that same way toward one another.

How is it with you? How do you feel toward the children in your program? Or for that matter, how do you feel about yourself?

ACCEPTING YOURSELF PERSONALLY

Before adults in the classroom can have a positive effect on the self-esteem of the children, they must feel good about themselves. What about you? What do you like about yourself as you are now? Think about it for a minute, and list some of your positive qualities: your features, your health, your sense of humor, the sound of your voice, the way you interact with children, your creative ideas for children's activities. What else? Can you respond positively to any of these qualities?

Now make another list. No, not your negative qualities, for that is not the way to bring about acceptance of yourself and others. Instead, make a list of qualities you would like to possess: an even temper, a more positive outlook on life, a way of getting along better with family members, better organizational skills. Put the two lists side by side and consider the things you might do to change items from the "qualities desired" list over to the "positive qualities" list. Try working on one item at a time and see what happens.

As you help the young children in your program to grow and develop, you can grow along with them. Teaching, as you may have discovered, is truly a reciprocal occupation. As you teach, you also learn. As you accept yourself, you also accept the children and help them to accept one another more positively. So start with yourself, and be as honest as you can in outlining your qualities. Then keep a check on yourself as you progress through the year. Are you growing and changing just as your children are? Are you better able to accept yourself and them?

ACCEPTING THE CHILDREN

In order for young children to accept themselves as worthy individuals in your classroom or center, they must first be accepted by you and your co-workers. Are they? Talk about it with your staff. Spend one of your early planning sessions listing the names of each child and what you and the others like about him or her. If anyone mentions not liking a child or not knowing anything positive to list about a child, have that person spend a few days informally observing the child and jotting down each positive action the child accomplishes. It can be quite ordinary things such as "hangs up her jacket" or "always says 'hi.'" Add these comments to the list at the next staff meeting and ask whether the staff member has changed his or her attitude toward the child.

Make "accepting each child" your most important goal for every staff member at the beginning of the year, because, as Asa Hilliard, African American university professor, notes, it is "that attitude of the educator toward diversity that creates problems in the education setting" (King, Chipman, & Cruz-Janzen, 1994, p. x). Hence, it is imperative that every staff member honestly examine his or her own attitude toward each child at the outset, so that necessary changes in attitude can be made.

It is not the differences in the children—their skin color, hair styles, clothing, or cultural background—that create most of the self-image problems in the early childhood classroom; rather, it is the attitude and treatment of the youngsters by those who interact with them. This treatment and those attitudes affect the development of the children's most important feelings about themselves, their self-esteem.

Young children look to you and your co-workers when they first enter your classroom. Most of their peers around them are strangers. They *all* look different to the new child, no matter what their race, culture, or background happens to be. They are, in fact, all different. Are all unique individuals who have come from their own families and their own neighborhoods to be a part of this group.

On the other hand, they are also all alike. They are all children with common bonds who have come to your program to grow and learn together. If you show your acceptance to each of these different-looking youngsters, if you treat each of them with equal respect, then the other children will follow your lead.

This means that you look at all of them as children, not as children with different racial characteristics, physical abilities, or psychological temperaments. It means that you do not make a fuss or do not point out to the others who has a white skin, black skin, or brown skin, or who has to wear a hearing aid or use a leg brace. If Jamie has a "bad temper" or Maria is "too shy to talk," you do not make statements about these differences. Instead, you accept each of the children as they are and help them to accept one another.

SHOWING YOUR ACCEPTANCE

In order for children to know they are accepted, you must show them that they are by the way you look at them, talk to them, and interact with them. Ask your co-workers how they show acceptance. Do any of them use any of the ideas presented in Figure 3.1? For instance, do they take care to call a child by his or her accurate name?

FIGURE 3.1 Developing Self-Esteem Through Acceptance

1. Accept yourself personally.
2. Accept each child as a worthy person.
3. Show your acceptance by:
   • Calling the child by his or her accurate name.
   • Making eye contact and smiling.
   • Greeting each child daily.
   • Having a personal conversation with each child daily.
4. Promote children's acceptance of themselves and of other children through picture book stories and activities.

Names

◆ *Angel Child, Dragon Child* (Surat, 1983)
◆ *Tikki Tikki Tembo* (Mosel, 1968)
◆ *Cleversticks* (Ashley, 1991)
◆ *Little Eagle Lots of Owls* (Edmiston, 1993)
◆ *Jafta* (Lewin, 1981)
◆ *Sabrina* (Alexander, 1971)

Of course, you and your co-workers call the children by their names, but do you pronounce each child's name correctly? Do you use the name or nickname the child hears at home? How does the child want to be called? Ask the child or ask his or her parent. Names are important to their bearers. Isn't yours to you? Young children, in fact, seem to believe that they *are* their names. It is often confusing for them to be in a class where more than one child has the same name. If you have more than one Shaneika or José in the group, ask them whether they would like to be called in a special way so they will know you are talking to them and not to someone else. As noted by Robert D. Morrow (1989):

> Most of us consider our name uniquely ours; we take pride in it and have preferences as to how we want to be addressed. Research suggests that our names have a strong influence on our self-image, which in turn affects how we function in life. (p. 20)

Children from most cultures are usually called by their given name rather than their family name. For teachers who are not familiar with a culture's language and customs, it is important to determine what that name is and how it should be pronounced. Ask the child or parent. Vietnamese names consist of three words in a particular order: the family name first, then the middle name, then the given name. A Vietnamese child is usually called by the given name, which is the third of the three names. For example, a child whose whole name is Nguyen Van Hai would be called Hai, or by a nickname.

Be sure to pronounce the name correctly, as well. Many Asian names are not pronounced the way English phonetics seem to indicate. For example, Nguyen is pronounced "new-yen." Ask the child or a family member how the child's name should be spoken.

Vietnamese given names are often carefully chosen to reflect the parents' aspirations for a child (Morrow, 1989, p. 20). However, children from large families may be given numerical names to make identification quicker. For example, children may be named Hai meaning "two," Ba, meaning "three," Tu meaning "four," or Nam meaning "Five" (Lewis & Roelen, 1982). Often there are also the personal nicknames that children may be called within the family.

The Vietnamese girl in *Angel Child, Dragon Child* (Surat, 1983) is called Nguyen Hoa (new-yen hwa) or Hoa by her American teacher, but she tells us in her narration that: "Hoa is my true name, but I am Ut. Ut is my at-home name—a tender name for smallest daughter."

Cambodians may have more than one given name, such as Sa Mol. Other Southeast Asian immigrants to the United States include people from Laos, whose names are usually made up of more than one syllable and written in the same order as American names. For example, Thongphoun Sourivong would be addressed by the given name Thongphoun, or by a shortened form of it, Phoun.

Another group of immigrants are the Hmong people from the hill country of Laos. Hmong children receive their given name in a ceremony three days after birth. They are called by that name (e.g., Sao) until they can socialize, and after that by their clan name (e.g., Thao), or in some cases still by their given name (Morrow, 1989, p. 22). Thus, it is important for early childhood classroom workers to find out how family members want their children and themselves to be addressed, since names are used in such different ways by different cultures. Teachers and other adults should never Anglicize children's names to make them easier to pronounce, nor give children nicknames.

The same respect for names should be afforded to all children in your class. Find out from family members how their children's American given names should be used, as well. Do not assume that a boy named James should be called Jimmy or that a girl named Candace should be called Candy. Ask and find out. Acceptance of a child's name is your first step toward acceptance of the child.

Children understand that names are important. They enjoy doing all sorts of activities that feature names, especially their own names. To get your children involved effortlessly in name activities, read them a name story about a child from another culture.

A light-hearted story about names is the classic Chinese folktale *Tikki Tikki Tembo* (Mosel, 1968), about a little Chinese boy with a name so long that it almost costs him his life. Being the first and honored son, this boy's whole name is: "Tikki tikki tembo - no sa rembo - chari bari ruchi - pip peri pembo," which means "the most wonderful thing in the whole wide world." His brother, being the second son, is called only Chang. While playing with their kites around an open stone well, first Chang falls in and is rescued, and then Tikki Tikki Tembo falls in. But it takes so long for his brother to say his tremendous name while calling for help, that he nearly drowns before Chang can persuade help to come. From that day on, Chinese children have been given little, short names.

Children enjoy sitting close to the teacher while the story is being read in order to see the Chinese folk-style illustrations, especially of the paper butterfly and bird kites the boys play with. This is an appropriate time for your children to make and decorate their own similar cutout paper kites to be flown on sticks or strings, as the Chinese boys did. The kites can be small in size for classroom use, or large for outdoor play. Some children may want to print their names on their kites in letters, or even scribbles if this is what they make.

Take time also to talk about folktales and legends. Tell the children that they are stories from long ago, and that today Chinese people dress and live differently. Folktales are kept alive by many people to help them remember their past and the lessons their ancestors wanted them to learn. As a balance, be sure to read a picture book with modern Chinese characters so that your children can visualize the difference between children from long ago and today.

This may be the time to read *Cleversticks* (Ashley, 1991) a story about a modern Chinese boy named Ling Sung who has trouble adjusting to his multi-ethnic American nursery school. He can't seem to do what the other children accomplish so easily, like fastening their jackets, putting on their paint aprons, or making the letters of their names, after which everyone claps. His chance to be recognized finally comes when he drops cookies by accident and picks them up Chinese fashion with two inverted paintbrushes used like chopsticks. The teachers and children alike want him to teach them how to do it. When his dad hears about his finally doing something that made the others clap, he calls him "Cleversticks."

To help make this story meaningful to your children, bring in several pairs of chopsticks for them to practice with. Put them in the housekeeping area along with the play silverware. On another day, have cracker pieces for snack, and provide enough chopsticks for each child to experiment with. Can any of the children pick up a cracker piece with chopsticks and put it in their mouth? Can you?

Names like "Cleversticks" may come to children because of something they do or say. On the other hand, children are sometimes given names that they don't really understand. In *Little Eagle Lots of Owls* (Edmiston,

1993), an old-time Native American story, a little Indian boy has a name "as long as it takes the moon to walk across the sky," says his grandfather, who decides to call him by the shortened form: Little Eagle. To help the boy remember his full name, his grandfather sends him the gift of a strange creature in a basket. Little Eagle turns the basket this way and that but can't figure out what it contains because the creature seems to be sleeping. Nothing he tries will wake the creature. But when the sun goes down, it suddenly comes to life as three fat owls that had been huddling together—the second part of Little Eagle's name.

As an extension activity to make this book meaningful, bring in a basketful of stuffed animal toys. Have children make up names for themselves according to what the basket contains. Make it a game that is fun for all.

African American names often reflect the people's unique heritage. According to Faulkner (1994), "three-syllable names beginning with *La* for girls are popular because they are soft-sounding" (p. 6). They may be names like Ladonna, Latasha, Latoya, or Lavonne. Two-syllable names beginning with *Ja* "are chosen for boys because they are strong-sounding" (p. 7). They may be Jamal, Jamon, Jareem, or Jafta. Of course, many children are named for someone in the family, or for an African American sports hero, television personality, or historically famous person. Faulkner also notes:

> *Parents in Africa and in the United States may name their children after a mountain range or a river or a city because the city means something special, or the river is important to the family.* (p. 72)

In Africa itself, the first-name tradition "looks at the circumstances surrounding the child's birth." In other words, the child is named according to what was going on in the world or in the community when he or she was born. What was happening within the home or with the parents is also sometimes a part of the naming. Finally, some names indicate what the parents hope the child will become (Faulkner, 1994, 78–79).

Three simple African stories about the little village boy named Jafta are done in brown-and-white, reflecting his strong masculine name. Your youngest children may get a good feel for village life and African mothers and fathers as they bond with Jafta in *Jafta, Jafta's Mother,* and *Jafta's Father* (Lewin, 1981). Afterwards, you can ask the children to pretend to be Jafta and to go around naming the various plastic or stuffed animals you have with African names. Be sure to have some African animals such as lions, hippos, rhinos, elephants, zebras, and giraffes available in the block area. You might also use animal puppets for this game.

An American name story that has characters with whom your children may want to bond with is **Sabrina** (Alexander, 1971). Sabrina is a Caucasian girl who doesn't like her name. When she goes to school the first day, the teacher calls the names of all the children in her multi-ethnic class. There are three Michaels, two Lisas, two Susans, a David, and an Amy—but no name as strange as Sabrina, she notes. When two little African American girls look at her and whisper, Sabrina is so unhappy she wants to cry. Before the week is out, Sabrina tells her teacher that she wants to change her name. But then she hears the two girls quickly say they'll take her "princess name," and suddenly her name sounds good to her, too.

Now is the time to make name cards for each of your children, perhaps as placecards for lunch or snack. Make the cards one at a time with the child beside you, and then have the children put their cards at their places at the lunch table. Another day put all the cards out on a table and have the children try to find their own names. It may be easier for the youngest children if you also place a different peel-off sticker on each card to give them a symbol as well as letters to look for.

Children also enjoy playing with computer name programs. *Early Games* (Queue, 1984) contains nine separate games, one of which is "Names." The child at the keyboard enters the letters of his or her name, presses "return," and then watches while the screen fills and flashes with highlighted versions of her name in different colors.

What other use can you make of young children's strong interest in their own names? Why not play name-guessing games, or make lotto cards for children to match with similar names, or sing name songs such as "Where Is Thumbkin?" substituting your children's names. Children also enjoy drawing names out of a hat for turn-taking with favorite toys or activities. Finally, you can substitute the names of storybook characters with your own children's names when it seems appropriate and not disrespectful of another culture.

We all have names that are a part of us. Accepting a person's name is the first step in accepting each of us as a worthy person.

Eye Contact and Smiles

◆ *Will You Come Back for Me?* (Tompert, 1988)

Another important way you and your co-workers can accept each of the children is by making eye contact with them and then smiling. These are nonverbal cues that tell children you really care about them. Some children are shy about strange, new adults when they first enter the classroom. Bend over or squat down so you are not towering over them. When they finally make eye-contact and see you smiling at them, it helps to diffuse their unsure feelings and lets them know you are happy to see each of them. Children, especially young children, can quickly tell how you feel about them by looking at you. Or as Dorothy Briggs says in her now-classic book *Your Child's Self-Esteem* (1970):

Mirrors create self-images. Have you ever thought of yourself as a mirror? You are one—a psychological mirror your child uses to build his identity. And his whole life is affected by the conclusions he draws." (p. 9)

What will your children see when they look at you? Smiles? Frowns? Sparkling eyes? Nonverbal cues like this are more powerful than words for young children—especially young children from other cultures who may not understand your words. Smiles speak a universal language of happiness.

On the other hand, things may be different at home. Some cultures teach their children that it is disrespectful to look an adult in the eye when they are being addressed. Traditional Hispanic people, for instance, may give such instruction to their children. If these children seem embarrassed to look at you, let them know that "it's okay at the center to look at the teachers." But don't make a fuss about it and embarrass the children further. They will soon come to recognize your friendly nature and feel good about your smiling at them.

Talk with their parents about such customs. Ask them how they expect their children to behave toward the teachers. Tell them what your expectations are. Let the parents know that their children will be learning American customs in school, if this is the case, but that their own cultures will still be respected and they can follow their traditional practices at home.

If the family is newly arrived in the United States and the parents do not understand English, they may be too proud to let the teacher know this. Try contacting the family's sponsor for help. Many Southeast Asian families, for example, have been sponsored by individuals, groups, or churches. Some Hispanic families have also been sponsored by friends, relatives, or churches. These sponsors can help if communication between home and school is not working well (Sholtys, 1989, p. 76).

Sometimes reading storybooks can help diffuse the situation for children new to the class. ***Will You Come Back for Me?*** (Tompert, 1988), mentioned in Chapter 1, is a tender story of an Asian American mother who takes her daughter Suki to visit a child care center for the first time. They stay only long enough the first day for Suki to see what is happening and for her mother to talk to the teacher. When they are ready to leave, the teacher bends over, looks Suki in the eye, and says, "I hope I'll see you soon." The story then describes Suki's fears about going to the center as expressed through her stuffed bear, Lulu. Her mother cuts out a big red paper heart to help Suki learn that her mother will really come back for her every day.

After reading the story, talk about it with your preschool children. It is a good way to help them express their own fears about starting school for the first time. They are often surprised to learn that other children feel the same way they do. In addition, invite parents or other family members to stay for a short time at the beginning of school if they or their children are experiencing separation anxieties. They will learn how you and your staff behave toward each of the children, and their children will learn how much you care for each of them and their families through your nonverbal cues such as eye contact and smiling.

For day care or preschool children who want to act out this story, have them pretend to be Suki and take their stuffed animals to preschool for the first time. Or have them choose one of the center's stuffed animals and talk to it about going to school for the first time, and what it will be like.

Greetings and Farewells

◆ *Rise and Shine, Mariko-chan!* (Tomoika, 1992)

◆ *Mcheshi Goes to the Market* (Jacaranda Designs, 1991)

◆ *Jambo Means Hello, Swahili alphabet book* (Feelings, 1974)

◆ *Where Are You Going Manyoni?* (Stock, 1993)

You will be expressing your acceptance of every child through greetings and goodbyes, as well. Young children from every culture learn best how others feel about them through nonverbal cues such as smiles, nods, and body language. But they also soon come to understand the words you use in greetings and goodbyes. Be sure that every child is included every day. If you miss a child by accident, you may not realize it, but the child will feel it. Keep a list of your children's names handy the first days of school and check them off to make sure each child has been greeted personally by you or one of the teachers. Then be sure to say goodbye to each child at the end of every day.

If you have recent immigrants to the United States in your program, you may want to greet these newcomers in their native language in order to have them feel more at home. Ask their parents or sponsors what to say. As noted by Browne, Howard, and Pitts (1984):

> *Developing esteem can begin for child and parent when first entering a group. When a refugee Vietnamese family enrolled Thuy (Twee) in the day care center, the caregiver greeted the parents and child each day in their native language: "chao ong" (cha/oo ohm) to the father, "chao ba" (cha/oo bah) to the mother, and "chao em" to the child. By showing affection toward the children and encouraging their mutual affection for each other, the caregiver communicates that each child is liked, and therefore, that each child should like himself.* (p. 2)

Many cultures use greetings and farewells in a more formal manner than Americans do. Sometimes a handshake, a nod, or a bow is part of the greeting. Your children may enjoy hearing about another culture and its method of greeting through your reading of a storybook such as **Rise and Shine, Mariko-chan!** (Tomoika, 1992). Little Mariko-chan, the youngest daughter in this Japanese family, enjoys greeting everyone with her cheery good-mornings and goodbyes as the family goes off to school and work. She stands by the door every morning to shake hands with her sisters as they leave for school. As her mother leaves for work, Mariko-chan links pinkies with her to remind her of her promise to bring home strawberries. And finally Mariko-chan runs over to her own school bus, singing her good morning song to the bus driver as loud as she can.

Your youngest children may want to try some of Mariko's greetings themselves. Or they can put on a brief role play of Mariko-chan saying "good morning" and "goodbye" to members of her family with figures of people from the block area. Be sure that your block people represent different races for the children to choose from. Children can choose any figures they want to represent Mariko-chan and her family.

Another book for the younger children is **Mcheshi Goes to the Market** (Jacaranda Designs, 1991), discussed in Chapter 2, a colorfully illustrated story used in the schools of Nairobi, Kenya, in Africa, but also distributed in the United States. The story is written in both English and Swahili. Try using both languages as you read it. But first have Mcheshi introduce herself: "Hello! My name's Mcheshi. What's your name? Today's market day and I'm going with my Mummy. Do you want to come with us?" Your children may be surprised to hear that Kenyans sometimes say their hello greeting almost the same way we do: "Halo!"

The entire story is told through the conversation of the two speakers, Mcheshi and her mother. As the story ends Mcheshi says goodbye to the egg man, the chickens, and the market with the Swahili word *kwaheri*. Try using this farewell yourself with the children on the day you read this story. How do they answer back to you?

If your children show an interest in learning more about the Swahili language, read them the Caldecott Honor Book **Jambo Means Hello, Swahili Alphabet Book** (Feelings and Feelings, 1974). It presents an African word for each letter of the English alphabet, along with its pronunciation, its meaning, and a double-page drawing from village life illustrating the meaning. The children will also enjoy learning the words "Hello", "Goodbye," "Please," "Thank you," "Yes," "No," and "Happy Birthday" from the tape cassette *Jambo, Hola, Hello! (Vol. 1)*, with greetings in ten languages: Cambodian, Cantonese, English, Farsi, French, Korean, Russian, Spanish, Swahili,

---

 Good source for multicultural speaking and music tapes:

Claudia's Caravan
Multicultural/Multilingual Materials
P. O. Box 1582
Alameda, CA 94501

> *Jambo, Hola, Hello! Volumes 1 & 2*, greeting tape cassettes

> *Jambo & Other Call Response Songs & Chants*, Ella Jenkins

and Vietnamese; or singing along with Ella Jenkins on her cassette *Jambo and Other Call Response Songs and Chants* from Kenya and Tanzania.

Another African story that is becoming popular with American children is **Where Are You Going Manyoni?** (Stock, 1993). Beautiful double-page illustrations show a slightly older African girl named Manyoni getting up, getting ready, and walking from her village in Zimbabwe across the ridge, through the wild fig trees, across the fever tree pan, past the red sandstone koppies, over the hot, dry plains until she finally reaches a village school. Then the first thing she does before the story ends is to greet her teacher: "Good morning, Mrs. Dube." Although African words are not used, your children should sit close to the reader of this book to view the detailed watercolor forests and plains that Manyoni crosses.

Can they find the little girl walking among the vegetation of the tropical forest? What about the animals? Can such a story motivate your children to tell their own detailed descriptions of getting up, getting dressed, eating breakfast, and trekking to their own school? They may want to record their stories on a cassette recorder. Then they can end each one with their own greeting to you. It might even be in Swahili!

Personal Conversations

◆ *Louie* (Keats, 1975)

Not only are the words of greetings and goodbyes important for all the children, whether or not they speak English, but you should also be sure that each child receives personal conversational attention from one of the teachers every day. What you talk about is not so important as the personal attention you bestow on each child with your friendly words. This is still another way to show that you accept the child. It is another important brushstroke in the picture of self-esteem you and the child are creating together.

If you feel there is not time enough to talk with each child, keep a list of their names handy and check off each youngster with whom you and your co-workers converse. It need not be a long conversation—just a few words are enough, perhaps about the interesting clothing or shoes the child is wearing, or how well the child worked on painting, block building, or number games. If your children stay for lunch, that is another opportunity for the adult at each table to carry on a brief conversation with each of the youngsters. Be sure your talk is not a quiz about what foods they like. Make it informal and fun just as you would with a friend you are having lunch with. Did you converse with every child on your list? If not, be sure to start the next day with any child who was omitted.

Talk with each child, whether or not he or she speaks English. The child will eventually learn the language, and in the meantime you can learn some words of the child's language. Through sign language and pointing you can always find a way to make yourself known. Try learning at least one new word from the child's language, as well. How does she say "shoes" in her language, for example? Learn her word as she learns yours, and then use the word in a conversation with her the following day. This is still another way you can show her that you accept her.

Conversation involves speaking and then listening while the other person speaks. Be sure you take your turn to listen to the child. Whether or not you understand what he is saying, it is polite to listen. It is not so polite to make him repeat his part of the conversation over and over until you get it. Just continue to chat until you do pick up a word or two that you can respond to.

When you are not used to hearing a particular child speak, sometimes the child's accent or babytalk make it difficult to understand him. You may need to practice listening closely to your children until you begin to pick up their words. They may need to do the same thing with you. This is part of the excitement that makes teaching and learning so fascinating. What new words or ideas did you learn from your children today? Different cultures and their unique child representatives should make your classroom a beehive of exciting conversations and activities.

If you have no children from different cultures in your class, it is more important than ever to involve the children in the storybooks and activities suggested in this text. Otherwise they will miss out on the stimulation that children from other cultures bring with them. Bring in posters and dolls from different cultures. Have the youngsters take on character roles from the books you read. Play tape cassettes of songs and languages from these cultures. All of our children need to be prepared for the multicultural America they will be living in as adults. (This issue is covered in greater depth in Chapter 7.)

Louie (Keats, 1975) tells the story of Louie, a nonverbal little boy who says his first word, "hello," in response to a puppet show that the multicultural neighborhood children put on. You may decide to read this story and then use a puppet yourself for children to talk to. Have two puppets, one for a child and one for yourself, and let them carry on a conversation. Shy children like Louie are sometimes able to talk through a puppet when they are afraid to express themselves directly.

As you plan your curriculum, especially at the beginning of the year, have your staff—and the children, too—help create a web of activities about names and greetings. An example is shown in Figure 3.2.

CHILDREN'S ACCEPTANCE BY OTHER CHILDREN

Whereas it is important that classroom adults show their acceptance of each child in the program, acceptance by the other children is even more crucial to a child's development of positive self-esteem. That is the true test of a child's self-worth, or so it seems to the child. Do the other children like

FIGURE 3.2 **Curriculum Web**

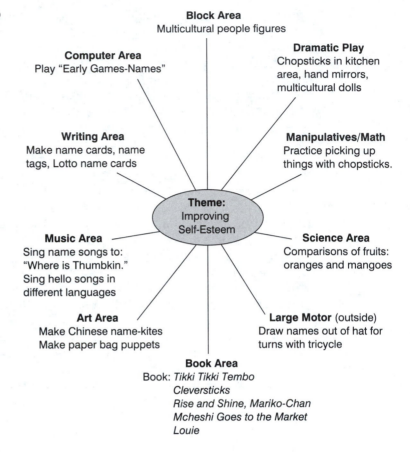

Block Area
Multicultural people figures

Computer Area
Play "Early Games-Names"

Dramatic Play
Chopsticks in kitchen
area, hand mirrors,
multicultural dolls

Writing Area
Make name cards, name
tags, Lotto name cards

Manipulatives/Math
Practice picking up
things with chopsticks.

Theme:
Improving
Self-Esteem

Music Area
Sing name songs to:
"Where is Thumbkin."
Sing hello songs in
different languages

Science Area
Comparisons of fruits:
oranges and mangoes

Art Area
Make Chinese name-kites
Make paper bag puppets

Large Motor (outside)
Draw names out of hat for
turns with tricycle

Book Area
Book: *Tikki Tikki Tembo*
Cleversticks
Rise and Shine, Mariko-Chan
Mcheshi Goes to the Market
Louie

the child? Will they play with her or him? Will they invite the newcomer into their group? Does skin color make a difference about whom children will play with?

As a teacher of young children, you need to consider these factors. You may wonder whether children as young as 3 years old are aware of differences in the race of other children. Cognitive psychologists have made the point that young children see things first in a general holistic way and later note specific details. For instance, they may recognize that Caucasians and African Americans look different, but not know exactly why at first. Early childhood specialist Ramsey (1987) points out:

> By age three to four, most children have a rudimentary concept of race and are quite accurate in the application of the socially conventional racial labels of black and white to pictures, dolls, and people. It is not known exactly when children first observe racial cues, but it is presumed to be early in the child's life. (p. 17)

Racial Attitudes of Children

However, teachers have found that it is not so much children's awareness or recognition of racial differences that has the most serious effect on children's self-esteem, but their *attitude* toward people of races different from their own. Researchers such as Katz (1976, 1983) have found that children acquire racial attitudes towards people in a developmental sequence such as that shown in Table 3.1.

All sorts of attitudes about people develop in children in much the same sequence. This does not mean that over time children become racist in their thoughts and actions. Children's attitudes about race are just as often positive ones, depending on how the significant persons around them respond to people of different races. If their parents, teachers, and caregivers react positively to people of every race and background, then most children will do likewise. The importance of Katz's "attitude sequence" to you should be that children's racial attitudes up to about age 7 are still not crystallized and rigid. Thus, your respectful behavior toward all of the children has a very significant effect on their own development of attitudes.

TABLE 3.1   Acquiring Racial Attitudes

Age	Attitudes
Infants and Toddlers 0–3 yrs.	Sometimes act with surprise when they see a person who is different racially from them.
Preschoolers 3–5 yrs.	Have a rudimentary concept about race. May repeat comments they hear about race. Do not understand meaning of such comments.
Early Elementary Children 5–7 yrs.	Clarify which physical characteristics belong to a particular race. Learn that racial characteristics are permanent in people.
Middle Elementary Children 7–10 yrs.	Develop concepts and feelings about their own and other races. Crystallize attitudes about race and become more resistant to change. Often reflect viewpoint of families and communities about race.

Source: Ramsey, P. G. (1991). *Making friends in school: Promoting peer relationships in early childhood.* New York: Teachers College Press, p. 55

Determinants of Friendship

◆ *Crow Boy* (Yashima, 1955)

Factors other than race seem to make more of a difference in determining whom young children will accept or reject as friends or playmates. Ramsey (1987) notes:

I found that, among children aged three through six, gender was a stronger determinant of friendship choice than was race. (p. 22)

Most teachers of preschool children will agree. Girls who band together in the housekeeping areas sometimes try to keep out a boy who tries to join them, while boys in the block area may try to prevent girls from entering.

It is also true that children of either gender or any race may find themselves rejected at first if they are newcomers to the program. If a new child acts like an outsider, he or she will often be prevented from joining in group play. It is not so much that the child may look different in skin color or clothing or speak a different language. Instead, it is the child's different behavior to which the other children respond, often in negative ways.

An outsider of any culture may be shy or withdrawn. If the child is a preschooler, he or she may not have previously developed the social skills for entering a new group. On the other hand, the new child may be more aggressive than the other children, using belligerence as a strategy to enter the group. Either way, the other children often close ranks against the newcomer.

Teachers, of course, can force the issue and insist that the children include the newcomer in their activities. But that does not mean the child will be accepted. There are subtle differences in what a teacher requires and how children actually respond to a child they do not know or have not accepted.

A better strategy on the teacher's part may be to let the child find his or her own way. Many preschoolers learn to socialize in groups in the manner observed by Mildred Parten (1932): by going through a progression of sequences from onlooker behavior to solitary play, then parallel play next to others, and finally to cooperative play with other children (pp. 248–251). In other words, children do better finding their own level of interaction with peers in the classroom. Preschoolers often play parallel to other children for weeks and even months before they are ready to interact in cooperative play.

Teachers can, however, help young children who seem to have trouble entering dramatic play with others by coaching them or playing a role alongside them when the time seems right. For instance, if Mariko does not know how to enter the housekeeping play with the others, but shows every indication that she would like to, you might say to her, "Mariko, shall we take our purses and go knock on Angela's door to see if she is home?" Most children enjoy having the teacher play a role with them, and will therefore accept a child partner that the teacher brings along. Once the play is proceeding smoothly, the teacher can unobtrusively withdraw.

With kindergartners, the teacher might suggest a child partner for the newcomer, who can help the newcomer become involved. It is sometimes overwhelming for a new child to enter an entire classroom full of strange children, but a single partner can help to break the ice.

There are a number of picture storybooks about children who have not been accepted by their classmates. Use your own judgment about reading them to the entire group, especially if you have one child that the others have not accepted, as it could be an embarrassment to the child. On the other hand, you might read such a book to a small group of children or individuals, and then discuss its implications. Leave the book in your library area for others to look at and talk about.

Crow Boy (Yashima, 1955) is a story from Japan about Chibi, the "tiny boy," who was afraid of the teacher and the other children and didn't seem to be able to learn anything. Year after year, Chibi was made fun of and left alone by everyone in the classroom and on the playground. Finally, Chibi's sixth-grade teacher took an interest in him because he knew about all the living things that the class visited on their field trips.

When it came time for the class talent show at the end of the year, everyone was amazed when Chibi participated. He imitated the voices of the crows that he heard every day on his long walk to school. He performed the voices of newly hatched crows, the mother and father crow, the way crows cried in the early morning, and how they sounded when they were happy and unhappy. His performance carried the audience with him in their minds into the country, the trees, and the sky. After that, no one ever called him Chibi again. From then on he was known and respected as someone very special: "Crow Boy."

After reading *Crow Boy*, put out animal hand puppets—several alike and one different—and ask who wants to play the roles of the Japanese children and who will be Crow Boy, the different one. They can play their parts like the story or any way they want. Can any of the youngsters imitate a crow?

CHILDREN'S ACCEPTANCE OF THEMSELVES

◆ *The Best Bug To Be* (Johnson, 1992)

◆ *Amazing Grace* (Hoffman, 1991)

◆ *I Want To Be* (Moss, 1993)

How well do children accept themselves in your classroom? This is the final measure of their self-esteem. If they feel good about themselves as worthy human beings, then they will be relaxed enough in the classroom to let go of their parents upon arrival, to let go of the adult staff, and to enter into the program activities without being urged. They may soon find friends among the other children and become a part of the group.

In a multicultural class like the one Mrs. Gonzales teaches in *The Best Bug To Be* (Johnson, 1992) the children try to outdo one another, as early

Good source for multicultural puzzles, flannelboard figures, dolls, block people, puppets:

Constructive Playthings
1227 East 119th St.
Grandview, Missouri 64030-1117

Multi-ethnic children (puzzles, flannelboard figures)

Multi-ethnic dolls (white, black, Hispanic, Asian, Native American)

Flexible Families (block people: white, black, Hispanic, Asian)

Multi-ethnic family puppets; worker puppets

elementary children often do. Kelly, an African American girl, wants to be the star of the school play, but she ends up as a lowly bumblebee, one of five. Her friend Megan, an Asian girl, is picked to play the cymbals in the ladybug band. Another friend, Sharon, is chosen to be Queen of the Butterflies, and just knows there will be a talent scout in the audience to sign her up for her own TV show. Robert is picked to be the only toad in the froggy pond, and he promises to give Kelly warts. Kelly finally accepts her minor role and decides to practice poses and buzzes. Then, on the night of the play, Sharon trips, Robert falls, and Megan drops the cymbals, but Kelly outdoes herself in a sparkling performance. Everyone has to agree that the role of the bumblebee is truly "the best bug to be."

Read the story to older children, but stop before the end to have them choose a pretend role for themselves. How would they handle the bumblebee role if they were Kelly? Does the story eventually turn out like they thought it would? If the children are interested in putting on their own bug play or dance, they can make bug hats out of construction paper like the ones in the book and try dancing to a recording of the "bug music" that you provide.

The moral to such a story is not always clear to young children. Do any of the youngsters understand that this story is about being the best you can be, no matter what your role? What would they like to be? The moral is the same for you and your co-workers: each child in the class can be "the best bug to be" if he or she chooses to. Your acceptance of them and their acceptance of themselves can make such outcomes possible.

Another story with a similar theme is the popular *Amazing Grace* (Hoffman, 1991), about an African American girl named Grace, whose Nana tells her thrilling tales about Joan of Arc, Anansi the Spider, Hiawatha, Aladdin, and many other heroes. Afterwards, Grace acts out the adventures, giving herself the most exciting part. When it comes time for the children in her class to try out for parts in their school play *Peter Pan*, Grace, of course, wants to be Peter. But the children in her multi-ethnic class are against it at first. Raj says she can't be Peter Pan because she's a girl. Natalie says she can't because she's black. Then Grace's Nana takes her to the ballet *Romeo and Juliet*, where she sees a wonderful black ballerina perform the role of Juliet. Afterwards, Grace gives a fantastic performance at the tryouts for the play, and gets everyone's vote as Peter Pan. As Nana tells her mother: "If Grace put her mind to it, she can do anything she want."

Your children will want to try out some of Grace's roles after they see the striking illustrations. Bring in props for the various roles shown in the pictures. Although Grace is older than a preschooler, even the youngest children are attracted to these exciting illustrations and gripping story. A cloth doll that looks exactly like Grace is also available from the publisher of the book. Your children can make up their own adventures for Grace as a doll.

Children can try out a character's role with dolls.

As a follow-up story, read to the children *I Want To Be* (Moss, 1993). In this book, several neighbors and friends ask the young African American girl narrator what she wants to be. Then, in poet Thylias Moss's words and Jerry Pinkney's full-page illustrations, the girl skips and twirls through page after page acting out her wishes: "I want to be tall but not so tall that nothing is above me. . . . I want to be green but not so green that I can't also be purple. . . . " And finally, "I want to be life doing, doing everything. That's all."

What do your children want to be? Can they be their own wonderful selves and still have dreams of being more and better? The time they spend in your classroom or center should inspire them first of all to accept themselves no matter who they are, and then go on from there with the confidence and self-esteem to become whatever they want to be.

◆ **Activities To Promote Self-Esteem** ◆

For the Teacher

1. List your own positive qualities.
2. Jot down positive things you see about a child to help change your attitude about the child.
3. Ask parents which name you should call their child.
4. Call children by accurate names and pronounce their names correctly.
5. Make name cards and name tags for each child.
6. Talk with parents about how they expect their children to behave toward adults.
7. Make eye contact and smile at each child.
8. Invite family members to stay for a short time at the beginning of school.
9. Talk with children about feeling like Suki in *Will You Come Back for Me?*
10. Greet each child every day.
11. Use the Swahili word for goodbye when your children leave.
12. Have a personal conversation with each child daily.
13. Listen and learn new words from children who speak another language.
14. Bring in posters, dolls, and tapes about other cultures.
15. Help a new child enter group play by playing a role with him.
16. Use puppets to converse with children as in *Louie*.

For the Children

1. Draw names from hat for turns.
2. Use chopsticks to pick up cracker pieces as in *Cleversticks*.
3. Play an animal naming game with a basket of stuffed animals, as in *Little Eagle Lots of Owls*.

4. Give African names to African animal toys or puppets after reading the *Jafta* stories.

5. Have children find their own name cards.

6. Play computer name games, sing name songs, use lotto name cards.

7. Pretend to be Suki bringing her stuffed animal to preschool for the first time.

8. Role-play Mariko-chan saying goodbye to her family using figures from the block area.

9. Learn Swahili words from books, language tapes, or songs.

10. After reading *Where Are You Going Manyoni?* record children's own stories about getting up, coming to school, and greeting the teacher like Manyoni.

11. Use animal puppets to reenact *Crow Boy*.

12. Put on a dance or play as in *The Best Bug To Be* and have children choose a bug to play.

13. Play roles with the Grace doll from *Amazing Grace*.

 ## LEARNING ACTIVITIES

1. List in two columns the personal qualities that you accept in yourself and those that you would like to possess. What can you do to acquire the desired qualities?

2. Make a list of the children in your class and after each write something positive about the child. If you have any blanks, observe that child and find something positive to list.

3. Talk to the children about how they got their names. Tell how you got your name. Can any of their family members visit the class and tell a naming story?

4. Are you able to make eye contact with each of your children? If not, might the problem be a cultural difference? Talk with a family member about how that particular culture teaches children to show respect for an adult. Record the results.

5. Make a list of expressions for saying hello and goodbye in other languages. Use some of them with the children. Can they tell you any others?

 ## REFERENCES

Briggs, D. C. (1970). *Your child's self-esteem.* Garden City, NY: Doubleday & Co.

Browne, G., Howard, J., & Pitts, M. (1984). *Culture and children.* Austin, TX: Texas Department of Human Resources.

Faulkner, B. (1994). *What to name your African-American baby.* New York: St. Martin's Press.

King, E. W., Chipman, M, & Cruz-Janzen, M. (1994). *Educating young children in a diverse society.* Boston: Allyn & Bacon.

Katz, P. A. (Ed.). (1976). *Towards the elimination of racism.* New York: Pergamon Press.

Katz, P. A. (1983). Developmental foundations of gender and racial attitudes. In R. L. Leahy (Ed.), *The child's construction of social inequality.* New York: Academic Press.

Lewis, M., & Roelen, G. (1982). *In-service handbook for educators of Indochinese students,* Costa Mesa, CA: Orange County Superintendent of Schools.

Morrow, R. D. (1989). What's in a name? In particular, a Southeast Asian name?" *Young Children, 44*(6), 20–23.

Parten, M.B. (1932). Social participation among pre-school children. *Journal of Abnormal and Social Psychology, 27,* 243–369.

Ramsey, P.G. (1987). *Teaching and learning in a diverse world.* New York: Teachers College Press.

Ramsey, P.G. (1991). *Making friends in school: Promoting peer relationships in early childhood.* New York: Teachers College Press.

Rudman, M. K. (1984). *Children's literature: An issues approach.* New York: Longman.

Sholtys, K. C. (1989). A new language, a new life. *Young Children, 44*(3), 76–77.

 ## ADDITIONAL READINGS

Barrera, R. M. (1993, March). Retrato de my familia; A portrait of my Hispanic family. *Child care information exchange,* 1993 (March), 31–34.

Buckleitner, W. (1993). *High/Scope buyer's guide to children's software.* Ypsilanti, MI: High/Scope Press.

Carter, M. (1993). Developing a cultural disposition in teachers. *Child Care Information Exchange, 3,* 52–55.

Fu, V. R. (1993). Children of Asian cultures, *Child Care Information Exchange, 3,* 49–51.

CHILDREN'S BOOKS

Names

Alexander, M. (1971). *Sabrina.* New York: Dial.

Ashley, B. (1991). *Cleversticks.* New York: Crown Publishers.

Bayer, J. (1984). *A my name is ALICE.* New York: Dial Books for Young Readers.

Caseley, J. (1991). *Harry and Willy and Carrothead.* New York: Greenwillow Books.

DePaola, T. (1983). *The legend of the bluebonnet.* New York: Putnam.

Edmiston, J. (1993). *Little Eagle Lots of Owls.* Boston: Houghton Mifflin.

Lester, H. (1986). *A porcupine named Fluffy.* Boston: Houghton Mifflin.

Lewin, H. (1981). *Jafta.* Minneapolis: Carolrhoda Books.

Lewin, H. (1981). *Jafta's Father*. Minneapolis: Carolrhoda Books.

Lewin, H. (1981). *Jafta's Mother*. Minneapolis: Carolrhoda Books.

Lund, J. (1993). *Way out west lives a coyote named Frank*. New York: Dutton.

Martin, B., & Archambault, J. (1986). *White Dynamite and Curly Kidd*. New York: Henry Holt & Co.

Mosel, A. (1968). *Tikki Tikki Tembo*, New York: Scholastic Publications.

Surat, M. M. (1983). *Angel child, dragon child*. New York: Scholastic Publications.

Greetings

Cooney, N. E. (1993). *Chatterbox Jamie*. New York: Putnam.

Corrigan, K. (1984). *Emily Umily*. Toronto, Canada: Annick Press.

Feelings, M. (1974). *Jambo means hello, Swahili alphabet book*. New York: Dial.

Keats, E. J. (1975). *Louie*. New York: Scholastic Publications.

Mcheshi goes to the market. (1991). Nairobi, Kenya: Jacaranda Designs.

Stock, C. (1993). *Where are you going Manyoni?* New York: Morrow Junior Books.

Tomoika, C. (1992). *Rise and shine, Mariko-chan!* New York: Scholastic Publications.

Tompert, A. (1988). *Will you come back for me?* Morton Grove, IL: Whitman & Co.

Self-Esteem

Carlson, N. (1988). *I like me!* New York: Penguin.

Hoffman, M. (1991). *Amazing Grace*. New York: Dial.

Johnson, D. (1992). *The best bug to be*. Upper Saddle River, NJ: Macmillan.

Little, L. J. (1978). *I can do it by myself*. New York: Crowell.

Marton, J. (1989). *I'll do it myself*. Toronto, Canada: Annick Press.

Minarik, E. H., & Abolafia, Y. (1992). *Am I beautiful?* New York: Greenwillow Books.

Moss, T. (1993). *I want to be*. New York: Dial.

Williams, V. B. (1983). *Something special for me*. New York: Mulberry Books.

Winter, S. (1993). *I can*. New York: Doring Kindersley.

Yashima, T. (1955). *Crow Boy*. New York: Viking.

 ## CHILDREN'S COMPUTER PROGRAMS

Queue, Inc.
338 Commerce Drive
Fairfield, CT 06434

Early Games (Apple, IBM, Mac)

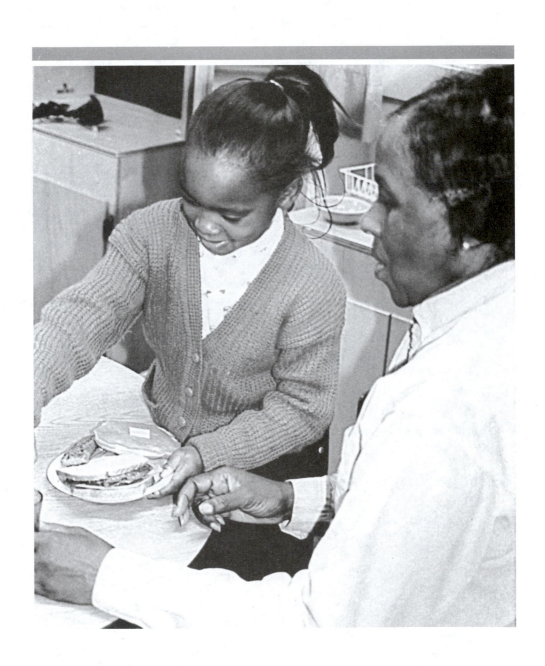

Relating to Family Members

4

All children are individuals with unique family backgrounds. . . . No child or family should be responded to
as part of a group—all are individuals with individual
needs. (Wardle, 1990, p. 44)

MULTICULTURAL FAMILY ROLE MODELS

Each child in your program comes first of all from a family, not a culture.
Each child looks first to someone in that family—a mother, father, grandmother, or other primary caregiver—as his or her most important role
model. That is the reason young children relate so well to picture books
about family members. They can easily identify with the characters in a
family setting because most of them are presently involved in such an experience themselves. When the books feature children and their families from
another culture, all children have the opportunity to put themselves in the
roles of the multicultural characters. As Ramsey (1987) has noted:

By involving the children with characters and situations that they can identify with, books increase children's appreciation of other ways of life and
help them see unfamiliar people as individuals. (p. 69)

This means you will want to fill your books shelves with stories featuring
various multicultural children interacting with mothers, grandmothers,
fathers, grandfathers, sisters and brothers, uncles, aunts, and cousins. The
cultures they represent may be very different from one another, but the family members will be most familiar. Starting with "mothers," let's look at
what popular picture books can show young children about this important
role in different cultures.

Mothers
◆ *Mama, Do You Love Me?* (Joose, 1991)
◆ *On Mother's Lap* (Scott, 1972)
◆ *On a Hot, Hot Day* (Weiss, 1992)
◆ *Tucking Mommy In* (Loh, 1987)
◆ *Laney's Lost Momma* (Hamm, 1991)

Children from every culture feel closer to Native Americans after experiencing this book.

In the vibrantly illustrated story *Mama, Do You Love Me?* (Joose, 1991), a little Inuit (Eskimo) girl challenges her mother with the title question, but then presses on with question after question ("How much? How long? and What if I . . . ?") to test the limits of her mother's love. For each question the girl asks, the daughter and mother are shown clothed in bright, home-sewn dresses—a different one for every question. Each answer involves the birds, mammals, and fish of the Arctic, some of them draped in colorful blankets as well.

Read this simple story to a few children at a time so they can see the pictures and try to put themselves in the same situation. Bring in blue, purple, red, and green dresses of large and small sizes, and ask your listeners to match the dresses in the book with ones you have brought. Would they like to put them on and play the roles of mother and daughter? Bring several small blankets, too, and perhaps a fake fur cape, so that children can pretend to be the animals, as well. Let the children act out the parts as you read the story. Can one of your children wrap up in white as the polar bear, become "the meanest bear you ever saw," and scare the mother with his sharp teeth? You can calmly reply in the mother's words of unconditional love: "Still, inside the bear, you would be you, and I would love you."

Not only does such a book demonstrate mother love at its finest, but it also depicts people in a very different culture from mainstream America expressing these universal sentiments. Children of every race and background can feel closer to the Native Americans of the north because of it. If you are prepared with props and dress-up clothes as suggested, some of your children may make this their favorite story by acting out the roles again and again. They may even make up their own game of Mama Do You Love Me?, asking their own "what if I. . . . ?" questions. For example, "What if I turned into a spider—would you still love me?"

Another way to help children bring this story into their own lives is through dolls or puppets. An Inuit girl doll made to look exactly like the book character holding her own little Inuit doll is available commercially. Or children can pretend by using their own dolls. Because stories present concepts in an abstract way, young children need to convert them into concrete, three-dimensional representations, with themselves performing the actions, to make the stories meaningful.

As you can see, this is not just another unit on Eskimo life. Instead, the book and activities focus on a mother's love for her child, a common bond most of us share no matter where we live or which culture we come from. For children 3 to 5 years old, this is enough. They begin to understand that people who fish from skin boats called *umiaks* and wear snow boots called *mukluks* also have mothers who love them. For teachers of young children, it is a topic that can easily be incorporated into a unit on "the family," often at the beginning of the year.

Can boys also experience unconditional love from multicultural mothers, you may wonder? If gender is more important than race to these youngsters, as discussed in Chapter 3, then you need to have books on hand with a balance of both girl and boy characters. In **On Mother's Lap** (Scott, 1972), a little Inuit boy named Michael wants his mother to rock him while baby lies quietly on a bed nearby. But then Michael hops off Mother's lap to get Dolly to join them in the rocking chair. In another minute he stops the

 Good source for multicultural dolls:

Demco's Kids & Things
Box 7488
Madison, WI 53707

Culture Kids dolls

Mama Do You Love Me?
(book and doll)

rocking to get Boat, then once again to get Puppy, and finally to get his reindeer blanket. It is really a test of the breadth of his mother's love, similar to the girl's in *Momma, Do You Love Me?*

Then when Baby starts crying and Mother wonders if she'd like to rock, too, Michael demurs saying, "There isn't room." "Let's see," counters Mother as she swoops them all up together: Michael and Baby and Boat and Dolly and Puppy under the reindeer blanket on Mother's lap. It is important for Michael to learn that there is always room for everyone on Mother's lap.

Children of either gender can role-play this story, too, if you have a rocking chair in the book area. Put a collection of dolls, stuffed animals, and toys in the area, and let children take turns being Michael in the rocking chair. Every time he stops rocking he can pick up one more item. How many can he hold? If he uses a blanket can he add just one more?

Hispanic mothers also display deep caring for their children, as shown in *On a Hot, Hot Day* (Weiss, 1992). In this story, a mother looks out of her apartment window onto a city street lined with stores such as El Bodegero, the grocery store, and Pepe's Luncheonette. She takes her child Angel down on the street in every season of the year, telling him to think cool in the summer, sip slow from the hot chocolate in Pepe's Luncheonette in the fall, bundle up in the winter, and breathe deeply the breezy air of spring.

Whatever the weather when you read this story, take the children for a walk around the building and have them also think cool, or bundle up, or breathe deep. Then bring them back inside for a slow sip of hot chocolate or cold lemonade. Have them tell how they felt as they were doing these things.

Sometimes family roles are reversed. In *Tucking Mommy In* (Loh, 1987), a hard-working Asian mother comes home one night exhausted. Because Mommy is "too tired to think," daughter Sue volunteers to tell the bedtime story after Mommy has tucked in Sue and her sister Jenny. But it is Mommy who falls asleep on Jenny's bed during the story, and the two girls who end up tucking her in and telling the story one more time. Can one of your children pretend to be Mommy and fall asleep on the pillows of your book area? Then have someone volunteer to be Sue and tell a bedtime tale while everyone listens. If this activity catches on, have other children take these roles and tell another story. Someone may want to pretend to read a story from one of the book area books, as well.

In another role reversal, or so it seems, *Laney's Lost Momma* (Hamm, 1991) is nowhere to be found in the department store where she and Laney are shopping. Frantically the little African American girl looks everywhere, and finally remembers that Momma told her to go to someone who works behind a counter if she ever needs help. It is the shoe department clerk who eventually locates Momma, who has also been searching frantically for her little lost girl.

Besides showing a mother and daughter's concern for one another, this story is an excellent lead-in to a discussion on what to do if anyone gets lost. Have children tell what rules their mothers have made about what they should do or how to find help. Read the story again before you take the children on a city field trip. As African American educator Walter Gill (1991) declares:

> *Mothers teach. The impact minority mothers and grandmothers have, and can have on children is immeasurable. These sacred women, traditionally, have been about survival. Their spiritual and functional energy should be experienced and acted out more by minority youth because these women teach survival and lifelong learning skills.* (p. 120)

Whoever hears and sees these picture-book stories about mothers and grandmothers from different cultures will also understand that these women function from a common ground of love, concern, and protection for their children. As your children identify with the characters in these stories, they begin to understand that mothers and grandmothers everywhere are very much like their own.

Grandmothers

◆ *Halmoni and the Picnic* (Choi, 1993)

◆ *Two Pairs of Shoes* (Sanderson, 1990)

◆ *Abuela* (Dorros, 1991)

Grandmothers of every background and ethnic group also love their grandchildren. Your picture books can reflect this concept as a common bond across all cultures. Most of the stories portray these women sharing their love and wisdom with their grandchildren. A few books show a reciprocal sharing: that is, a grandchild helping the grandmother feel at ease. This is the case in **Halmoni and the Picnic** (Choi, 1993), about a Korean grandmother who immigrates to New York City and finds it difficult to adjust. Halmoni's granddaughter Yummi invites her to come along on a school picnic in Central Park. When the children taste the delicious Korean *kimbap* the grandmother has prepared, they take her into their games, their songs, and their hearts. Although this book is for older children (kindergarten and above), preschoolers can enjoy the pictures in this story, and teachers can tell them what is happening without reading the long text.

In **Two Pairs of Shoes** (Sanderson, 1990), Maggie's Native American grandmother, her Kokum, is blind but can "see" very well by touching. She feels Maggie's new patent leather shoes, and then asks Maggie to get out the "special box" under her bed. In it Maggie finds a pair of wonderful beaded moccasins that her Kokum has made for her. How could she have beaded the shoes in such beautiful flower designs when she couldn't see? Your children can cover their own eyes and feel the shoes you have brought in. Can they tell what the shoes look like by touch alone?

Abuela (Dorros, 1991) is a Hispanic grandmother in New York City who takes her granddaughter Rosalba all around the city to see the sights—at first by bus, but then by imagination. On this particular day they go to the park. The grandmother speaks a line of Spanish on almost every page, and Rosalba translates as she narrates the tale. They do ordinary things like feeding the pigeons, but then Rosalba's imagination takes them off into an extraordinary adventure. What if the pigeons should pick them up and carry them high over the park? she wonders. In the next scene, Rosalba and Abuela are flying free over the park, then the city, and finally across the harbor to the Statue of Liberty. Full-page illustrations show tiny detailed people in the windows of colorful buildings and on busy sidewalks below, joyously pursuing everyday living. It is an entirely different perspective of life in a large city. "Vamos a otra aventura," declares Abuela on the last page. She wants to go on another adventure, and that's what Rosalba loves about her grandmother.

USE OF DOLLS TO FACILITATE BONDING

Your children may want to take an imaginary adventure, too, if you have planned for it. Bring in multicultural child dolls like those available in the set called Culture Kids. Realistic cloth dolls with ethnic hair styles, skin colors, and bright clothing that reflect their heritage are exciting for young girls and boys alike to play with. These 13-inch dolls represent girls from France, China, Italy, United States (African American), and a boy from Australia.

Some psychological research seems to indicate that young children from all backgrounds prefer to play with white-skinned dolls (Hopson & Hopson, 1993, p. 12), supposedly because they see the white culture as the dominant one. Children, however, often respond differently in real-life play situations than they do when they are being tested by psychologists. Whatever the case, we must be sure that multi-ethnic dolls are available in every classroom. Try these Culture Kids dolls with your children and watch what happens.

The youngest children like dolls of any kind. Just as racial features do not seem to matter much in their choice of classroom playmates at this age, 3- and 4-year-olds will choose almost any doll to play, with no matter what their race or the doll's skin color. Five-year-olds begin to select more realistic dolls to go with the stories they are hearing. For *Abuela*, they may well choose the Hispanic doll from the Culture Kids set who looks like Rosalba with her white blouse, colorful skirt, and black hair.

Be sure to have a number of dolls of different skin colors, whether or not your classroom contains multicultural children. This is another important method for integrating cultural material into the curriculum. As young children play with dolls of different races, they are subconsciously learning to accept children from these different races, as well.

Book character dolls help children extend the book experience through pretending.

Most school supply companies now stock multicultural baby dolls, realistic child dolls in ethnic costumes, as well as doll-house and block-building figures of men, women, and children with Caucasian, Hispanic, African American, Native American, and Asian American features. Boys as well as girls should be encouraged to play with them. As Frank and Theresa Caplan (1974) note:

> *Dolls should be freely played with by boys without adult snickering or criticism. Homemaking play in childhood and housekeeping in adulthood require interchangeable participation of both female and male members of the family.* (p. 224)

If you are reading *Abuela* to a small group, have one of your listeners at a time pick a doll and then pretend to be Abuela with her little granddaughter doll, soaring over the classroom. Have them hold the doll high like a plane as they fly over every curriculum area, and then return to the book area to tell the others what they saw from so high above. Record the stories on a cassette player so children can replay their adventure later. Some may tell a realistic story about Ramon piling up blocks in the block area or Becky putting the dolls to bed in the housekeeping area. Others may fill in with imaginary details of visiting their fathers at work, as Rosalba does in the story. Use a Hispanic people figure from the block area if you do not have a Culture Kids doll.

Some children may not want to participate. They can be the audience for the others. Never force a youngster to take part in an activity they are uncomfortable with. The fun and enthusiasm of the others may eventually convince unsure children to try this new experience themselves.

CREATING A CURRICULUM WEB BASED ON A STORYBOOK THEME

A book like *Abuela* (or any of the books mentioned) can lead into an entire curriculum of activities. Look through this story page by page and see what topics emerge. Then try arranging your ideas on a curriculum web like the one in Figure 4.1.

FIGURE 4.1   Curriculum Web

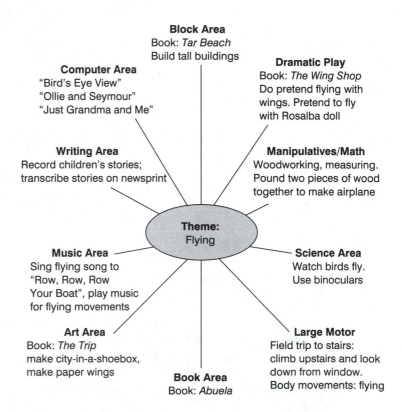

Block Area
Book: *Tar Beach*
Build tall buildings

Computer Area
"Bird's Eye View"
"Ollie and Seymour"
"Just Grandma and Me"

Dramatic Play
Book: *The Wing Shop*
Do pretend flying with wings. Pretend to fly with Rosalba doll

Writing Area
Record children's stories;
transcribe stories on newsprint

Manipulatives/Math
Woodworking, measuring.
Pound two pieces of wood together to make airplane

Theme: Flying

Music Area
Sing flying song to
"Row, Row, Row
Your Boat", play music
for flying movements

Science Area
Watch birds fly.
Use binoculars

Art Area
Book: *The Trip*
make city-in-a-shoebox,
make paper wings

Large Motor
Field trip to stairs:
climb upstairs and look
down from window.
Body movements: flying

Book Area
Book: *Abuela*

Following are some curriculum topics from *Abuela*:

Traveling by bus.
Visiting a park.
Feeding the birds.
Flying with birds.
Watching the children in a park below.
Looking down at city streets and buildings.
Racing with sailboats.
Watching men on ships unload fruit.
Visiting the Statue of Liberty.
Visiting an airport.
Visiting uncle's store.
Resting in grandmother's arms.
Looking at father in his office.
Getting in a boat on the lake.

The topics seem to center on the idea of flying over a city and looking down on buildings and people below. It is such a different perspective that it can easily attract the children's attention. What can they see if they are up high and look down? Let them try it by going on field trips to different high locations and looking down. If you are in a multi-story building, take small groups upstairs one at a time and have them look out a window. How is it different from being at the ground level? Take a camera and tape recorder along to capture the moment.

What other books do you know that feature this same imaginative topic? Read such stories in various curriculum areas on different days to stimulate children's participation in activities. *Tar Beach* (Ringgold, 1991), mentioned in a previous chapter, is about a little African American girl named Cassie who picnics on top of her New York apartment building in the summer and flies in her imagination over the city. A wonderful cloth doll of Cassie is also available from the publisher. The Hispanic boy Louie in *The Trip* (Keats, 1978) takes his friends on an imaginary ride over the streets of Manhattan on his little red airplane. Your children can make his plane in the woodworking area. Older children can enjoy Matthew, the Caucasian boy who doesn't like where he has moved, and who finally flies to his old location with imaginary wings from *The Wing Shop* (Woodruff, 1991). Can your children also make wings?

Computer programs can support your theme, as well. For older children, *Bird's Eye View* (Hartley, 1987) shows bird scenes and asks children to choose which view the bird sees from its location. In *Ollie and Seymour* (Hartley, 1984), children use an arrow key to move Ollie around a park and through street scenes as shown from above. Don't forget grandma as your

Good sources for computer programs:

Broderbund Software
500 Redwood Boulevard
P. O. Box 6121
Novato, CA 94948-6121

> *Just Grandma and Me* (1992;
>   CD-ROM)

Hartley Courseware
133 Bridge
Dimondale, MI 48821

> *Bird's Eye View* (1987; Apple,
>   IBM)

> *Ollie and Seymour* (1984; Apple)

ideas expand. *Just Grandma and Me* (Broderbund, 1992) is an interactive CD-ROM story about a little boy getting on the bus and going to the beach with his grandma. Although these two do not fly, they become involved with 10–20 animated objects in each scene which your children can activate by clicking a computer mouse. The program is available in English, Spanish, and Japanese (Buckleitner, 1993).

One thing leads to another in an early childhood classroom. You can begin to be prepared if you brainstorm ideas with your staff and outline them on a curriculum web.

If some of your children do not have grandmothers close at hand, invite retired persons from the community to visit your program to read a story or sing a song with the children. Perhaps your class can become involved with a Foster Grandparents Program or RSVP (Retired Senior Volunteer Program) that will place a volunteer grandparent in your center or class on a permanent basis.

Fathers

◆ *At the Crossroads* (Isadora, 1991)

◆ *Hue Boy* (Mitchell, 1993)

◆ *Friday Night Is Papa Night* (Sonneborn, 1970)

◆ *The First Pink Light* (Greenfield, 1976)

◆ *The Best Time of Day* (Flournoy, 1978)

◆ *Carousel* (Cummings, 1994)

◆ *Daddy* (Caines, 1977)

Fathers should play as important a role as mothers in the family, so that children will grow up with a male as well as a female role model to emulate. Unfortunately, many single-parent families today contain only a mother as head of household. Be sure, then, to have available numerous stories about fathers and their children from many cultures.

"Waiting for daddy," seems to be the most common theme across all cultures found in children's picture books. Many of these daddies are at work during the day, during the week, or sometimes for many months at a time. We have already met, in Chapter 2, the South African fathers coming home from working in the mines who meet their children in *At the Crossroads* (Isadora, 1991). *Hue Boy* (Mitchell, 1993), the little Caribbean boy who doesn't seem to grow, suddenly feels taller when he meets his papa coming home after a long sea voyage.

Pedro, the little Hispanic boy in *Friday Night Is Papa Night* (Sonneborn, 1970) waits up all night for his father, who is delayed coming home from his week of work. The youngster is the only one still awake when his father finally returns, and is rewarded by his father declaring: "My Pedro was at the door waiting for me. And suddenly I was not tired any more."

Tyree, the little African American boy in *The First Pink Light* (Greenfield, 1976) is determined to stay up all night until his daddy comes home at daybreak after being away for a month. In *The Best Time of Day* (Flournoy, 1978), another African American boy, William, goes through an entire day of activities before his favorite time rolls around: when daddy comes home from work.

If this is a favorite theme with your children as well, they may want to reenact one of these stories. Bring in father-type clothes for them to dress up in: jacket, vest, hat, pants, shirt, and briefcase or bag. Have the children take turns playing the roles of the father, the children waiting for him to come home, and the mother. Children who do not have a role can be the audience. As you read the story, the role-players can act it out in any way they want. Repeat the reenactment as many times as you have characters who want to play a role.

What about girls? Aren't they concerned about their fathers, too? Of course. They can also play the role of a child waiting for daddy. Or they can be a particular character such as Alex, the 5-year-old girl in *Carousel* (Cummings, 1994) who is so upset over her father's absence from her birthday party that she accidently breaks the little carousel toy he has sent her. That night she dreams that the carousel animals have come to life. In the morning she awakes to find her father home.

Your children may want to reenact this story with hand puppets. Hot-pad gloves come in all sorts of animal heads, including the giraffe, elephant, frog, and zebra from Alex's carousel. The African American doll from the Culture Kids set makes a perfect Alex. Have different children put on each of the gloves while one takes the role of Alex with a doll. The child who plays Alex can be from any culture, not just African American. In this way, children not only bond with the book character, but also come to recognize the common bonds of all children everywhere.

Some fathers have remarried and live with other families. That is the case with *Daddy* (Caines, 1977), who comes to get his little African American girl, Windy, every Saturday and take her over to his apartment for the weekend. There they play their pretend games together and with daddy's new wife, Paula. They go shopping, cook, and finally come home again on Sunday. Windy knows she'll see her daddy next Saturday, but each time before he comes she gets "wrinkles in her stomach." This may be a story to talk about with the children rather than reenact. Children of every culture find it difficult when the parents they love live apart.

Grandfathers

◆ *When I Am Old with You* (Johnson, 1990)

◆ *Storm in the Night* (Stolz, 1988)

◆ *Knots on a Counting Rope* (Martin & Archambault, 1987)

◆ *Grandpa's Town* (Nomura, 1991)

◆ *Pablo's Tree* (Mora, 1994)

A little African American girl's feelings for her granddaddy come through with great poignancy in *When I Am Old with You* (Johnson, 1990), as she sits next to him in their two rocking chairs to reminisce about the things they have done together. Every page shows the two of them in a different scene: fishing from a canoe, playing cards under a tree, looking through a trunk in the attic, roasting corn over a fire, and visiting the ocean. She looks up at her granddaddy when she has finished talking, but he is sound asleep.

Thomas, an African American boy, sits next to his grandfather too, in *Storm in the Night* (Stolz, 1988), but they are in the dark because the storm has put out the lights. It is Grandfather who is the storyteller in this tale: a story of when he was a boy Thomas's age during a storm in the night. This book is full of sound words—the *ping ping* of the chiming clock, the *ticki ticki* of the kitchen clock, and the *bong bong* of the church bells— because you can hear better in the dark. This is also a story about fear: of the dark and of the storm. When the lights finally do come on, Thomas and his grandfather turn them off and go to bed. Have your children cover their eyes and listen. Can they hear better with their eyes closed? What do they hear?

Both of these are also good stories to help your children feel what it was like when they were younger, or will be like when they will be older. Can they do it? Can they tell their own stories about what they were like when they were little? Can they imagine what it will be like when they are as old as their grandfathers? How will people get around? Will there be cars? What will people eat? Where will they live? What will they wear? Will they have grandchildren? Listening to the children's remembrances and imaginings can give you a better idea of their understanding about life as it is today. It will also help them and you to understand the common bonds we all have with grandfathers in every culture. Tape-record the stories they tell, and later transcribe them onto newsprint or into their own personal books.

Bonding with the Navajo boy who talks with his grandfather in *Knots on a Counting Rope* (Martin & Archambault, 1987) will take courage and resourcefulness on your children's part, for the boy is blind. He urges his grandfather to tell him one more time the story of his birth and how he got the name Boy-Strength-of-Blue-Horses. Dark canyon nights turn to dazzling days when the boy finally gallops bareback across the finish line in the tribal day horse race. "You have raced the darkness and won," says his grandfather, and ties another knot in the storytelling counting rope.

Can your children close their eyes this time and remember what is in the room around them without looking? Can they walk around the story area with their hands over their eyes without bumping into things? What do they think about the grandfather's words to his grandson: "You can now see with your heart, feel a part of all that surrounds you"?

Grandpa's Town (Nomura, 1991) will take your listeners across the sea to Japan, where a Japanese grandfather and his grandson Yuuta go to the public bath together. There they meet the fish store man, the vegetable man, the bathhouse attendant, the tatami-mat maker, the cabinetmaker, and the man from the plate-glass store. Illustrations help bring this unique culture to life. But the problem of an elderly person living alone is the same everywhere. Yuuta and his mother are trying to persuade the grandfather to leave his town and move in with them. In the end, he stays where he is, and Yuuta comes to understand that his grandpa is not really alone after all.

Read this story to one or two children at a time so they are close enough to see the pictures of Japanese life. Do they notice the Japanese writing on the side of every page? Do they think that the grandfather made the right decision to stay in his town? Do any of your children have grandfathers who live nearby? Perhaps they can visit the program and read one of these grandfather stories. If not, ask a Foster Grandparents program to lend you a grandfather.

Pablo's Tree (Mora, 1994) concerns the close relationship between a little Hispanic boy and his grandfather. When his newly adopted baby grandson is brought home, the grandfather buys a tree and decorates it with a different surprise every year on the boy's birthday. On this, his fifth birthday, Pablo goes with his mother to spend the night at grandfather's to see the new birthday decorations and reminisce about his other four birthdays around the tree.

This story is an excellent lead-in to an art project in which children make cut-paper decorations and hang them on their own "Pablo's tree" in the classroom. The tree can be a large tree mural on a bulletin board with the decorations stapled on, or a bare tree branch set in a planter. Leave the tree standing so that every time the children celebrate a birthday you can read them this story and have them hang a cutout number on the tree showing their name and age.

Brothers and Sisters

◆ *Do Like Kyla* (Johnson, 1990)

◆ *I Need a Lunch Box* (Caines, 1988)

◆ *Jamaica Tag-Along* (Havill, 1989)

It is somewhat easier for children to bond with a character who is closer to their own age. These next stories show brothers and sisters from different cultures interacting with one another within their families.

In ***Do Like Kyla*** (Johnson, 1990), a 3-year-old African American girl and her big sister, Kyla, spend a winter day together, from waking up until night time. The little narrator tells what her sister does on every page as they get dressed, eat breakfast, go to the store, walk in the snow, come home, and finally go to bed. She does exactly what Kyla does in every instance until bedtime, when she taps goodnight on her window to the birds below, and Kyla does the same.

This is a follow-the-leader story that you can easily act out together. Have someone in your small reading group be Kyla, the leader, and go around the room picking up and putting down toys, tapping on things, taking giant steps, sitting down and standing up, or any other appropriate motion. The others can follow, one behind the other, making the same motions as they go. This activity should be done in small groups; if you try to involve the whole class at once, the children at the end of the line often become confused because the leader is performing a new motion before they get to do the old one.

A miniature version of follow-the-leader can be done with block people figures. Have each child choose a block person and take turns being Kyla as she leads the parade of little people around the block area, making various motions that others can follow.

In ***I Need a Lunch Box*** (Caines, 1988), the littlest child is an African American boy who feels bad when his big sister, Doris, gets a new lunch box because she is starting first grade. But Mommy says no lunch box for him until he goes to school. He looks at lunch boxes in the store, all in vain. He even dreams of lunch boxes—a different one for every day in the week. In the end, as Mommy hands Doris her full lunch box for school, Daddy has a surprise for the little brother: his own lunch box.

Before you read this story, be sure to have enough empty shoe boxes for every child in the class. Parents can help you collect them ahead of time. After looking at the pictures of the imaginary lunch boxes that this boy dreams up, put out shoe boxes for your small reading group along with colored construction paper, scissors, glue, peel-off stickers of all kinds, and markers. A basket of collage materials can also add to your children's own creative lunch box inventions. This is also the time for a picnic on the playground, with lunch boxes full of sandwiches, fruit, cheese, and crackers that the children helped to prepare.

Not every brother-sister relationship goes so smoothly. In *Jamaica Tag-Along* (Havill, 1989), one of the popular Jamaica books, a little African American girl named Jamaica wants to play basketball in the park with her bigger brother, Ossie, but he won't let her. She ends up building a castle in the park sandpile, but a little Hispanic boy, Berto, begins to bother her. When she shoos Berto away, his mother tells him that big kids don't like to be bothered by little kids. This strikes a familiar chord with Jamaica, and soon she has Berto helping her build the biggest sand castle ever. She even lets Ossie join them when he has finished playing basketball.

Can your children respond to this common conflict among big and little kids? What do they do when they are prevented from tagging along? Do they ever stop smaller children from playing with them? How do they think the children feel? What other kinds of things can cause hurt feelings? If this discussion strikes a common chord with the children, perhaps they can make up a group tag-along story that you can record on a newsprint pad as they tell it.

Families With Adopted Minority Children

◆ *Angel Child, Dragon Child* (Surat, 1983)

◆ *Through Moon and Stars and Night Skies* (Turner, 1990)

◆ *We Adopted You, Benjamin Koo* (Girard, 1989)

◆ *If I Ran the Family* (Johnson & Johnson, 1992)

An increasing number of families have adopted children from other cultures or countries. This is especially the case with children from Asia. Early childhood programs need to be aware of such families in order to lend their support both to the children and their parents. As noted by Wardle (1990):

> *Minority children who are foster or adopted children in White homes have very special needs. Programs must respond to them and to those of the parents, who bring strengths, diversity, and opportunities to the program.* (p. 44)

Support can be in the form of encouraging adoptive families to endorse their child's national origin and cultural background. Your program can help parents find information about the child's country of origin to help them give the culture's unique language, food, and customs a place in their family. Perhaps they can join a support group for adoptive parents or a church group that sponsors families from other countries. You also can learn more about the culture. What beliefs and values does it emphasize?

The Vietnamese, for example, respect authority and age, teaching their children to be polite and obey their elders. The family is considered more important than an individual; therefore, children are taught not to call attention to themselves or to bring shame on the family by their behavior. In

Angel Child, Dragon Child (Surat, 1983), little Ut has great difficulty not showing anger when the other children tease her about her clothing and her speech. She wants to run home, but her older sister holds her steady, saying: "Children stay where parents place them, Ut. We stay."

On the other hand, we need to avoid making generalizations about children from particular cultural backgrounds. Some educators have suggested, for instance, that a highly structured curriculum would be most appropriate for Vietnamese children who are taught to value obedience; or that imitation and modeling are the best approaches for teaching Hispanic children. We need to remember that all children are individuals, and so are their families (Coleman, 1991, p. 19). As Wardle (1990) notes:

> *The foreign child's identity is almost always national and cultural, often not ethnic. She may well belong to the majority group in her native country. A Spanish-speaking child from Peru does not have the same cultural background as an American Hispanic child; a Black child from rural Kenya has a very different background from an American Black child. We must be vigilant in never stereotyping any of the children we serve.* (p. 45)

What should our attitude be toward the foreign adopted children in our classes? It is our behavior toward such youngsters that sets the tone for their acceptance or rejection by the other children, as well as their own acceptance of themselves as worthy individuals. If we focus on their differences, so will the other children. On the other hand, if we treat them just as we do the others, then we can celebrate their uniqueness when the occasion arises. We need not gloss over the children's differences, but should help them to understand those unique characteristics they possess that are strengths. For example, once a child like Ut has been accepted as one of the group, then the fact that she can count in a different language can be celebrated: "Isn't it wonderful that Ut knows how to say the numbers in another language as well as in English? Maybe she can teach us how. Can anyone else count in another language?"

Children's picture books can help, as well. More books are being published about adopted foreign children. Whether or not there are such children in your program, be sure to read stories about them to the youngsters. One of the special joys of early childhood teaching is your opportunity to open all children's hearts and minds to the fascinating cultural images reflected in American society today. This is the time to do it. As noted by early childhood specialists Clark, DeWolf, and Clark (1992):

> *The early years are an especially sensitive period for imprinting language, visual, and other sensory stimuli, and for developing lifelong attachments. We ought to imprint our children with a variety of people. Their teachers and peers, as well as pictures on the walls, books on the shelves, and babies in the play areas, should all reflect cultural diversity. If your center has enrollment of primarily one ethnic or racial group, you should work doubly hard to bring this diversity in.* (p. 8)

Multicultural picture books can initiate such imprinting. ***Through Moon and Stars and Night Skies*** (Turner, 1990) tells the tender story of a Southeast Asian boy who needs a poppa and momma of his own, but has to take a scary flight for a day and a night to get to his new American family. The little boy tells his new mother how he carried all their pictures with him: of his new poppa and momma, of the red dog, of the white house with a green tree in front, and of a bed with a teddy-bear quilt waiting just for him.

Read this story to one or two children at a time so that they can see each illustration clearly and identify the little boy's feelings: first of fear, then, little by little, of acceptance and love—especially when the big red dog licks his hand. Put out one of your block people families with a dog figure on one table. On another table across the room, put a boy figure and an airplane. Can one of your children pretend to be the boy and fly across the room to his new family? What will he say to them? How will they answer? You can speak for the family members and ask him what he saw as he looked out the windows of his airplane, and what he would like to do in his new home.

Pretending like this with three-dimensional people figures helps young children bond more closely with book characters, as well as with real-life multicultural children. Be sure that all of the children, both boys and girls, get a chance to be the adopted child flying to his new home. In this way they will begin to imprint with children different from themselves.

We Adopted You, Benjamin Koo (Girard, 1989) may be a bit old for your children, but could be a book for you to lend to the family of an older adopted foreign child. The tale is narrated by 9-year-old Benjamin Koo Andrews, who tells how his birth mother left him on the doorstep of an orphanage in Korea, and how he came to be a part of the Andrews family in America. It is not until second grade that Benjamin first realizes how different he looks from the other children, and he wants to go back to Korea to find his real mother. A wise African American school counselor finally helps him to resolve his dilemma.

If I Ran the Family (Johnson & Johnson, 1992) does not focus on adoption, but on the family, which consists of a Caucasian mother and father, a Caucasian girl and little boy, an Asian boy, and an African American girl. For all we know, all of the children may be adopted. It is a story told in rhyme of a close-knit family whose oldest child, Debbie, tells what it would be like if she ran the family. She would make sure that they all had some say-so each day; that they could cry all they wanted to when necessary, and then get a big hug when they were through, but not be forced to be hugged when they didn't want to; that they shouldn't be afraid to talk about anything; that they could pick what to eat or to skip; that they didn't always have to play or to smile; that how they felt inside was just right for them.

Then Debbie asks the readers how it is with their families. Ask your children what they would do if they ran their families, even just for a day. Large, bright illustrations showing each of these multiethnic youngsters in action make this book highly attractive. And the theme is one that many children like to pretend about. What about your children?

Bi-Racial Families

◆ *Black Is Brown Is Tan* (Adoff, 1973)

◆ *You Be Me I'll Be You* (Mandelbaum, 1990)

◆ *Black, White, Just Right!* (Davol, 1993)

The term "bi-racial family" often refers to families where the mother and father are of different races and the children are of a mixed background. As with families with adopted minority children, bi-racial families also have differences among their members to consider. The way in which these mothers and fathers deal with racial attitudes has a strong impact on their children. If parents focus on common bonds and celebrate differences, then their children should also be accepting of themselves as worthy people, no matter what their race.

Outside of the family, attitudes toward race may be different. The sequence of children's development of racial attitudes was given in Chapter 3, Table 3.2. Ramsey (1987), found that although young children are capable of distinguishing skin colors and facial features, they do not always choose to make these distinctions.

> *Race is a category that children use, but the readiness to use it may depend upon their previous social contact, the kinds of distinctions that they are asked to make, and the immediate social situation. . . . Children may appear to be "color blind" because race is not significant in that particular situation; however, low prominence should not be confused with lack of awareness.* (p. 19)

Children's picture books about bi-racial families sometimes focus on race and how it is dealt with within the family. If this topic is important to you and the children in your class, you may want one or more of such books in your program. Before choosing to use these books with the children, however, consider carefully the messages different books about bi-racial families may convey.

Black Is Brown Is Tan (Adoff, 1973) is a classic story-poem about a family with a white father, black mother, and two children of varied skin color. Skin colors are lightheartedly compared with chocolate milk, white milk, coffee, and snow as the children are hugged and kissed, tickled and read to; or faces get ginger red when either mother or father puff and yell the children into bed. Although the book focuses on skin color, its message is one of happiness, delight, and love.

How will your youngsters respond to a book of this sort? If you treat all of the children as worthy individuals, and if you respond to any of their comments about race or skin color in a matter-of-fact manner, then they should react to such a story just as you do. On the other hand, you may

decide that there is a better way for you to approach multicultural consider-
ations than pointing out differences like this.

If this is the case, you may want to consider carefully whether to use a
book such as *You Be Me I'll Be You* (Mandelbaum, 1990), originally published in Belgium. It is the story of preschool-aged Anna, a black child with
a white father and black mother, who tells her father that she doesn't like
the color of her face and wants to be like him. Her father, an artist, helps
her make up in white face while she helps make him up in black face. Then
they go downtown to meet her mother. People who see them on the street
wonder if there is a circus in town. The mother is not pleased with what she
sees. Father and daughter look at women in a beauty parlor having their
hair permed and at a sign advertising suntan lotion, noting that no one
seems happy with the hair they have or the color of their skin.

Although racial differences are treated in a fun-loving manner, the overall
effect of making up in white and black face because you are dissatisfied
with your skin color is inappropriate. It implies that there is something
wrong with a person's skin color, and that you can change it if you want to.
Because the father and daughter turn out to look like clowns with dirty
faces, racial differences are accentuated in a manner that is disrespectful to
both races. If we want children to celebrate differences, then we should provide them with picture books that show children and parents having pride
in their differences.

Black, White, Just Right! (Davol, 1993), which was mentioned in Chapter 1, treats the same topic more sensitively. The little girl narrator has a
black mother and white father, while she herself is a little dark and a little
light, or as her parents say, "just right." The book shows her ballet dancing
with her mother, dancing to rap with her father, and proceeding through life
in a "just right" manner that leaves everyone satisfied. It is obvious that this
family considers its common bonds more important than its differences, and
that its differences are something to celebrate. The daughter not only knows
she is free to imitate either mother or father, but that either choice is "just
right." If you choose to use this book with your children, ask them what
they like to do like their fathers and what they like to do like their mothers.

MULTICULTURAL FAMILY INVOLVEMENT
IN EARLY CHILDHOOD PROGRAMS

Does your program encourage families to become involved in its activities
with their children? When we recall that it is parents who are their children's first and most important teachers, then we realize how important it
is to involve these significant people in their children's experiences with us.
Such support is even more crucial when the home culture and school culture are different.

Polly Greenberg (1989), one of the original designers of Project Head Start's parent involvement component, has this to say about the importance of parents' involvement in their children's programs:

When a member of a child's family takes part in his school life in a positive manner, even briefly and infrequently, the child's self-esteem appears to soar. Such positive participation sends a signal to the child. The family endorses this other world . . . a world very different from the world at home. (p. 62)

Even the youngest children see differences between home and school. They need to know that teachers support their families and cultures. They also want their parents to support their teachers and schools. It is up to the program to initiate contact and find ways to bring home and school together. Can the use of multicultural picture books help to bridge this gap?

FOLKTALES AS MULTICULTURAL BRIDGE BUILDERS

Folk stories have long served the purpose of expressing the traditions, beliefs, practices, and hopes of a culture. Oral tales often relate where the people came from or how they came to look the way they do. Such tales may describe the feats of folk heroes and the tricks of wily animals, as well as the hopes and dreams of ordinary people. Today, many of these traditional tales appear in children's picture books. Using such books with your children and their families can help to create a cultural bond between school and home. As Hopson and Hopson (1993) declare:

Folktales, we think, demonstrate that whatever our skin color or cultural background, we share many if not all the same values that from the dawn of humankind have enabled civilization to progress. Offering stories is a subtle yet effective way of teaching children that the rainbow generation of the twenty-first century has much to appreciate, enjoy, and share. (p. 146)

This belief in the power of folktales can also be applied to establishing a contact with children's parents and families. Make it a point to read or tell folktales from many cultures to the children. Lend folktale picture books for children to take home and share with their families. When families realize that you are interested in their culture and in a variety of different cultures, they may be willing to share folk stories that they know.

Have a weekly story time when you invite outside storytellers or readers to share a story with the children. Invite family storytellers to have lunch in the program and then tell their story. They can also read to the children from one of the folktale picture books you have sent home, if this is more comfortable for them. You may want to start with humorous folk stories that feature children or young people as well as animal tricksters. They can include some of the following:

African

Oh, Kojo! How Could You! (Aardema, 1984)

An Ashanti tale about the boy Kojo who spends his mother's money buying foolish animals until finally he is rewarded with a magic ring.

What's So Funny, Ketu? (Aardema, 1982)

A Nuer tale about a man who is given the magic gift of hearing what every animal thinks; but he cannot tell anyone, so he laughs.

Why Mosquitoes Buzz in People's Ears (Aardema, 1975)

A cumulative West African tale about a misunderstanding among the animals that prevents the sun from coming up until they find out what the mosquito said to cause this chain of events. This book is a Caldecott Medal winner.

Caribbean

The Banza (Wolkstein, 1981)

A Haitian tale about a little goat who becomes friends with a little tiger, and is rewarded with a "banza," a magic banjo that gives the goat courage to frighten away ten fat tigers.

Laotian

Nine-In-One Grr! Grr! (Xiong, 1989)

A Hmong tale about mother tiger who must remember the words in the sky god's song that tells how many cubs she will have. A bird makes her forget, so instead of nine tigers in one year, she has one in nine years.

Japanese

The Badger and the Magic Fan (Johnston, 1990)

In this story, a wicked badger steals a magic fan from *tengu* children and uses it to make a rich man's daughter grow a long nose. Her father has no luck getting her nose back to normal until the badger comes along. But the *tengu* have their revenge when the badger falls asleep.

Native American

Iktomi and the Berries (Goble, 1989)

In this Lakota tale, Iktomi, the trickster, disguised in a coyote skin, goes hunting for prairie dogs and ducks without any luck because of the tricks the animals play. Then he sees the reflection of buffalo berries in the water and dives down to get them. Once again, the trickster is tricked.

The Eye of the Needle (Sloat, 1990)

In this Yupik tale, hungry little Amik, an Inuit (Eskimo) boy who lives with his grandmother, goes hunting for food for both of them, but ends up eating everything he finds himself until he grows too fat to get in their house. He comes in through the eye of his grandmother's magic needle and coughs up all the things he has swallowed including a whale which they share with the everyone.

Coyote: A Trickster Tale from the American Southwest (McDermott, 1994)

In this story, blue coyote is also a trickster who gets tricked by a flock of crows when they try to teach him to fly.

STORYTELLING

Some of these tales may be too long for your youngest children to sit through while you read. Instead, try *telling* the tale to the children. Read the story to yourself several times until you know what comes next. Then practice telling it to your own family or even to a mirror. You may want to make a brief outline of the incidents of the story to help you remember them (Beaty, 1994, pp. 14–15). For instance, the coyote tale has the following incidents:

Sticks nose into badger's hole. Gets bitten.

Tries to get a flaming red head like woodpecker. Fur catches on fire.

Looks for snake. Finds trouble.

Tries to fly with crows. Loses balance and falls.

Tries to fly again. Falls in water and dirt after crows take feathers back.

Children will love hearing your tale if you make hand, arm, and head gestures for coyote's blundering actions. You will enjoy telling the story because of your children's rapt attention. Later they can look at pictures in the book and laugh over coyote's antics, which they already know so well from your telling of the story. You will realize how successful you have been when the youngsters beg you to "tell it again, teacher!" Would they like to try telling the story, too?

Such stories build bridges between cultures. Such oral telling by you, the children, and their family members demonstrates to everyone the common bonds we all enjoy.

◆ **Activities To Promote Good Family Relations** ◆

1. Have children match dresses you bring in with those in the story *Mama, Do You Love Me?*

2. Have children play roles of mother, daughter, and animals in this story.

3. Obtain Inuit girl doll for children to play with.

4. Role play *On Mother's Lap* with rocking chair and toys.

5. Take children for a walk around the building after reading *On a Hot, Hot Day.*

6. Role play *Tucking Mommy In* and have children take turns telling their sleepy mommy a bedtime story.

7. After reading *Laney's Lost Momma,* talk about rules mothers make so children won't get lost.

8. After reading *Abuela,* have a child choose a doll to be Rosalba and "fly" it across the room, then return and tell what she saw. Tape-record the story.

9. Read other books to support the theme of pretend flying: *Tar Beach, The Trip,* and *The Wing Shop.*

10. Use computer programs to support the theme of pretend flying, such as *Bird's Eye View* and *Ollie and Seymour,* and of going on a trip with grandma, such as *Just Grandma and Me.*

11. Invite retired persons to visit your program or become involved with a Foster Grandparents Program or RSVP.

12. Reenact waiting-for-father stories with dress-up clothes or hot-pad glove puppets.

13. After reading *When I Am Old with You,* have children tell and tape-record stories about what they were like when they were little and what they might be like when they are old.

14. After reading *Knots on a Counting Rope,* have children walk around room with their eyes closed.

15. After reading *Pablo's Tree,* make paper decorations to hang on a classroom "tree."

16. After reading *Do Like Kyla,* play follow-the-leader.

17. After reading *I Need a Lunch Box,* make lunch boxes out of shoe boxes.

18. After reading *Jamaica Tag-Along,* have group make up a tag-along story that you record on newsprint.

19. After reading *Through Moon and Stars and Night Skies,* make a block person figure "fly" across room to family and tell what he saw.

20. After reading *If I Ran the Family,* have children tell what they would do if they ran their families.

21. After reading *Black, White, Just Right!* ask children what they like to imitate about their fathers and what they like to imitate about their mothers.

22. Have a weekly storytime when you invite children's family members to visit the class and read or tell a folktale.

23. Learn to tell a folktale like *Coyote* orally and make hand and body gestures.

 ## LEARNING ACTIVITIES

1. Talk with your children about their family members after reading some of the books mentioned. Ask them how their own family members are like the characters in the books.

2. Family members of every race express love and affection toward their children. Ask the children how the book characters and their own family members express love toward their children.

3. Make a list of multicultural picture books for children of preschool or kindergarten age featuring boy characters and a list of books featuring girl characters. Be sure to use a balance of these books with your youngsters.

4. Choose one of the books from this chapter and make a curriculum web of activities that support the story in each of the learning areas in the classroom. Try one of the activities.

5. Obtain a collection of multicultural dolls that can be used with the family stories you read. Make a list of ways the children can use these dolls after hearing the story, and let them try some.

 ## REFERENCES

Beaty, J. J. (1994). *Picture book storytelling: Literature activities for young children.* Fort Worth, TX: Harcourt Brace.

Buckleitner, W. (1993). *High/Scope buyer's guide to children's software.* Ypsilanti, MI: High/Scope Press.

Caplan, F., & Caplan, T. (1974). *The power of play.* Garden City, NY: Doubleday.

Clark, L., DeWolf, S., & Clark, C. (1992). Teaching teachers to avoid having culturally assaultive classrooms. *Young Children, 47*(5), 4–9.

Coleman, M. (1991). Planning for the changing nature of family life in schools for young children. *Young Children, 46*(4), 15–20.

Gill, W. (1991). *Issues in African American education.* Nashville, TN: Winston-Derek Publishers.

Greenberg, P. (1989). Parents as partners in young children's development and education: A new American fad? Why does it matter? *Young Children, 44*(4), 61–75.

Hopson, D. P., & Hopson, D. S. (1993). *Raising the rainbow generation: Teaching your children to be successful in a multicultural society.* New York: Simon & Schuster.

Ramsey, P. G. (1987). *Teaching and learning in a diverse world: Multicultural education for young children.* New York: Teachers College Press.

Wardle, F. (1990). Endorsing children's differences: Meeting the needs of adopted minority children. *Young Children, 45*(5), 44–46.

ADDITIONAL READINGS

Allen, J., McNeill, E., & Schmidt, V. (1992). *Cultural awareness for children.* Menlo Park, CA: Addison-Wesley.

Berger, E. H. (1991). *Parents as partners in education: The school and home working together.* Upper Saddle River, NJ: Merrill/Prentice Hall.

Gonzalez-Mena, J. (1992). Taking a culturally sensitive approach in infant-toddler programs. *Young Children, 47*(2), 4–9.

Swick, K. J., Boutte, G., & Van Scoy, I. (1994). Multicultural learning through family involvement. *Dimensions of Early Education, 22*(4), 17–21.

CHILDREN'S BOOKS

Mothers

Hamm, D. J. (1991). *Laney's lost momma.* Morton Grove, IL: Whitman. (African American)

Joose, B. M. (1991). *Mama, do you love me?* San Francisco: Chronicle Books. (Inuit)

Loewen, I. (1986). *My mom is so unusual.* Winnipeg, Canada: Pemmican Publications. (Native American)

Loh, M. (1987). *Tucking Mommy in.* New York: Orchard. (Asian American)

Sardegna, J., & Hays, M. (1994). *K is for kiss good night: A bedtime alphabet.* New York: Doubleday. (Multicultural)

Scott, A. H. (1972, 1992). *On mother's lap.* New York: Clarion. (Inuit)

Smalls-Hector, I., & Hays, M. (1992). *Jonathan and his mommy.* Boston: Little, Brown. (African American)

Tomioka, C. (1986). *Rise and shine, Mariko-chan!* New York: Scholastic. (Japanese)

Tompert, A. (1988). *Will you come back for me?* Morton Grove, IL: Whitman. (Asian American)

Weiss, N. (1992). *On a hot, hot day.* New York: Putnam. (Hispanic)

Grandmothers

Choi, S. N. (1993). *Halmoni and the picnic.* Boston: Houghton Mifflin. (Korean)

Crews, D. (1991). *Bigmamma's.* New York: Greenwillow. (African American)

Dorros, A. (1991). *Abuela.* New York: Dutton. (Hispanic)

Miles, M. (1971). *Annie and the old one.* Boston: Little, Brown. (Navajo)

Nodar, C. S. (1992). *Abuelita's paradise.* Morton Grove, IL: Whitman. (Puerto Rican)

Patrick, D. L. (1993). *Red dancing shoes.* New York: Tambourine. (African American)

Sanderson, E. (1990). *Two pairs of shoes.* Winnipeg, Canada: Pemmican Publications. (Native American)

Fathers

Caines, J. (1977). *Daddy.* New York: Harper & Row. (African American)

Cummings, P. (1994). *Carousel.* New York: Bradbury. (African American)

Flournoy, V. (1978). *The best time of day.* New York: Random House. (African American)

Greenfield, E. (1976). *The first pink light.* New York: Scholastic. (African American)

Isadora, R. (1991). *At the crossroads.* New York: Greenwillow. (African)

Johnson, D. (1993). *Your dad was just like you.* New York: Macmillan. (African American)

Mitchell, R. P. (1993). *Hue Boy.* New York: Dial. (Caribbean)

Sonneborn, R. A. (1970). *Friday night is papa night.* New York: Penguin. (Hispanic)

Grandfathers

Cummings, P. (1994). *Carousel.* New York: Bradbury. (African American)

Greenfield, E. (1988). *Grandpa's face.* New York: Philomel. (African American)

Johnson, A. (1990). *When I am old with you.* New York: Orchard Books. (African American)

Martin, B., & Archambault, J. (1987). *Knots on a counting rope.* New York: Holt. (Native American)

Mora, P. (1994). *Pablo's tree.* New York: Macmillan. (Hispanic)

Nomura, T. (1991). *Grandpa's town.* Brooklyn, NY: Kane/Miller. (Japanese)

Orr, K. (1990). *My Grandpa and the sea.* Minneapolis, MN: Carolrhoda. (Caribbean)

Stolz, M. (1988). *Storm in the night.* New York: Harper & Row. (African American)

Brothers and Sisters

Caines, J. (1988). *I need a lunch box.* New York: Harper & Row. (African American)

Dale, P. (1987). *Bet you can't.* New York: Lippincott. (African American)

Havill, J. (1989). *Jamaica tag-along.* Boston: Houghton Mifflin. (African American; Hispanic)

Johnson, A. (1990). *Do like Kyla.* New York: Orchard Books. (African American)

Johnson, A. (1991). *One of three.* New York: Orchard Books.

Adopted Minority Children

Girard, L. W. (1989). *We adopted you, Benjamin Koo.* Morton Grove, IL: Whitman. (Korean American)

Johnson, L., & Johnson, S. K. (1992). *If I ran the family.* Minneapolis, MN: Free Spirit Publishing. (Multicultural)

Surat, M. M. (1983). *Angel child, dragon child.* New York: Scholastic. (Vietnamese)

Turner, A. (1990). *Through moon and stars and night skies.* New York: Harper-Collins. (Vietnamese American)

Bi-Racial Families

Adoff, A. (1973). *Black is brown is tan.* New York: Harper & Row. (Caucasian-African American)

Davol, M. W. (1993). *Black, white, just right!* Morton Grove, IL: Whitman. (African American-Caucasian)

Mandelbaum, P. (1990). *You be me I'll be you.* Brooklyn: Kane/Miller. (Caucasian-African American)

Folktales

Aardema, V. (1982). *What's so funny, Ketu?* New York: Dial. (African-Nuer)

Aardema, V. (1984). *Oh, Kojo! How could you!* New York: Dial. (African-Ashanti)

Aardema, V. (1975). *Why mosquitoes buzz in people's ears.* New York: Dial. (West African)

Aardema, V. (1989). *Rabbit makes a monkey of lion.* New York: Penguin. (African-Swahili)

Goble, P. (1988). *Iktomi and the boulder.* New York: Orchard Books. (Native American)

Goble, P. (1989). *Iktomi and the berries.* New York: Orchard Books. (Native American)

Goble, P. (1990). *Iktomi and the ducks.* New York: Orchard Books. (Native American)

Goble, P. (1994). *Iktomi and the buzzard.* New York: Orchard Books. (Native American)

Johnston, T. (1990). *The badger and the magic fan.* New York: Putnam. (Japanese)

McDermott, G. (1994). *Coyote: A trickster tale from the American Southwest.* San Diego: Harcourt Brace. (Native American)

McLellan, J. (1994). *Nanabosho: How the turtle got its shell.* Winnipeg, Canada: Pemmican Publications. (Ojibwa)

Sloat, T., & Huffmon, B. (1990). *The eye of the needle.* New York: Penguin. (Inuit)

Wolkstein, D. (1981). *The banza.* New York: Dial. (Haitian)

Xiong, B. (1989). *Nine-in-one Grr! Grr!* San Francisco: Children's Book Press. (Laotian-Hmong)

Other

Keats, E. J. (1978). *The trip.* New York: Greenwillow. (Hispanic)

Ringgold, F. (1991). *Tar beach.* New York: Crown Publishers. (African American)

Woodruff, E. (1991). *The wing shop.* New York: Holiday House. (Caucasian)

Getting Along with Other Children

5

As the world grows ever smaller in terms of the ease of interaction among peoples, . . . the need for cooperation among countries, concern for others, and mutual aid and support among different groups of people increases. If people do not learn to live together in harmony, the consequences promise to be disastrous for us all. (Eisenberg, 1992, pp. 148–149)

DEVELOPING EMPATHY: FEELING AS ANOTHER PERSON FEELS

Learning to get along with people—all sorts of other people—needs to start in early childhood. It should begin within the family and then spread to outsiders, starting with neighbors and relatives. Eventually this learning becomes the task of a child care center, preschool, or kindergarten. It is important that children learn at the outset the social skills of interacting with one another in harmony—taking turns, sharing toys, cooperating with adults, helping other children, and even resolving their own conflicts—if they are to grow and develop as whole human beings.

How does a young child learn such skills? We understand from Chapter 3 that he must first feel he is accepted before he can accept someone else. But how do young children learn to get along with another person, especially when that person is quite different from themselves?

Experience has shown us that for children to get along with peers in a classroom situation, they need to develop a feeling about their peers. This feeling does not arise from focusing on differences, but from the youngsters' ability to identify with or feel something in common with the other child. That something is *empathy:* the ability to feel as another person feels or to recognize how another person feels. Empathy is one of the initial moral emotions that is shaped by the child's earliest interactions with other people. It then influences how the child himself will act toward others. As psychologist William Damon (1988) notes:

Young children feel the sting of injustice and the pull of empathy. . . . Wherever there is human discourse and interpersonal exchange there will follow rules of conduct, feelings of care, and sense of obligation. Children participate in social relations very early, practically at birth. Their moral thoughts and feelings are an inevitable consequence of these early relations and the others that will arise throughout life. (pp. 1–2)

LEARNING EMPATHY FROM INTERPERSONAL CONFLICTS

The youngsters come to your program, then, with feelings about themselves as persons and some sort of feelings about others. How they are treated by you, your co-workers, and the other children will continue to shape their feelings. However, if the children are preschoolers, their strongest feelings will be about themselves. Children at age 3 and 4 are still egocentric beings who are just beginning to learn that the world does not revolve around them alone. Through their interactions with other children, through activities and materials, and especially through confrontations with their peers, they begin to learn that other children have feelings, too, and that other children's feelings may be just like theirs.

It is up to you, therefore, to make sure that they have such experiences, and to make sure that you do not take over their interpersonal dilemmas and resolve them yourself. *Young children learn social skills best through their own interactions with the children around them, not from adults resolving their conflicts.*

If yours is a preschool program for 3- and 4-year-olds, this may be the first time the youngster has experienced a group situation in which a classroom of toys and activities has been set up for her and her classmates. For example, Rhenika, an African American girl, may at first have the idea that everything in the room is for her alone. She soon learns differently. Another child, Melissa, a Caucasian girl, wants to play with the musical keyboard Rhenika is using, but Rhenika will not share it. Melissa grabs it out of her hand. Rhenika may cry, or hit Melissa, or run to the teacher for help. Melissa may run away with the keyboard, or may herself turn to the teacher. Thus begins the two girls' social learning about how to get along with one another.

Racial or cultural issues are not the point here. What is important is how you handle the conflict. How do you or your co-workers handle a conflict over common materials such as the one just described? You could take charge and settle it yourself, telling Rhenika she has to take turns and setting a kitchen timer for five minutes for each girl's turn. Or you could put the keyboard away until the girls can learn to play with it peaceably. Or you could make Rhenika sit in a "time out chair" until she understands that she can't hit others. Or you could put Melissa in the chair until she understands that she can't grab things from others.

Each of these strategies has been used by teachers of preschool children time and again when disputes over toys and materials arise. If you use one of these strategies, you will have halted the immediate conflict, it is true, but what social skills have the two girls really learned from this interpersonal confrontation? Without meaning to, you may well have taught the two girls that it is you and not they who will be resolving classroom disputes. This means that when a similar problem arises—and it will—they will come to you once again to referee their dispute rather than trying to work it out for themselves. It is only natural for young children to turn to an adult for help. But it is not always helpful for their social skills development.

Taking over the resolution of children's conflicts is a natural thing for you to do, too. But you should resist, because you will be short-circuiting the lessons that classroom conflicts can so effectively teach children about one another. As Crosser (1992) notes:

> *Conflict is a natural part of living and working together in groups. It is good that conflicts arise in the early childhood classroom because it is only through facing conflicts that children can learn the skills necessary to resolve real-life problems.* (p. 28)

Preschool programs offer young children exceptional experiences in learning to get along with their peers when conflicts occur. The lessons learned will last a lifetime. Thus, how adults deal with a situation is crucial if children are to learn to empathize with others. Think about your own goals for children. If your primary goal is to manage a smoothly running program, then you and your co-workers will undoubtedly intervene in children's conflicts and resolve them yourselves. Although this tactic may make things easier for you, it does not help the children develop important social skills. You will have missed a golden opportunity for the children to learn to resolve their own dilemma. If, however, your primary goal is *to help children learn how to get along with others*, then you will value classroom conflicts as opportunities for children to learn how others feel when things happen to them.

If you decide to intervene, your role should be to help the children *focus on the other child's feelings*, not to resolve the conflict yourself. We call this shifting of focus from the conflict to the other child's feelings "conflict conversion" as opposed to conflict resolution. This technique not only helps the children to take charge of working out their own solutions, but also helps them both to feel good about themselves and each other while doing so. In other words, it helps the two children to identify positively with one another. The next time they interact, the results should be much different because they now have come to understand one another's feelings.

Most of the brief confrontations that preschool children engage in over toys and materials can be settled by the children themselves. An adult should intervene only when someone gets hurt or when a child starts crying.

CONVERTING CONFLICTS TO POSITIVE FEELINGS

How can conflicts be converted to positive feelings in your classroom or center? When two children are experiencing conflict, an adult should calmly take them aside, help them to quiet down, and then ask them each in turn the following questions (Beaty, 1995):

1. What's happening, [child's name]?
2. How does [name of other child] feel about it?
3. What will make [name of other child] feel better?

The entire sequence is conducted in a nonthreatening, nonjudgmental manner if the teacher accepts the idea that "conflicts for children are social problems" (Shantz, 1987, p. 300), and that this conflict can be converted by the children to good feelings for one another.

For example, in the conflict described earlier, the teacher would ask each child the first question: "What's happening, Rhenika?" and then, "What's happening, Melissa?" In this way, the teacher gives each girl a chance to justify her own position. This is important for children in conflict: that the teacher know their side of the dispute. The teacher needs to listen carefully and withhold judgment. Rhenika may complain that Melissa grabbed the keyboard she was playing with. Melissa may respond that Rhenika wouldn't share and that she hit her.

The teacher then needs to restate each child's position matter-of-factly, without blaming either girl: "Rhenika, you say that Melissa grabbed the keyboard you were playing with. And Melissa, you say that Rhenika wouldn't share and that she hit you." This sort of restatement lets the children know that you have heard their justifications, but are not upset with them. Now it is time for the conversion to begin.

Next, the teacher asks, "How do you think Melissa feels about this, Rhenika?" This question may be a surprising one for Rhenika. She knows how she feels: she is angry because Melissa took her toy. She may answer, "It's Melissa's fault! She took my keyboard!" The teacher then replies, "Yes, you said that before. Now we're talking about feelings. How do you think Melissa feels about it, Rhenika?" Rhenika has to make the conversion from focusing on the incident to focusing on how the other child feels. She may answer inaccurately: "She feels good because she got my keyboard." To this, the teacher may respond by redirecting Rhenika to Melissa's appearance. "Look at Melissa, Rhenika, does she look like she feels good?" Since Melissa's frowning face tells a different story, Rhenika is likely to reply, "She looks like she feels bad."

Surprisingly, even young children can identify emotions in others by "reading" their facial expressions. All it takes is someone to redirect their attention. Camras (1980) found that:

Children as young as 5 and 6 years can identify facial expressions of emotions (e.g., happiness, sadness, fear, anger, disgust) with significant accuracy. (p. 879)

Preschool teachers agree that even 3- and 4-year-olds can tell how other children feel by looking at them.

Now it is Melissa's turn. When the teacher asks her how she thinks Rhenika feels about the situation, it is Melissa's turn to be surprised. She knows that she herself feels upset about being hit, but it is something quite different to consider how Rhenika feels. She is able, however, to make the conversion and reply, "I guess she feels bad, because she was crying." Both girls are on their way to developing empathy toward one another. The teacher can now ask each girl in turn the final question: "Rhenika, what do you think might make Melissa feel better?" and "Melissa, what do you think will make Rhenika feel better?"

Each has to come up with a solution that the other accepts. Rhenika suggests that it might make Melissa feel better if she had a turn at playing with the keyboard. Melissa accepts and they agree to set the kitchen timer for five minutes for each child's turn. Melissa suggests that it might make Rhenika feel better if she said, "I'm sorry I took the keyboard." Rhenika accepts Melissa's apology, and they shake on it. The teacher tells them both how happy she is that they could tell how the other one felt: "When we know how another person feels, then we try not to do things to make that person feel bad."

Yes, the teacher could have arrived at the same solution by herself and in much less time. But it would not have had the same positive effect. It would be the teacher's solution, not the girls'. Furthermore, the girls would not have had the opportunity to find out how each other felt. Rhenika, the African American girl, and Melissa, the Caucasian girl, were brought closer together when they realized how the other one felt about the incident. They had not known about the other's feelings before the conflict conversion. They also learned that the incident was not about their racial differences, nor was it about who was to blame. As the teacher pointed out, it was about feelings: how the other girl felt. And it was also about how the other person could feel better. All of them, including the teacher, ended up feeling better because they had taken the time to work out the solution. None of this would have been achieved had the teacher simply told them what to do.

Teachers who wonder about preschool children's reasoning ability, and whether it is really worthwhile to direct their thinking and feeling toward the other child, need not worry. The research of psychologists regarding children's "inductions" (reasoning in the service of discipline) shows positive results even with 1- and 2-year-olds. As Eisenberg (1992) notes:

Surprisingly, inductions appear to be effective with very young children. . . . Inductions that point out others' feelings and needs may be especially effective in promoting prosocial development. (p. 96)

USING CHILDREN'S BOOKS TO MOTIVATE CONFLICT CONVERSION

◆ *When Emily Woke Up Angry* (Duncan, 1989)
◆ *Double-Dip Feelings: Stories to Help Children Understand Emotions* (Cain, 1990)
◆ *Just Not the Same* (Lacoe, 1992)

Teachers who decide to introduce this simple but effective conflict conversion technique into their own classrooms often start with picture storybooks to set the stage for the children. Stories about feelings are especially appropriate. In order for children to tell how another child feels, they must be able to identify feelings.

A picture storybook about a single feeling, **When Emily Woke Up Angry** (Duncan, 1989), tells the tale of a preschooler who gets up "on the wrong side of the bed" and goes through the day trying to get over her negative mood. The cat, the dog, a hedgehog, a bee, a horse, a gull, a rabbit, a spider, a bull, and a mouse give her advice on how they get over being angry. Nothing works for Emily, until a frog suggests she jump up and down, and soon she is jumping for joy.

Younger children enjoy trying out the various animal movements. Ask them how they feel after each. Make a photocopy of each page showing the animal doing something to work off its anger. Mount the copies around the room for the children to imitate on their own.

A multicultural book for kindergarten youngsters is **Double-Dip Feelings: Stories to Help Children Understand Emotions** (Cain, 1990). Charcoal drawings show Asian, Caucasian, African American, and Hispanic boys and girls at home and at school experiencing double emotions—cheerful and sad, playful and mad, proud and scared, joyful and sad, silly and mad, happy and sad, brave and frightened, mean and friendly, thrilled and worried, glad and sorry, embarrassed and excited, and jealous and happy—with a brief text describing each. After reading this book, have two children at a time act out a pair of the emotions and let the others guess what the two feelings are.

Then read a story about actual interpersonal conflicts among children. **Just Not the Same** (Lacoe, 1992) tells the tale of girl triplets who constantly argue over who goes first and who gets what. Because they can never agree, their mother ends up deciding on the solution every time. But it is just not the same. For example, when they cannot decide on which apple slice each one should get, their mother takes back the three pieces and makes them into applesauce.

Read the book to small groups of children and ask them how they would resolve each of the conflicts in the story. Then do an informal puppet play with two or three of the children at a time, acting out each of the incidents with hand puppets. Do your creative youngsters think up solutions for the girls' conflicts that you never would have dreamed of?

DEVELOPING EMPATHY FOR CHILDREN WHO ARE DIFFERENT-LOOKING

◆ *Angel Child, Dragon Child* (Surat, 1983)

One of the powerful blocks to a young child's learning to get along with peers in the early elementary classroom (but not so much in preschool pro- grams) is fear: fear of other children because they do not look like him or her. This sort of fear tends to be reciprocal. Often when a particular child is afraid of the others, the other children carry out negative acts against that child because of their own fears.

For example, a new child to a class may be held up to ridicule at first because he or she looks different from the rest. If the child herself seems fearful, she is even more likely to be victimized. In the picture storybook **Angel Child, Dragon Child** (Surat, 1983), mentioned in a previous chapter, a Vietnamese girl named Nguyen Hoa (called Ut at home) and her sister come to an American school for the first time in their *ao dai* dresses with white cotton pants. Almost immediately the children on the playground, led by a red-haired boy, Raymond, make fun of them, shouting, "Pajamas! They wore white pajamas to school!"

His teasing continues into the winter season, when he hits the girls with a snowball. This finally makes Ut fight back. The principal marches both of them into an empty classroom where Ut must tell Raymond her story with English words, and Raymond must write it down. They sit doing nothing until finally Raymond begins to sniffle. Ut, who has been angry at him, sud- denly feels sorry and tells him not to cry. Raymond finally gets to know Ut by writing her story about how much she misses her mother left behind in Vietnam. In the end, Raymond leads the school in conducting a Vietnamese Fair to raise enough money to bring Ut's mother to America.

Stories like this one are important to every American class, whether or not foreign students are present. They set the stage for important learning about empathy toward others. What did Ut feel like when she first came to school? When the teacher called her Hoa instead of Ut? When Raymond hit her sister with a "snow rock"? When she had to tell Raymond her story? Just as important, what did Raymond feel like when he was forced to write Ut's story but could not understand her "funny" words?

Feelings about others are powerful motives behind the actions youngsters take. A child who is really different from the other children may provoke feelings of fear in those who have trouble accepting differences. On the other hand, when a child who is fearful is led into feelings of empathy for the other child, as Ut and Raymond were, he or she is suddenly on a com-

Children can reenact favorite stories with character dolls.

mon ground with the other. The child can feel the way the other child feels, and that kind of empathy is the beginning of learning to get along.

Story Reenactments

If your children like this story, they too can experience these feelings through a "story reenactment" of the tale. Story reenactments are on-the-spot impromptu plays put on by the youngsters themselves. Sign up children for each of the roles in *Angel Child, Dragon Child,* with more than one child playing the same role. As many children as want to should play a role. You be narrator, letting children reenact the story with actions and dialogue. You can prompt them or they can make up their own words if they are familiar with the story. This means you should read or tell the story more than once before the reenactment. It also means that the children will probably want to repeat the play more than once.

Young children especially will like to repeat story reenactments of their favorite tales. Ishee and Goldhaber (1990) report how their own preschool children performed *The Three Bears* 27 times in four days! The children who want to play different roles should all have a chance. Those who do not want a role can be the audience. Repeat performances are important for everyone to explore roles or to watch while they are being explored. As Ishee and Goldhaber (1990) state:

> *This is the most important part. Many repetitions help children. For many children it is necessary to watch a play numerous times before making that first gesture of pretense within a play. For others, repetition allows an opportunity to elaborate and expand on the story as presented, to take on a variety of roles, and to assume major responsibility for a role.* (p. 74)

For children who need to learn how to get along with youngsters who are different from themselves, such story reenactments give them the opportunity to feel real empathy for a character. They can play Raymond's role and see how it feels to tease someone who is different. Then they can play Ut's role as a newcomer and feel the way she does about being teased. They can also learn by being part of the audience. Learning how another feels is most effective when a child actually "stands-in" for the other child, but it can also be learned vicariously by watching how characters behave in a performance. Try it with your children. Since *Angel Child, Dragon Child* is too long for many preschoolers, you may want to simplify and shorten the story by telling it to them rather than reading it. Then, if they enjoy the tale, they can more easily play the roles with gusto.

Such plays are for the children themselves and not for an outside audience. The plays should be done in an impromptu manner, without costumes or memorizing of parts. But occasionally children feel so good about a particular drama that they want to make it more elaborate, with costumes and a more formal presentation to parents or other children. It is up to you and to the youngsters. Make sure it is fun for all.

If there are no Vietnamese children with an *ao dai* in your program, clothing like Ut wore can be made by parent volunteers from the pictures in the book or purchased from an educational supply company.

 Source for Vietnamese *ao dai* costume:

Write for catalog:

Lakeshore Learning Materials
2695 E. Dominguez St.
P. O. Box 6261
Carson, CA 90749

FIGURE 5.1 Story Reenactment

Source: Based on Beaty, J. J. (1994). *Picture Book Storytelling: Literature Activities for Young Children*, Fort Worth, TX: Harcourt Brace, p. 136.

1. Read or tell the story several times.
2. Sign up children to play the character roles.
3. Any role not chosen can be played by teacher.
4. Teacher narrates story while children play their roles.
5. More than one child can play each role at the same time.
6. Everyone else serves as audience.
7. Repeat reenactment as often as desired so everyone gets a chance to play different roles.

DEVELOPING EMPATHY FOR CHILDREN WITH BACKGROUND DIFFERENCES

◆ *Arrow to the Sun* (McDermott, 1974)
◆ *The Lost Children* (Goble, 1993)

Folktales from different cultures also tell stories about children who are rejected by their cultural peers because their background is somehow different. In **Arrow to the Sun** (McDermott, 1974), a Hopi tale, a boy is rejected by the other boys because he has no father. In **The Lost Children** (Goble, 1993), a Blackfoot Indian legend, six brothers are rejected by the rest of the tribe because their mother and father are dead.

We understand that just as in these Native American stories, children can come from the same culture but still be rejected because they are in some way different. They may look the same as the others, but something in their background makes them different in the eyes of their peers. With children, "different" usually means "lesser than" or "not as good." Such rejected children may eventually begin acting as if they are truly not as good as the others, or they may start fighting back and acting aggressively toward everyone.

Feeling-Faces

◆ *Kinda Blue* (Grifalconi, 1993)
◆ *Kelly in the Mirror* (Vertreace, 1993)

The lesson for us as teachers in any program is to make sure that we do not focus on differences in children. Children want to feel a part of the group. They want to be as much like the others as possible so that the others will accept them. Differences in children's background will not cause other youngsters to reject them if children learn that they are all alike in the way that they feel.

As humans, we all have feelings of joy and sadness, love and anger, or pride and disappointment. Can your children demonstrate such feelings?

Have children practice "feeling-faces" in a mirror.

Have them practice making "feeling-faces" in the hand mirrors you bring in for everyone to use. In small groups, let children practice until each one has a feeling down pat, then take an instant-print photo of each child's "feeling-face." Can the others identify the feeling from the photo? Does anyone make the same kind of face for the same feeling, or are there different ways to show joy or anger?

Read the picture storybook ***Kinda Blue*** (Grifalconi, 1993) about 6-year-old African American girl named Missy, who is feeling "kinda blue" and sorry for herself because she doesn't have a Daddy. Sensitive illustrations clearly show Sissy's facial expressions change from grumpy to giggly as Uncle Dan introduces her to the plants in his corn field and proves to her that plants, too, have feelings, and that people too, sometimes need watering when they're feeling sad.

Talk with your children about feeling "kinda blue." What makes them feel that way? What helps them to get over the feeling? If children want to do a story reenactment of this book, be sure to include several cornstalks as characters.

In the story ***Kelly in the Mirror*** (Vertreace, 1993), Kelly, another African American girl about the same age, is also sad, but it is because she doesn't think she looks like anyone in her family. But when she discovers an old photo album in the attic with pictures of her mother as a little girl, a smile lights up Kelly's face, for she sees that she looks exactly like her mother did as a little girl.

Make a feelings photo album of your children's pictures. Put one picture on a page and have each child add a line or two telling how they felt in their own photos. They can print it, scribble it, or dictate it for you to write. Put the album in the book center for everyone to look at.

DEVELOPING EMPATHY THROUGH HELPING OTHERS

◆ *Herman the Helper* (Kraus, 1974)

◆ *Daniel's Dog* (Bogart, 1990)

◆ *Tucking Mommy In* (Loh, 1989)

Our society expects its children to develop prosocial behaviors such as empathy, sharing, caring, cooperating, and helping. But we often spend more time teaching youngsters to share and cooperate than we do teaching the other behaviors. Some children learn to help their parents at home. Most youngsters are exposed to the idea of helping the teacher in school. But what about helping other children? Do young children help others naturally or do they have to be taught?

Some children pitch in to help when they see a peer struggling with something. Others do not. It is often friendship rather than cultural similarity that dictates who helps whom. Friends frequently come together to work on a task. However, certain cultures sometimes expect certain helping behaviors from their children as well. As Damon (1988) notes:

> *In many African and Asian communities parents expect daughters to spend much of their time helping with the care of younger siblings. They do not expect sons to do so.* (p. 101)

How is it with the youngsters in your program? All children can learn to help others, and to do it gladly. Teachers of young children in American classrooms should expect both girls and boys to help one another. This is part of their social development. To get them started, read a picture book about helping.

Herman the Helper (Kraus, 1974) features José Aruego and Ariane Dewey's distinctive drawings of the little green octopus, Herman, as he helps his underwater friends and family. He helps his father, who wants to be hidden by stones; his brothers and sisters, who need to be rescued from a big fish that swallowed them; his fish friends, who need to be pulled from the tentacles of sea anemones; and even his shark enemies, whom he camouflages with his ink when a sea monster appears. The youngest children especially need to sit close to the reader of this story to see the details of how Herman saves the day.

Good source for puppets to accompany picture books:

Write for catalog:

> Demco's Kids & Things
> Box 7488
> Madison, WI 53707

Buy or make several glove puppets of Herman and let children reenact their own Herman story right in the classroom. To make an octopus puppet, sew, staple, or glue three fingers cut from one glove to the sides of another glove. You will have an 8-fingered octopus puppet . . . an octopus with a child's hand inside that can help anyone who needs help! Have the gloved youngsters go around the classroom looking for ways they can be Herman, and help others to complete tasks. How do they feel after helping someone? How does the other person feel?

Daniel's Dog (Bogart, 1990) is the story of a young African American boy who feels left out since his baby sister arrived. But then he finds an imaginary ghost dog called Lucy, and all is well again. When his Hispanic friend, Norman, also feels lonely because his father is away on a trip, Daniel tells him that Lucy will send a friend to stay with him, a shaggy gray ghost dog named Max.

Children aged 3 and 4 often invent imaginary playmates when they feel lonely. Can a ghost dog really help? Ask your children about it. Would they like to have an imaginary animal helper of their own? Children can choose one of the animal figures from your block accessory shelves and trace around it on stiff paper. Then they can color it lightly in a pale color and cut it out. Have them name their ghost helper and tell what it can do. Did any of them choose a dog or cat? What about a dinosaur?

Jenny and Sue, the two Asian girls in *Tucking Mommy In* (Loh, 1989), have a Mommy who works hard all day. One night she is so tired when she tucks in the girls that they end up telling their own bedtime story and then tucking Mommy in. Sensitive illustrations portray tender feelings on the part of the girls, their Mommy, and finally their Daddy when he comes home from work. If your children like this helping story, let them do a story reenactment using people figures or dolls to play the roles. Have a child speak for each character as you narrate the story.

These days, toy stores and educational toy catalogs stock all kinds of people figurines as well as dolls of various ethnic makeups: white families, black families, Asian families, Hispanic families, and Native American families. Have each child choose a person figure from the story and enact his or

Good sources for multicultural dolls, puppets:

Write for catalog:

> Constructive Playthings
> 1227 East 119th St.
> Grandview, MO 64030-1117

her role as you narrate the story again. Don't forget the black cat, Mitzi, who has a prominent nonverbal role.

Activities of this sort should alert your children to the idea of helping one another. Do they? Listen to the children as they pretend or engage in dramatic play. Do any of them play helping roles? Commend them for their pretend actions. Also have them make up stories about people or animal helpers and record them on tape cassettes, or dictate them for you to record. Once children understand that the adults around them applaud helping actions, they are more inclined to be helpful. And the more they actually help the people around them, the more attuned they become to the feelings of others, no matter what their culture or background.

DEVELOPING EMPATHY THROUGH MAKING FRIENDS

◆ *Let's Be Enemies* (Udry, 1961)

◆ *Jamaica and Brianna* (Havill, 1993)

◆ *Margaret and Margarita* (Reiser, 1993)

◆ *The Yesterday Stone* (Eyvindson, 1992)

How young children make friends in early childhood programs has more to do with their ages and stages of cognitive development than with their attitudes toward other children of different cultures. Preschoolers, for example, are still at a concrete stage in their perceptions of the world around them. Thus, they tend to define friendships in very concrete ways. Ramsey (1991) describes a typical example of preschool friendship:

> *When Luz stomps off from Gabriela, she declares that the friendship ended. This announcement reflects the typical preschooler's view that "friends are the people I play with." . . . She does not understand that the underlying attraction and affection continues and that she and Gabriela will once again be friends as soon as they have gotten over their anger.* (p. 13)

The little picture book ***Let's Be Enemies*** (Udry, 1961) effectively demonstrates this same truth as John, the narrator, goes grumpily over to James' house to inform him that they are no longer friends because, among other things, "James takes all the crayons." When John finally gets to James' house they both agree to be enemies, but first they decide to roller-skate with one pair of skates between them, and then to share a pretzel.

Read the story to a small group of your preschoolers at a time and see what their reaction is. What do they think about these friendly enemies? What makes a person a friend? The race or culture of the children should have little to do with their formation of friendships in your classroom if your own attitude toward each of them is an accepting one.

Your other picture storybooks should reflect the same attitude. In ***Jamaica and Brianna*** (Havill, 1993), the friendship breaks down between the little African American girl, Jamaica, and her Asian friend, Brianna, over the snow boots each must wear, not over their cultural differences. After reading this book, bring in several pairs of boots (including cowboy boots) and have the youngsters take on the roles of Jamaica and Brianna. How will they choose which boots to wear? Young children especially enjoy playing with shoes and boots. Give everyone who wants to—girls and boys alike—a chance to be Jamaica or Brianna and choose the boots. It is the boots, not the culture, that makes the difference to these children.

Through this sort of role-playing, children learn another important social skill: taking another child's point of view. In the *Jamaica* story, it is an African American or Asian child's perspective. Psychologist Damon (1988) notes:

> *Although empathy is experienced as a feeling state, it has a cognitive as well as affective component. In order to resonate to another's feelings, a child first must recognize accurately the other's feelings. The cognitive ability to discern another's inner psychological states is called perspective taking.* (pp. 14–15)

"How can children learn perspective-taking of an ethnic child's feelings if all their peers are Caucasian?" you may wonder. Some creative teachers have developed a Sister Schools Program in which two preschool classes with different ethnic populations exchange letters, pictures, samples of art projects, language experience stories, videotapes, and audio tapes with one another. According to Koeppel and Mulrooney (1992):

> *In addition to sharing aspects of their school culture, the children learn about each other's home, family, and community life. Through a combination of careful teacher planning and spontaneity on the part of the children, each school sends the other a monthly package containing elements of the children's lives to be shared with the children in the other school.* (p. 44–47)

Other programs having few children of different cultural backgrounds stock their classrooms with multiethnic picture books, posters, toys, dolls, and figures of different kinds of people. They read the stories to the children and encourage them to look at the books on their own. In this way, everyone is given the opportunity to see the pictures and hear the words about children of different backgrounds as they interact with one another in common social situations. In addition to this vicarious experience, the youngsters can also play the actual roles of the other children through story reenactment and pretending, as this text suggests. Pretending to be a character in the story of another ethnic or racial group helps your youngsters to develop their own perspective-taking. According to Damon (1988):

> Perspective taking is a powerful capacity. . . . Through social experience, especially in peer relations, children acquire more information and greater understanding of these matters. . . . Children are able to act more effectively on their moral insights, thus helping others in more realistic ways. (p. 93)

The book *Margaret and Margarita* (Reiser, 1993) shows two little girls, one Caucasian and one Hispanic, going to the park with their mothers. English and Spanish words appear on opposite pages. Neither girls wants to go to the park because there is no one to play with. When they see one another, they realize that the other one does not speak their language. But they begin trying to communicate with "hello" and "hola" and soon have a conversation going in two languages. A friendship soon blossoms as their toy rabbit and toy cat join in.

Bring in two similar toy animals and have them each speak the English and Spanish words from the book. If you have trouble pronouncing the Spanish words, ask someone who speaks Spanish to do it for you. Or perhaps a high school language student will tape-record the Spanish from the book so that you can play it for your children at the appropriate times.

Another friendship book about two girls from different cultures, *The Yesterday Stone* (Eyvindson, 1992), involves Anna, a Native American, and Molly, a Caucasian, who become friends because they believe in and trust one another. The other children at school laugh when Anna tells them to smile at the dandelions and they will smile back. But not Molly. She believes. Wonderfully sensitive illustrations show Anna with her grandmother, who helps her find her "yesterday stone," so full of magical adventures, although her grandmother warns Anna that not everyone will believe in it. But Molly believes. Your mature 4-year-olds and most kindergarten girls will enjoy this story. Can they find their own "yesterday stones"? What stories will they tell?

As a teacher you realize that the young children in your classroom are as different in their social skills as they are in their looks. Some youngsters really do have special friends in the adult sense of the word. But, generally speaking, most preschoolers are still more egocentric than socially aware in their thinking and behavior. Their friends tend to be their playmates, and they continually change playmates. These friends are sure to be of as many different racial and ethnic backgrounds as you have cultures in your program. By experiencing feelings in common, these children will learn first-hand that friends can be anyone—and everyone.

◆ Activities To Promote Getting Along With Others ◆

1. Focus on others' feelings to convert conflicts.

2. Learn to feel how the other child feels during conflict.

3. Mount photocopies of the animals working off anger in *When Emily Woke Up Angry* for children to imitate.

4. Try out various animal movements to get over being angry.

5. Do a story reenactment of *Kinda Blue*.

6. Talk about feeling "kinda blue."

7. Make "feeling-faces" in pocket mirrors.

8. Take photos of children's feeling-faces.

9. Have children identify feelings from the "feeling-faces" photos.

10. Make a "feeling-faces" photo album with your children's photos. Have each child add words to tell how he felt.

11. Have two children act out a pair of emotions and others try to guess what they are.

12. Read *Let's Be Enemies* and ask the children: What is an enemy? A friend?

13. Simplify *Angel Child, Dragon Child* for preschoolers by telling rather than reading it.

14. Do a story reenactment of *Angel Child, Dragon Child*. Repeat it until everyone who wants gets to play a role.

15. Make up stories about people or animal helpers. Record them on tape or paper.

16. Make a ghost animal helper by tracing around an animal figure from the block corner.

17. Have two or three children do a puppet play of each incident in *Just Not the Same* showing how they would resolve the conflicts.

18. Have parent volunteers make Vietnamese outfits for a play.

19. Make glove octopus puppets and have a child pretend to be Herman helping others in the class.

20. Commend children whenever they help each other, even in play.

21. Do a story reenactment of *Tucking Mommy In* using figures of people or dolls.

22. Bring in several pairs of boots and have children play the roles of Jamaica and Brianna in choosing which boots to wear.

23. Develop a relationship with a sister school.

24. Stock classroom with multicultural books, dolls, toys, and people figures.

25. Pretend to be a character from another ethnic or racial background.

 ## LEARNING ACTIVITIES

1. Intervene in two children's interpersonal conflict if one is crying or being hurt. Use the conflict conversion questions. Record the results.

2. Make photocopies of pictures of animals working off anger, or other pictures showing emotions, and mount the pictures in the classroom. Have some children imitate the pictures and others guess the emotion being shown.

3. Have children do a puppet play with hand puppets acting out conflicts from one of the books mentioned. Record the results.

4. Do a story reenactment with the children based on one of the books about conflict mentioned in this chapter. Record the results.

5. Have children practice making "feeling-faces" in a mirror. Take a photo of each child's emotion and have the others guess which emotion is being shown.

 ## REFERENCES

Beaty, J. J. (1994). *Picture book storytelling: Literature activities for young children.* Fort Worth, TX: Harcourt Brace.

Beaty, J. J. (1995). *Converting conflicts in preschool.* Fort Worth, TX: Harcourt Brace.

Camras, L. A. (1980). Children's understanding of facial expressions used during conflict. *Child Development, 51,* 879–885.

Crosser, S. (1992). Managing the early childhood classroom. *Young Children, 47*(2), 23–29.

Damon, W. (1988). *The moral child.* New York: The Free Press.

Eisenberg, N. (1992). *The caring child.* Cambridge, MA: Harvard University Press.

Ishee, N., & Goldhaber, J. (1990). Story re-enactment: Let the play begin! *Young Children, 45*(3), 70–75.

Koeppel, J., & Mulrooney, M. (1992). The Sister Schools Program: A way for children to learn about cultural diversity—when there isn't any in their school. *Young Children, 48*(1), 44–47.

Ramsey, P. G. (1991). *Making friends in school: Promoting peer relationships in early childhood.* New York: Teachers College Press.

Shantz, C. U. (1987). Conflicts between children. *Child Development, 58,* 283–305.

ADDITIONAL READINGS

Burgess, R. (1993). African American children. *Child Care Information Exchange*, 3, 35–38.

Fu, V. R. (1993). Children of Asian cultures. *Child Care Information Exchange*, 3, 49–51.

Sample, W. (1993). The American Indian child. *Child Care Information Exchange*, 3, 39–40.

Shaffer, D. D. (1993). Making Native American lessons meaningful. *Childhood Education*, Summer, 201–203.

 ## CHILDREN'S BOOKS

Empathy

Baker, K. (1990). *Who is the beast?* San Diego, CA: Harcourt Brace. (animals)

Johnson, A. (1990). *Do like Kyla.* New York: Orchard Books. (African American)

Lionni, L. (1970). *Fish is fish.* New York: Knopf/Pantheon. (animals)

Feelings

Brandenberg, A. (1984). *Feelings.* New York: Mulberry Books. (multicultural)

Cain, B. S. (1990). *Double-dip feelings: Stories to help children understand emotions.* New York: Magination Press. (African American and Caucasian)

Duncan, R. (1989). *When Emily woke up angry,* Hauppauge, NY: Barron's Educational Series. (Caucasian)

Goble, P. (1993). *The lost children.* New York: Bradbury Press. (Native American)

Grifalconi, A. (1993). *Kinda blue.* Boston: Little, Brown. (African American)

McDermott, G. (1974). *Arrow to the sun.* New York: Viking Press. (Native American)

Murphy, J. B. (1985). *Feelings.* Windsor, Canada: Black Moss Press. (Caucasian)

Vertreace, M. M. (1993). *Kelly in the mirror.* Morton Grove, IL: Whitman. (African American)

Conflict

Carle, E. (1977). *The grouchy ladybug.* New York: Crowell. (animals)

Havill, J. (1986). *Jamaica's find.* Boston: Houghton Mifflin. (African American)

Keats, E. J. (1979). *Maggie and the pirate.* New York: Scholastic Publications. (multicultural)

Lacoe, A. (1992). *Just not the same.* Boston: Houghton Mifflin. (Caucasian)

Surat, M. M. (1983). *Angel child, dragon child.* New York: Scholastic Publications. (Vietnamese and Caucasian)

Udry, J. M. (1961). *Let's be enemies.* New York: Scholastic Publications. (Caucasian)

Zolotow, C. (1969). *The hating book.* New York: Scholastic Publications. (Caucasian)

Helping

Bogart, J. E. (1990). *Daniel's dog.* New York: Scholastic Publications. (African American and Hispanic)

Kraus, R. (1974). *Herman the helper.* New York: Simon and Schuster. (animals)

Lester, H., & Munsinger, L. (1992). *Me first.* Boston: Houghton Mifflin. (animals)

Loh, M. (1989). *Tucking Mommy in.* New York: Orchard Books. (Asian)

Friends

Bogart, J. E. (1990). *Daniel's dog.* New York: Scholastic Publications. (African American and Hispanic)

Carle, E. (1971). *Do you want to be my friend?* New York: Thomas Y. Crowell. (animals)

Cohen, M. (1967). *Will I have a friend?* New York: Collier Books. (multicultural)

Cohen, M. (1971). *Best friends.* New York: Collier Books. (multicultural)

Eyvindson, P. (1992). *The yesterday stone.* Winnipeg, Canada: Pemmican Publications. (Native American)

Havill, J. (1993). *Jamaica and Brianna.* Boston: Houghton Mifflin. (African American and Asian)

Henkes, K. (1989). *Jessica.* New York: Penguin Books. (Caucasian)

Hoban, R. (1969). *Best friends for Frances.* New York: Harper & Row. (animals)

Mayer, M. (1989). *Little Critter's This is my friend.* New York: Golden Book. (animals)

Reiser, L. (1993). *Margaret and Margarita.* New York: Greenwillow Books. (Caucasian and Hispanic)

Engaging in Physical Expression

6

Every child's body is different, but all bodies share the same need to climb, balance, and stretch. A child with superior athletic skills will enjoy an obstacle course because moving is his specialty. A child with special needs will love it because it is a challenge he can meet in his unique style. Preschoolers with special needs are so adept at making accommodations for their differences that they can teach their peers new ways of overcoming obstacles. (Carol Stock Kranowitz, 1987, pp. 26–27)

EVERY BODY IS DIFFERENT

Look at the children in your class or center, at their arms and legs, their torsos, their heads, their height, their weight, their movement. Yes, every child who passes your way is different in his or her own physical development. "Different" with young children means "unique," as you have come to realize. These physical differences in youngsters have to do with genetic makeup, not their race or culture. Some will be tall, others short. Some will be extremely active, others sedentary. In terms of physical characteristics, you will have as many different examples in your class as you have children. But while children's physiques may differ, their needs remain the same.

What is your role, then, in promoting young children's physical development? If such growth is dependent upon a child's genetics, does it matter what you do or don't do to address children's motor skills in your program? As you may surmise, your role in this area is just as crucial as it is with children's cognitive or language development. Although children's physical growth will continue whether or not you encourage it, their large motor skills can be developed and strengthened through the activities you provide.

It is this involvement with movement that makes the real difference in the motor development of preschool and kindergarten children. As Sinclair notes:

The receptors in the muscles, tendons, and joints are activated whenever movement occurs, and they are doubtless functioning before birth. They are thought to constitute the earliest input system of the body. This sensory-motor mechanism, activated through movement, thus provides the first

111

learning or experience system and is of prime importance in maturation and growth during infancy and early childhood. (Sinclair, 1973, p. 3)

Your task as a teacher in an early childhood program is to provide activities, equipment, and time for children to experience this large-motor practice, both within the classroom setting and outdoors. It is easy for children to run, jump, throw, and climb on an outside playground. But youngsters also need this practice on a daily basis, whether or not they have access to the outdoors. Rainy weather, for instance, should not prevent children's large-motor activities. It is important that the classroom itself provide space and equipment for large-motor practice anytime.

INCORPORATING LARGE-MOTOR EQUIPMENT IN THE CLASSROOM SETUP

At least one piece of large-motor equipment should be available at all times. A loft with steps, ladder, or slide is always an excellent addition to a classroom because it also provides two extra spaces, one on top and one underneath. An indoor climber is another good possibility. Many wooden climbers also include a ladder and slide. Teachers can construct their own large-motor equipment with plastic snap panels. These play sets come with slides and steps, as well as openings in the panels for children to crawl through.

Because space is usually at a premium in classrooms, teachers need to use their creativity to accommodate large-motor equipment so that it does not interfere with other classroom activities. Installing a small set of climbing bars in a corner from one wall to another is a possibility. Be sure a mat is permanently positioned underneath. Some programs have cleverly converted a closet to a climbing/jumping room by removing the door, installing climbing bars on one wall, and covering the floor with an inflated mattress or vinyl cushioning. Other programs use a child's indoor basketball hoop, either free-standing or attached to a wall in a corner, for youngsters to use with sponge balls that do not bounce. Other useful equipment includes: a wooden rocking boat that becomes steps when inverted, a beanbag board and beanbags, a fabric tunnel for crawling, a balance beam or boards, large plastic blocks or hollow wooden blocks, and wooden riding vehicles. Which pieces of equipment can you make room for in your program?

MULTICULTURAL BOOKS THAT PROMOTE WALKING

◆ *Father and Son* (Lauture, 1992)
◆ *Mirandy and Brother Wind* (McKissack, 1988)
◆ *Jonathan and His Mommy* (Smalls-Hector, 1992)
◆ *Gilberto and the Wind* (Ets, 1963)

Walking is a locomotor skill that all young children seem to do well. Even 3-year-olds walk in adult fashion, without watching their feet or balancing with their arms as they did at age 2. But you will notice that some children are more awkward in their movements than others, and that walking down stairs with alternating feet is a skill that many 3-year-olds have not yet learned. Although physical growth occurs in a predictable chronological sequence, we realize that some youngsters are less advanced than others at every age. Can practice in a particular large-motor skill help?

Research shows that children between the ages of 2 and 6 show observable improvement in their basic motor patterns after repeated practice accompanied by adult encouragement. Instruction alone for certain movements does not seem to help, but repeated practice does (Flinchum, 1975, p. 28). Thus, it is important that teachers provide many opportunities for their children to practice all kinds of large-muscle experiences.

The idea of using children's multicultural picture books as a lead-in to large-motor activities may be a new one, but it should soon become a favorite with your children. They may even seek out in the library corner themselves books whose characters can get them going with large-motor games. One such book can be *Father and Son* (Lauture, 1992), about an African American boy and his father from the low country of South Carolina who work and play, walk and ride together, side by side. The characters are not named in this simple touching poem, but the feeling behind the words is reflected in the texture and motion of the bright illustrations.

This is a story of parallels, as the boy and man go side by side carrying wood, flying kites, riding horses, building sweet-potato huts, walking on the sidewalk and on the beach, carrying a bucket, and rowing and poling a boat. Can you and the children make up your own curriculum activities based on the story? What about a parallel obstacle course, through which children follow parallel footprint steps you have laid out two by two? Let the children help you make parallel trails around the room. Another day the children can simply walk with partners imitating each action of the father and son as you read the story. Can they demonstrate the difference between walking on a sidewalk and on a beach? They may want to chant as they walk and do the actions:

Carry wood,   Fly kites,   Ride horses.
Carry wood,   Fly kites,   Ride horses.
Carry wood,   Fly kites,   Ride horses.

Follow-the-leader walking activities make fine transitions between times when the children may be waiting for lunch, for the bus, or for something new to begin. With you as the leader the children can follow you, walking one by one or two by two, imitating any movements or motions you make as you walk. Any time the children seem restless, you can spark their interest easily by saying, "Come on, everyone, let's go for a father-and-son walk around the room." They should already know the motions for "carry wood," "fly kites," and other actions from earlier activities.

Or how about a singing game to a folksong such as, "Here We Go 'Round the Mountain, Two By Two"? First, have partners walk around a circle swinging hands and singing:

> Here we go 'round the mountain, two by two,
> Here we go 'round the mountain, two by two,
> Here we go 'round the mountain, two by two,
> Rise up sugar, rise.

Next, choose one pair of partners to stand in the center of the circle while everyone else faces the center and claps as they sing:

> Give us a little motion, two by two,
> Give us a little motion, two by two,
> Give us a little motion, two by two,
> Rise up sugar, rise.

The two in the center need to make a motion for the others to follow. It can be anything from hopping up and down to slapping their sides to twirling around. The others then imitate this motion while singing:

> That's a very fine motion, two by two,
> That's a very fine motion, two by two,
> That's a very fine motion, two by two,
> Rise up sugar, rise.

The partners in the center then choose another pair to stand in the center, while everyone else begins walking two by two around the circle and repeating the first verse.

Older children can strut with Mirandy and Ezel, the African American girl and boy who compete for a prize cake at the junior cakewalk competition in *Mirandy and Brother Wind* (McKissack, 1988). This is a longer story for kindergartners and older children, taking place at the turn of the century. The dress and speech of early 1900's country people sets the tone for a different kind of dance contest. African American contestants must strut to fiddle music around a chalk square drawn on the schoolhouse floor. Mirandy knows she can win if only she can catch Brother Wind ahead of time and make him do her bidding.

All your children will be winners when partners strut around a large square you create on the classroom floor. What kinds of steps can the partners take in unison? Can they amble, stroll, stride, strut, stomp, saunter, tread, tramp, trudge, twist, twirl, tiptoe, march, hike, plod, wade, and zigzag? Put on a square dance tape and let the children try out their own cakewalking.

Younger children can walk like the African American boy in *Jonathan and His Mommy* (Smalls-Hector, 1992) as they zigzag, take giant steps, take itsy-bitsy steps, do bunny hops, run fast like the wind, do ballet steps, do crisscross steps, do reggae steps, and finally do backward steps all along the city streets. Read the book to small groups until everyone has a favorite step they would like to try out. Let each group do a different step as everyone else claps. Later when everyone has tried out all the steps, take the class for a walk around the school yard and call out the steps for them to do as they walk one behind the other.

The wind plays a starring role in the classic movement story *Gilberto and the Wind* (Ets, 1963). The main character in this story is Gilberto, a little Hispanic boy who moves with the wind, trying to get it to fly his kite, sail his toy boat, twirl his pinwheel, and blow his bubbles up in the sky. This is a book to be read on a windy day when children can go outside like Gilberto and challenge the wind face to face. With your help, preschoolers can make a pinwheel. Take a square of paper, cut four diagonal lines from the corners to near the center, then roll the corners over and pin them loosely at the center to the end of a stick or drinking straw. Or children can make a little paper kite on a string and run with it in the wind. Cut stiff paper into a kite-shape, then tie a cloth tail to the back and a pulling string to the front.

MULTICULTURAL BOOKS THAT PROMOTE EXERCISING, STRETCHING, LIFTING, CARRYING, AND PULLING

Exercising and Stretching
◆ *Hue Boy* (Mitchell, 1993)
◆ *So What?* (Cohen, 1982)

Hue Boy (Mitchell, 1993), the story of a little Caribbean boy who does not seem to grow "at all, at all," can engage the children in the fun of exercising and stretching, just as Hue Boy does in the book's large and striking illustrations. First, read the book to individuals and small groups so that everyone is familiar with the story and knows what the different fruits and exercises look like. Then do an "action chant" in which everyone stands in a circle to chant and imitate Hue Boy's actions. You can make up your own chant, such as the one that follows:

> Eat pumpkin soup, yum-yum,
> Eat mangoes and melons, mum-mum,
> Eat pineapples and sapodillas, sap-sap
> Eat craboos and cashews, rap-rap,
> Eat guavas and tamarinds, tall-tall,
> But Hue Boy doesn't grow at all, at all.

Children can pretend to be Hue Boy or Jim when they play on outdoor equipment.

Now exercise with Carlos:

> Arms up, arms down,
> Arms up, arms down, str-r-retch!
> Arms right, arms left,
> Arms right, arms left, str-r-retch!
> Now stand up tall and measure all.

Do it once again. [repeat actions]

If your children enjoy this story and the action chant, consider doing it once every three months, and actually measuring each child afterwards on his or her own height chart. Each time the children say the chant, have one child drop out to be measured by the co-teacher or assistant while the rest continue repeating the chant. Or ask a parent volunteer to come in and help during "measuring day." It will mean more to the children if you also bring in some of the Caribbean fruits mentioned in the book for snack or lunch on measuring day. And don't forget to play some reggae or calypso music during the chanting to give it a real island flavor. Hue Boy may be different

Good source for music for physical movement:

Kimbo Educational
Department S
P. O. Box 477
Long Branch, NJ 07740-0477

"Shake It To the One You Love Best" (Cassette: African, Creole, Caribbean; reggae)

"Raffi in Concert" (cassette: "Day-O," apples and bananas, etc.)

"Square Dance Fun for Everyone" (record, cassette)

from your children, but nevertheless they should be able to bond with gusto to this island boy who has the same growth concerns as they have.

Be sure to talk to the children about the meaning of this story. Is it true that Hue Boy really does not grow taller? What do the pictures really show? Why do the other children tease him? Why does Hue boy not feel small when his father comes? Do your children show an increase of growth on their own charts every three months? Growth often occurs in spurts. They may be like Hue Boy in their own physical development.

Older children may be interested in *So What?* (Cohen, 1982) one of the little books in Miriam Cohen's "Jim" series that shows first-grader Jim, a Caucasian boy, outside on the school playground with his multicultural friends. Children are throwing balls, climbing on a climber, shooting baskets, jumping rope, and swinging. Inside, the nurse is measuring each child's height. Jim tries to hang from his legs upside down on the climber, but is afraid to let go with his hands and stretch out his arms like the other children. Jim finally learns from one of the girls not to take the things that go wrong so seriously. Then he, too, can say, "So what?" and let go with his hands.

Do any of your children have trouble accomplishing physical challenges on the playground? Physical feats such as hanging upside down take courage. Help them to get over their fears, let go, and accomplish the feat as Jim does.

Lifting and Carrying
◆ *Bet You Can't* (Dale, 1987)
◆ *The Day of Ahmed's Secret* (Heide, 1990)

In the picture book ***Bet You Can't*** (Dale, 1987), two young African American children, a big sister and her little brother, challenge one another to pick up their toys at bedtime and carry them in a basket. This is a good book to read as a transition between activities and cleanup time in preschool programs. Have several baskets of varying sizes ready for your own children to use for cleanup. Another time, have two large clothes baskets and ask for two volunteers for each basket to pick up and carry all the blocks, for instance.

Play a "Who's Under the Basket?" guessing game after cleanup. Have children form a circle and close their eyes while you tap someone to scrunch up under the basket like the children in the story, and then have the children guess who it is. Use a blanket or sheet to cover the child if you need to.

In ***The Day of Ahmed's Secret*** (Heide, 1990), Ahmed is an Egyptian boy who delivers bottles of cooking fuel from his donkey cart to people in Cairo. This longer story for older children can be shortened for preschoolers by telling it instead of reading it. Be sure to use as many of the original words from this beautifully written story as you can remember: how Ahmed's secret is to him the loudest sound in the noisy city: "the silent sound of my secret which I have not yet spoken." As you read or tell the story, have the children repeat the sound that Ahmed's cart makes: *karink rink rink.*

Have a small group of listeners at a time sit close enough to the reader to guess what other sounds the objects in the illustrations might make. The double-page pictures of Cairo's streets and people have little resemblance to an American city. Can the children pick out any objects they recognize?

After reading the story choose a child to be Ahmed and have him or her carry a fuel bottle (a large hollow block) around the room on his shoulder as Ahmed does, and finally deliver it to another child. Have that child pick it up and carry it to another child, and so on. Why do they think that Ahmed is not able to carry the fuel bottles at first? Why is he able to do it later?

Do any of the children have the same secret to tell as Ahmed does: that they can write their own name? Does anyone notice that the letters Ahmed uses are different from the letters they use? Children can try writing their own names, if they want. Does anyone notice that some of them use different kinds of writing than others? Encourage the youngest children who may be in a scribble or mock-writing stage to write their names in their own "personal script." Although American children may have little in common with the life of a child in Egypt, they can nevertheless bond with this boy who is proud to be strong enough to help his father and clever enough to write his own name.

Pulling

◆ *Coconut Kind of Day* (Joseph, 1990)

Coconut Kind of Day (Joseph, 1990) describes one day in the life of a little girl and her friend, Jasmine, who live on the Caribbean island of

Trinidad. In a series of short rhythmical poems on double-spread illustrated pages, all kinds of physical activities are portrayed: from her brother's diving in the sea and playing cricket, to her own help in pulling in the fishermen's seine net. The poem "Pullin' Seine" has the two girls "Grab! de nets like we big and strong," and "Pull! and tug and pull some more," in island idiom.

Have a large fishnet available when you read this book, and have the youngsters pretend to be the island children pulling in a heavy load of fish. Your "fish" can be blocks from the block center that need picking up, or toys scattered around the room waiting for cleanup to begin. Some children can drag the net around the room while others fill it with blocks and toys to be pulled over to their shelves for cleanup.

MULTICULTURAL BOOKS THAT PROMOTE HOPPING, JUMPING, AND LEAPING

Hopping

◆ *Hopscotch Around the World* (Lankford, 1992)

Hopping is a bounding skill in which a child takes off and lands on the same foot. Children need to be able to balance before they can hop well. They also need to have developed length and strength in their legs. Most children do not hop well before age 4. Girls tend to develop this skill before boys, perhaps because they are a bit more physically mature than boys, but also because hopping is considered a girl's skill in our society. Games such as hopscotch and jump rope are played principally by girls rather than boys. Thus, 5-year-old girls can usually outperform boys in hopping, whereas boys this age show superiority in throwing and catching, at least partly because of practice. Nevertheless, you should encourage all of your children to develop each of these large-motor skills.

Hopscotch Around the World (Lankford, 1992), is full of fascinating descriptions about how this game is played in 16 different countries. Illustrations show boys and girls from Aruba to China, to Russia, to the United States playing similar hop-over-the-lines games with names like "Pele," "Jumby," or "Gat Fei Gei." Many children's games like this are surprisingly similar around the world, making our common human bonds seem stronger than ever.

Although hopscotch is usually considered an outdoors sidewalk game, educational supply companies now make indoor hopscotch carpets with colored squares and non-skid backing. You can also make your own game using masking tape for lines. The youngest children may not be ready yet for "games with rules" or even for hopping, but they nevertheless enjoy trying to hop on one foot and sometimes landing on two. Older children who know the rules for American hopscotch can have fun learning other versions of the game from this book. If the assessment of your children's large-motor skills shows that they need practice hopping, leave out the hopscotch carpet for everyday use.

Jumping

◆ *Moon Jump* (Matura, 1989)

◆ *No Jumping on the Bed!* (Arnold, 1987)

Can your children jump? This skill involves taking off with one or two feet and landing on both feet, whereas hopping, as noted above, is done on one foot. Children learn to jump in a variety of ways: springing up with both feet and landing in the same place, jumping forward and landing on both feet, jumping over an obstacle, or jumping from a height and landing on the floor (Beaty, 1994, p. 169).

For Cayal, the East Indian boy in **Moon Jump** (Matura, 1989), all of life is a trampoline. He jumps out of bed, into the bath, into his clothes and shoes, from chair to floor, from floor to sofa, and all the way to school. But most of all, he likes to jump on his parents' bed. One night he jumps so high he goes all the way up to the moon. This simply written book, with its large illustrations of Cayal nearly jumping off every page, can easily motivate your children to develop a new large-motor skill.

Youngsters who want to imitate Cayal can jump in the classroom on inflated mats or vinyl-covered foam mats attached to one another by Velcro tabs. All of these materials are available commercially from educational supply companies. This kind of jumping, however, needs built-in safety provisions. Children who jump high may fall hard, so cushioning material should be placed under and around the jumping surface and an adult should be nearby to supervise at all times.

For children who wonder what might happen if they jump just one more time on their beds after they have been told not to, read **No Jumping on the Bed!** (Arnold, 1987). In this book, Walter, a little Caucasian boy, learns the hard way as he and his bed fall through the floor of their apartment and on down through each apartment below, taking the occupants with them in

Good source for physical education equipment:

ABC School Supply
3312 N. Berkeley Lake Road
P. O. Box 100019
Duluth, GA 30136-9419

hilarious splendor. Your children can bond in more than imagination with Walter if you provide a grand jumping-jack fest, set up carefully and supervised prudently by you and your co-workers. Have masking tape lines to jump across, circles to jump into, and contact paper footprints to jump on, as well as inflated mats and other jumping surfaces.

Leaping

◆ *Pretend You're a Cat* (Marzollo, 1990)
◆ *Jafta* (Lewin, 1993)

Many children can leap before they can hop or jump. Leaping consists of taking off on one foot and landing on the other. Young children usually learn to leap as an aspect of running. Have the children run across the room or playground and leap across a pretend river you have made with two lines or masking tape strips.

Young children especially like to practice leaping by pretending to be particular animals. Read them **Pretend You're a Cat** (Marzollo, 1990,) and have your children imitate the African American, Hispanic, Asian, Native American, and Caucasian children moving like animals in this book. Can they climb, leap, and stretch like a cat? Roll over like a dog? Leap and swim like a fish? Fly and soar like a bird? Run, twirl, and leap like a squirrel?

The real-looking children in this book, caught in the middle of an animal movement by Jerry Pinkney's talented paintbrush, are not named. Your children should sit close as you read the words in order to see these vivacious pretenders. Would they like to name these book children, perhaps with their own names? If each of your youngsters wants to take on a book character's animal role, you will need some face paint to make them up like their animal, as shown by the illustrations of "tiger cat boy" and "holstein cow boy" in the book. Others may want paper bag masks like the "horse boy." Be sure to take photos of your child-animals. These can then illustrate your youngsters' own imaginative stories on what it feels like to leap like their animal.

In **Jafta** (Lewin, 1993), the first book in the Jafta series, a small African boy imitates the animals in his environment. He skips like a spider, jumps like an impala, dances like a zebra, wallows like a hippo, stamps like an elephant, runs like a cheetah, swings like a monkey, and stands on one leg like a crane. After a trip to the zoo, read this story again and have each child choose a zoo animal to imitate. Can the others guess what it is?

MULTICULTURAL BOOKS THAT PROMOTE BALL PLAYING

Ball playing is a skill that needs to be practiced in a gym or out on the playground for the most part. Occasionally teachers allow playing with sponge balls that the children toss at a beanbag target or shoot into a basketball hoop in the classroom. But most children love to play with balls anytime, so be sure that your program provides them with the opportunity.

Rolling, Catching, and Throwing

◆ *Darlene* (Greenfield, 1980)

Starting with the youngest preschoolers, have children sit on the floor of your room while you roll a large ball to them. They can catch it with their legs or arms if it rolls up on them. Then have them roll it back to you. Once children are used to handling the ball, have them stand in a circle while you bounce it to them. Can anyone catch it on one bounce? Have them try to bounce it back to you. Finally, try throwing the ball to each child. It may take a while for some of them to develop the coordination to catch and throw a ball. Others seem to know how intuitively.

Catching is more difficult than throwing. Children must possess both large-muscle maturity and eye-hand coordination in order to catch balls with their hands. Three-year-olds often try to catch a ball by holding their arms straight out in front of them. Even 5-year-olds can catch a chest-high ball only 60%–80% of the time (Cratty, 1982, p. 126).

In the book *Darlene* (Greenfield, 1980), a little African American girl named Darlene is confined to a wheelchair, but nevertheless is able to play catch with a large rubber ball and turn one end of a jump rope. Bring in a child's wheelchair and have children take turns playing catch with another child while sitting in the chair. If you cannot obtain a wheelchair, pretend a regular chair is a wheelchair and let the children take turns "being Darlene." Can they catch better in or out of the chair? Differently abled children often can show others how to perform physical feats in original and creative ways.

It takes not only maturity but a great deal of practice to throw and catch balls successfully. Use large, light balls at first and gradually introduce smaller, heavier ones.

Basketball

◆ *Jamaica Tag-Along* (Havill, 1989)

Young children see a variety of ball games on television these days, and want to participate themselves. They can, with the lightweight versions of basketballs and soccer balls that are available. Picture books with multi-ethnic characters are thus excellent lead-ins for youngsters to bond with their counterparts from different cultures who are practicing their own ball handling skills.

For example, the book *Jamaica Tag-Along* (Havill, 1989) is about a little African American girl, Jamaica, who says she knows how to shoot a basketball, but her older brother won't let her tag along when he goes to shoot baskets with his multicultural friends. When Jamaica finally settles down to building a castle in the sandpile, a small Hispanic boy named Berto tries to help, but Jamaica shoos him away. When Berto's mother tells him that big kids don't like to be bothered by little kids, Jamaica realizes that she is acting just like her big brother. After that, she invites Berto to help her build a really big sand castle.

This book is a good lead-in to dribbling and shooting basketballs. Preschool-size hoops and balls are available for both indoor and outdoor play. Can any of the children make a basket? Can anyone dribble first and then shoot? It is very difficult for a 3-year-old, but some 4-year-olds and many 5- and 6-year-olds can become agile enough with practice. Most children merely approach the basket or stand almost under it, jump up, and shoot. With practice, they can make a basket. Both girls and boys should be encouraged to try.

Soccer

◆ *Northern Lights, Soccer Trails* (Kusugak, 1993)

Older children can also begin learning to control a soccer ball. Have children stand in a row while you kick the ball to them. Let them try to stop the ball with their legs or feet. Have them kick the ball back to you, but not too hard.

If the children show an interest in soccer, you can consider reading the book **Northern Lights, Soccer Trails** (Kusugak, 1993). It is a modern version of an old Inuit legend that calls "northern lights" by the word "aqsarniit" or "soccer trails." These far-northern people believe that the lights in the sky are the souls of the departed who come out at night to indulge in a lively game of soccer, just as they did when they were living.

Stunning illustrations depict the girl Kataujaq when she is little and playing with her mother, and later when she is older and her mother has passed away. Her grandmother tells her the legend of the departed ones who love to play soccer across the sky at night, and Kataujaq seems to see her mother up in the sky, smiling.

This is an excellent story to introduce older children to a way of life completely different from theirs, lived by people who nevertheless have the same common human bonds: love for their parents, interest in having fun and doing things together with their parents, grief for a departed parent, and excitement over playing ball games with other children. Can your children find other common bonds they have with the Inuit people, either from the story or the illustrations? Would they like to live in the far north like Kataujaq? What would they especially like about it?

Baseball

◆ *Harry and Willy and Carrothead* (Caseley, 1991)

Baseball is the ball game featured in **Harry and Willy and Carrothead** (Caseley, 1991). Harry, who was born without a left hand, wears a prothesis that he can use "just like a regular kid." He makes friends with Willy and Oscar, called Carrothead, and is soon playing ball with them out on the playground. Some of your older children may want to practice throwing and catching a softball out on the playground just like Harry and Willy. Others may want to make up a story about it, just as Oscar does.

Although this story features Caucasian children, it takes place in a multi-cultural classroom showing children from different racial backgrounds engaged in playing games on the playground and in the classroom. Is there anything really different about "differently abled" Harry as he participates in activities just like the others? When children feel the same as the others around them, they tend to act the same. And when they act the same as everyone else, then they are treated the same. This should be your goal for all the children in the program.

MULTICULTURAL BOOKS THAT PROMOTE SWINGING, SKATING, SKIING, AND SWIMMING

Swinging

◆ *Swinging on a Rainbow* (Perkins, 1993)

Swinging is a large-motor skill most children learn to enjoy if they have access to a playground. Three- and 4-year-olds may need an adult to get their swings started, but older children soon learn how to start themselves. All children need to be reminded not to walk behind swings when they are in use. But everyone should experience the excitement of flying high up in the air and down again. How high can your children make the swing go without someone pushing?

In *Swinging on a Rainbow* (Perkins, 1993), a little African American girl named Patrice wants to go as high as a rainbow. Her friends have their doubts, but Patrice persists and finally realizes her dream. A brilliant bow of colors bathes her rainbow collection of friends and arches over Patrice's fanciful dream, finally coming to rest on the swing in her own backyard.

Let this book be a lead-in to swinging activities on the playground. At first children may want to talk more about rainbows: what makes rainbows and whether a person can really swing on one. Bring in a prism and let sunlight shine through it to show its rainbow colors. Then have the children tell what they can see from the highest point of their swinging that they cannot see from the ground. Can anyone see things in their imagination like Patrice does?

Skating

◆ *Wait, Skates!* (Johnson, 1983)

Roller skating is another large-motor activity enjoyed by children, but usually at home rather than school. In the simple book *Wait, Skates!*

(Johnson, 1983), a little African American boy tries out his first pair of skates on the sidewalk, with mixed results. The skates go every way but straight, and simply will not wait for him until he finally tames them by shouting "Wait, skates, wait!" Preschool children can pretend to be this boy by skating around the room on two unit blocks. Their sense of balance as well as their large muscles are strengthened by such an activity. You will find that some children can move with ease standing on the blocks while others do not seem to have the strength or coordination.

Skiing

◆ *Trouble with Trolls* (Brett, 1992)

Using unit blocks as classroom skis is another way to improve children's large-muscle coordination. Children love to "ski" around the room by standing on two large unit blocks and walking with them. Waxing them will make them more slippery, but try them out first with the children to see whether they work better on a carpeted or uncarpeted floor.

Children who have seen skiing in person or on television may want to build a low ski ramp with unit blocks after hearing you read ***Trouble with***

Children love to "ski" around the room on unit blocks.

Trolls (Brett, 1992). In this story, a Scandinavian girl named Treva climbs up Mount Baldy to go skiing with her German Shepherd dog, Tuffi. On the way up she is waylaid by trolls from underground who, one by one, try to steal her dog. She finally outwits them all as she skis down the mountain with the dog in her arms.

Read the story to a small group at a time, and have them gather close enough to see the underground haunts of the trolls on every page. Can they tell what is happening underground as Treva and Tuffi make their way up the mountain above ground? Why do the trolls want Tuffi? What happens at the end when they can't get Tuffi? Young children are especially good at picking out details. Let them have a close look at the parallel underground story of the trolls told wordlessly in pictures as the text describes Treva's adventures above ground. Read the story more than once at a sitting if the children like it. This gives them—and you—a chance to pick out even more of the details.

This is an excellent tale for a story reenactment, with the children playing the roles of Treva, Tuffi, the five trolls, and a hedgehog. As you narrate the story, the children can act it out, repeating their own lines with your prompting. Children playing the role of Treva can use either real or pretend articles of ski clothing to foil the greedy trolls in their attempt to steal Tuffi. You may need to have two "stages": one for Treva and Tuffi and another for the underground trolls. If this is a favorite story, the children will want to repeat the reenactment again and again.

Swimming
◆ *Mermaid Janine* (Thomas, 1991)
◆ *Gregory Cool* (Binch, 1994)

Young children can learn to swim, too, if they have the opportunity. In *Mermaid Janine* (Thomas, 1991), Janine is an African American 6-year-old who is determined not only to learn to swim, but to swim the length of the pool. In *Gregory Cool* (Binch, 1994), an African American boy named Gregory visits his grandparents and cousin on the Caribbean island of Tobago. Gregory tries to act "cool" as a swimmer but is scared by the "sharks," which turn out to be dolphins. After hearing these stories, your children can also pretend to be swimmers in the classroom by packing a pretend bag and going to the beach in a pretend bus they make out of chairs. How can they do pretend swimming? Ask them.

MULTICULTURAL BOOKS THAT PROMOTE BICYCLE RIDING

◆ *A Bicycle for Rosaura* (Bardot, 1991)
◆ *The Bicycle Man* (Say, 1982)

Many programs have equipment that children can ride, often large wooden vehicles to ride inside and tricycles to ride outside or in a gymnasium. The ability to turn the wheels with their feet and to steer with their arms and hands gives children practice at coordinating more than one large-motor skill. The youngest children may not at first have the leg strength to make the wheels turn, whereas the oldest children may already be trying out bicycles with training wheels at home. Be sure to have more than one trike for children to enjoy. Multicultural books can be a lead-in to this activity too.

In the imaginative tale *A Bicycle for Rosaura* (Bardot, 1991), Señora Amelia lives in a village in Venezuela with a household full of pets who talk. Her handsome hen, Rosaura, informs the señora that she wants a bicycle for her birthday, so off goes Amelia to the city to look for one. Light-hearted illustrations show the Venezuelan city and countryside as Amelia pursues her futile quest. Then a strange-looking man appears in the village with singing spoons and chocolate rocking chairs for sale. Yes, he will build such a bicycle, and he does. At last Rosaura has her bike, but watch out! The strange man forgot to put in brakes!

This is another fine story to reenact if the children respond to it well. Inside the classroom, the children can use wooden riding vehicles to represent Rosaura's bicycle. Children playing the role of the strange-looking man can practice their lifting and carrying skills by picking up a bagful of toys as they proceed through the "town" (the room). Children who play the role of Rosaura riding her new bicycle should use their feet as brakes and only pretend to crash into people as the hen does.

The Bicycle Man (Say, 1982), on the other hand, is a realistic story about two American soldiers, one black and one white, who visit a small Japanese school in the mountains shortly after the end of World War II. The narrator, a little first-grade boy, tells the story of the annual sports day, when all of the children compete for prizes in various races while their parents cheer them on and then provide lunch at noon. Afterwards the children engage in a tug of war, piggyback races, and watching the adults in a three-legged race.

Unexpectedly, the two American soldiers appear at the sports day festivities, at first watching and then asking the principal in sign language to borrow his bicycle. When he agrees, the tall African American soldier begins to perform astonishing feats on the bicycle, doing "wheelies," riding it backward, and standing on the seat. The second soldier acts as ringmaster, waving the bicycle man around and around with his jacket. The children, never having seen American soldiers up close, are at first afraid and then entranced. At the end, the principal awards the bicycle man the largest box from the prize table. The man bows and says "ari-*ga*-tow" (thank-you), and the two walk back down the mountain road arm-in-arm, waving and laughing.

The human bonds of physical accomplishment and good sportsmanship by people of different races have seldom been so sensitively portrayed. It is physical skill and not nationality that makes the difference here. After hearing this story, kindergarten children may want to put on their own sports day to display some of their own skills as discussed in this chapter. Be sure that the sports are noncompetitive and that everyone is awarded some sort of prize or ribbon—even the spectators.

For children to develop large-motor skills successfully, their only competition should be themselves. Having some children be winners necessarily means that the rest of the children are losers. When children compete against one another, those children who need the most large-motor practice usually are the losers. As a result, those children who most need to improve their skills often give up trying.

For children around the world, physical growth is a major developmental aspect of their early years. Thus, it makes perfect sense to focus on the common cultural bonds of all races and nationalities in developing such skills. Picture books whose multicultural characters strive for physical accomplishments can serve as models for your youngster's own striving. As children bond with these book characters, they can begin to see that all people everywhere experience the same needs and interests, tasks and triumphs, as they walk and climb, throw and catch, run and ride through life.

◆ Activities To Promote Physical Expression ◆

1. Have children walk with partners imitating a motion while *Father and Son* is being read.

2. Have two children pick up and carry blocks or toys in a large clothes basket.

3. Play the "Who's Under the Basket?" guessing game after cleanup.

4. Make a parallel obstacle course for partners based on *Father and Son* story.

5. Have each child go through a fun obstacle course you have set up while you observe and record their movements.

6. Have a follow-the-leader activity based on *Father and Son*.

7. Do a chant as children demonstrate different motions from *Father and Son*.

8. Have a child pick up and deliver a "fuel bottle" (large hollow block) to another child.

9. Have children pull a fishnet full of blocks or toys.

10. Have an indoor hopscotch carpet for children to use.

11. Jump on inflated mats or tire tubes.

12. Roll a large ball to children sitting on the floor.

13. Bounce a ball to children standing in a circle.

14. Have a child sit in a wheelchair (or chair) and try to catch a ball you throw.

15. Have children shoot a child-size basketball into a hoop.

16. Have children stand in a row while you kick a soccer ball to be caught with their legs or feet.

17. Throw a soft ball for children to catch.

18. Have children skate around the room on two blocks.

19. Have children ski on the floor or on a block ramp on two unit blocks.

20. Put on a sports day as in *The Bicycle Man*.

21. Measure the height of each child every three months. Have island fruit and play calypso music.

22. Do an action chant imitating Hue Boy's actions.

23. Pretend to be a moving/leaping animal.

24. Visit the zoo and look for animal motions.

25. Have children make up stories about what it feels like to be a leaping animal.

26. Make animal faces or masks for each child.

27. Have children tell what they can see from highest point in their swinging.

28. Play the singing game "Here We Go Round the Mountain, Two by Two."

29. Strut around a square to square-dance music.

30. Make pinwheels and kites and run in the wind.

31. Make up a story about playing ball.

32. Do a story reenactment of *Trouble with Trolls*.

33. Do a story reenactment of *A Bicycle for Rosaura*.

 LEARNING ACTIVITIES

1. Assess each of the children's large-motor locomotion skills by setting up an obstacle course and observing and recording children's progress as they go through each part of it.

2. Read one of the books mentioned that promotes a different sort of walking skill, and follow up with a walking activity. Record the results.

3. Read *Hue Boy* and then measure the height of each child.

4. Read one of the hopping, jumping, or leaping books and follow up with a movement activity. Record the results.

5. Read *Darlene* and then have children pretend to be Darlene sitting in a wheelchair (or chair) and catching a ball you throw to them.

REFERENCES

Beaty, J. J. (1994). *Observing development of the young child.* Upper Saddle River, NJ: Merrill/Prentice Hall.

Cratty, B. J. (1982). Motor development in early childhood. In B. Spodek (Ed.). *Handbook of research in early childhood education* (pp. 27–46). New York: Free Press.

Flinchum, B. M. (1975). *Motor development in early childhood: A guide for movement education with ages 2 to 6.* St. Louis: Mosby.

Kranowitz, C. S. (1987). Obstacle courses are for every body. In B. Neugebaurer (Ed.), *Alike and different: Exploring our humanity with young children.* Redmond, WA: Exchange Press, 24–35.

Sinclair, C. B. (1973). *Movement of the young child ages two to six.* Upper Saddle River, NJ: Merrill/Prentice Hall.

 ADDITIONAL READINGS

Allen, J., McNeill, E., & Schmidt, V. (1992). *Cultural awareness for children.* Menlo Park, CA: Addison-Wesley.

Andress, B. (1991). From research to practice: Preschool children and their movement responses to music. *Young Children, 47*(1), 22–27.

Benzwie, T. (1987). *A moving experience: Dance for lovers of children and the child within.* Tucson, AZ: Zephyr Press.

Cartwright, S. C. (1990). Learning with large blocks. *Young Children, 45*(3), 38–41.

Cherry, C. (1971). *Creative movement for the developing child.* Belmont, CA: Fearon.

Cratty, B. J. (1986). *Perceptual and motor development in infants and children.* Upper Saddle River, NJ: Prentice Hall.

 CHILDREN'S BOOKS

Arnold, T. (1987). *No jumping on the bed!* New York, Dial. (Caucasian)

Bardot, D. (1991). *A bicycle for Rosaura.* Brooklyn: Kane/Miller. (Hispanic)

Binch, C. (1994). *Gregory Cool.* New York: Dial. (Caribbean)

Brett, J. (1992). *Trouble with trolls.* New York: Putnam. (Scandinavian)

Caseley, J. (1991). *Harry and Willy and Carrothead.* New York: Greenwillow Books. (Caucasian, Multiethnic)

Cohen, M. (1982). *So what?* New York: Dell. (Caucasian, Multiethnic)

Dale, P. (1987). *Bet you can't.* New York: Lippincott. (African American)

Dorros, A. (1991). *Abuela.* New York: Dutton. (Hispanic)

Ets, M. H. (1963). *Gilberto and the wind.* New York: Viking. (Hispanic)

Galdone, P. (1994). *Jack and the beanstalk.* New York: Clarion. (Caucasian)

Garland, S. (1993). *Why ducks sleep on one leg.* New York: Scholastic Publications. (Vietnamese, Animals)

Greenfield, E. (1980). *Darlene.* New York: Methuen. (African American)

Havill, J. (1989). *Jamaica tag-along.* Boston: Houghton Mifflin. (African American and Hispanic)

Heide, F. P. (1990). *The day of Ahmed's secret.* New York: Lothrop, Lee, and Shepard. (Egyptian)

Johnson, M. D. (1983). *Wait, skates!* Chicago: Children's Press. (African American)

Joseph, L. (1990). *Coconut kind of day.* New York: Lothrop, Lee and Shepard. (Caribbean)

Kusugak, M. A. (1993). *Northern lights, soccer trails.* Toronto, Canada: Annick Press. (Inuit)

Lankford, M. D. (1992). *Hopscotch around the world.* New York: Morrow Junior Books. (Multiethnic)

Lauture, D. (1992). *Father and son.* New York: Philomel Books. (African American)

Lewin, H. (1993). *Jafta.* Minneapolis: Carolrhoda Books. (African)

Maris, R. (1986). *I wish I could fly.* New York: Greenwillow. (Animals)

Marzollo, J. (1990). *Pretend you're a cat.* New York: Dial. (Multiethnic; Animals)

Matura, M. (1989). *Moon jump.* New York: Alfred A. Knopf. (East Indian)

McKissack, P. C. (1988). *Mirandy and Brother Wind.* New York: Alfred A. Knopf. (African American)

Mitchell, R. P. (1993). *Hue Boy.* New York: Dial. (Caribbean)

Perkins, C. (1993). *Swinging on a rainbow.* Trenton, NJ: African World Press, Inc. (African American)

Say, A. (1982). *The bicycle man.* Boston: Houghton Mifflin. (Japanese)

Smalls-Hector, (1992). *Jonathan and his mommy.* Boston: Little, Brown. (African American)

Thomas, I. (1991). *Mermaid Janine.* New York: Scholastic Publications. (African American)

Speaking Other Languages

7

A major goal of multicultural education is to prepare children from all language backgrounds to participate fully in every aspect of our society. (Ramsey, 1987, p. 147)

SPEAKING OTHER LANGUAGES IN THE PRESCHOOL CLASSROOM

In most early childhood classrooms in the United States, the teacher speaks English as a first language, but may speak another language. The assistant teacher also speaks English, but may have been hired because she or he is also fluent in a second language, perhaps Spanish. The children speak the language they hear spoken at home. With the majority of children this may be English, but more and more youngsters who speak other languages are coming to preschool.

If children's families are immigrants from Asian or Latin American countries, their first language may be Vietnamese, Cambodian, Laotian, Tagalog, Japanese, Chinese, Korean, or Spanish. If the children themselves are recent immigrants, they may not speak English at all. If the preschool program is situated in a locality where families from different cultures live, then the majority of the children may speak a language other than English.

"What a babble!" you may say to yourself. "I speak only English. What am I as a teacher supposed to do?" The answer, of course, lies in your goals for children: to support them in their development of physical, cognitive, emotional, social, language, and creative skills; to help them feel good about themselves as this development occurs; and to help them learn to respect and get along with the other children around them.

Your commitment to language learning should be the same as your commitment to other areas of your children's development. This means that your classroom setup, materials, and activities should be designed to help youngsters teach themselves about languages and spoken words through exploratory play. Your classroom should be full of spoken language—dramatic play, mealtime conversations, visiting speakers, oral book-reading, storytelling, chanting, tape recorders and blank tapes, language tapes, play telephones, computer software—in as many languages as you deem appropriate.

What if you have no children who speak a language other than English? That is all the more reason to introduce them to a new language, especially during these early years, when children learn language most easily. Speaking a second language is a great benefit for everyone. In addition, learning new sounds, new words, and new symbols helps youngsters in the acquisition of their own language. More importantly, it helps them appreciate and bond with people who speak another language.

LANGUAGE ACQUISITION IN PRESCHOOL CHILDREN

Preschool children are at the language-acquisition stage of their development. Between birth and age 6, children acquire an entire native language from scratch. If they are from bilingual or multilingual families, they may acquire more than one language. This natural language acquisition in young children is so commonplace that we tend to take it for granted. We seldom stop to think what a miraculous accomplishment it is to go from having no spoken language at birth to speaking an entire native tongue by age 6!

The years from 2 to 5 are especially crucial in this process. During this period, a child's vocabulary expands from about 250 to 2,000 words, and he learns by himself the rules for putting words together to speak in sentences. Because children are often in early childhood programs during these years, the language environment you provide can have a profound effect on their language development.

Bilingual children are especially fortunate to attend a preschool like yours—one that recognizes their native language as well as English—because they will have the chance to become fluent in both languages during this period of natural language acquisition. At no other time in their lives will they be able to acquire another language so easily.

How do they do it? Not through formal language lessons, but in the most informal and spontaneous way imaginable: by hearing it spoken around them, by trial and error in speaking it among themselves, and by subconsciously extracting the rules of the language. Their brains are programmed to learn language this way—any language.

The process of introducing a new language to children in your class or center should follow the same principles. Rather than attempt formal teaching of the language, you need simply to provide opportunities for the children to be exposed to the language and allow them to acquire it naturally. For example, if Spanish is a first or second language for many of the children in your class, then you or your coworkers should speak Spanish as well as English at a certain time during the day. For full-day programs, you may want to have a Spanish hour during which nothing but Spanish is spoken. For half-day programs, have a Spanish half-hour. If you yourself do not know Spanish, have one of your co-workers do the speaking, and pick up a few words yourself as you listen to what is going on around you. Read, or have someone read, children's books in Spanish; sing songs in Spanish; do painting, block building, number games, or dramatic play in Spanish. Have a wonderful time during this Spanish hour, and soon most of the children, even Anglo children, will be saying a few Spanish words. A second language is truly a gift that everyone should feel good about receiving: both the Hispanic children whose language you have recognized, and the non-Hispanic children who have learned to say and understand simple phrases in this new language.

STAGES IN LEARNING A SECOND LANGUAGE FOR YOUNG CHILDREN

The early childhood teacher should recognize that the acquisition of a second language by young children seems to occur in stages. As Ramsey (1987) notes:

> To reduce anxiety and to provide an optimal balance of familiarity and challenge, it is useful to keep in mind the stages of second language acquisition. In games and tasks and in casual conversations, teachers can modify their expectations and questions according to the following stages. (pp. 157–158)

The Preproduction Stage
When children first hear a new language, they often respond by being silent. Then they concentrate on trying to understand what is being said rather than trying to repeat it. You can encourage children to point to objects when you say the name in another language, but don't expect every child to want or be able to repeat the name at first.

The Transition Stage
As children begin to try out words in another language, be sure to accept what they say. The words may not sound anything like they should, but do not correct their pronunciation. After all, many preschoolers' vocal development is not yet complete, so they do not and cannot pronounce all English words as they should. Instead, repeat the word many times yourself and encourage them to try again. Do it as a game or chant.

The Early Production Stage
Finally, children are able to respond to questions or activities that require a single-word or a short-phrase response. They may be able to sing the words of a simple song or do a finger play. Since you are not teaching the children a second language, this stage will be the final one for most preschool children.

USING MULTICULTURAL PICTURE BOOKS
TO PROMOTE SPEAKING OF SPANISH

◆ *Abuela* (Dorros, 1991)

◆ *Abuelita's Paradise* (Nodar, 1992)

◆ *Margaret and Margarita [Margaret y Margarita]* (Reiser, 1993)

◆ *This House Is Made of Mud [Esta Casa Esta Hecha de Lodo]*
   (Buchanan, 1991)

◆ *Uncle Nacho's Hat [El Sombrero del Tio Nacho]* (Rohmer, 1989)

The book *Abuela* (Dorros, 1991), also discussed in Chapter 4, is the story of Rosalba and her *abuela*, the Spanish word for grandmother. The two of them spend a day in the park feeding the pigeons and then suddenly fly high above the park, the city, the airport, and the Statue of Liberty. Her grandmother, who speaks only Spanish, calls her "*Rosalba el pajaro*," which means "Rosalba, the bird." Rosalba says to her, "*Ven, Abuela*," which means "Come, Abuela." She translates the simple Spanish words as they are spoken.

After you read this book, invite your children to play the Abuela game, and challenge each child who plays the role of Abuela or Rosalba to say at least one word in Spanish as they "fly" around the classroom. Can they say *mira*, meaning "look," as they zoom around? If they are using one of your Hispanic cultural dolls for this game, be sure to have them speak for her in a Spanish word or two. Do the other children understand what the doll is saying? If you have Spanish-speaking children playing this game, have them try speaking a word or two in English.

Do any of your Spanish-speaking children have an *abuela* who would come to the class and read this book to the children? Or, if not read the book, perhaps tell a story? The story could be in either Spanish or English—or both. Asking family members to share their language with the class is yet another way to cement relations between home and school, as well as demonstrate to all of the children your respect for their families and languages.

In *Abuelita's Paradise* (Nodar, 1992), a rocking chair and purple blanket help little Marita remember her deceased grandmother and all the stories she told her while holding Marita on her lap. Spanish words are interwoven throughout the story and interpreted by Marita. The purple blanket, for instance, has the word *paraiso* on it, which means "paradise." In lyrical prose, Marita's grandmother describes life as a little girl on a farm in the highlands of Puerto Rico: how she would go out to the sugar cane fields with their family's oxen, Pedrito and Pablito; how she would dance with the sugar cane stalks swaying in the wind; how the honeycreeper bird would fly through the kitchen window looking for bits of sugar.

When Abuelita rocks her chair fast, it seems as though the two of them are flying through the air in Puerto Rico like the soaring flamingos. Now, with her grandmother gone, Marita's mother sits in the rocking chair and holds Marita on her lap, and they wrap the purple blanket around them. Watercolor illustrations portray Puerto Rico as the paradise Abuelita describes. Some of the Spanish words she uses are:

little girl:	*niñita* (nin NYEE tah)
straw hat:	*sombrero* (som BRER oh)
sugar cane knife:	*machete* (mah SHEH tee)
nap:	*siesta* (see ES tah)
tree frog's song:	*coq-ui, coq-ui* (coh-KEE, coh-KEE)

If you have a rocking chair in your room, bring in a small blanket or shawl and read this story to the children one at a time, just like Marita's grandma. Can they "fly" around the classroom with the blanket afterwards, coming back to you and telling what sights they saw? If they imagined a scene from the book, have them show you that page in the book. Reading to children on a one-on-one basis like this helps them really understand stories and books. The closer they can get to the reader, the more meaningful books become.

Margaret and Margarita [Margaret y Margarita] (Reiser, 1993), also discussed in Chapter 5, is a story about two girls who go to the park with their mothers and meet one another. The story is presented in English and in Spanish on opposite pages. The girls try to speak with one another, but "Oh dear, they do not speak English" and "*Oh no, no hablan español*." But they do manage to say "Hello" and "*Hola*." Then the girls introduce their stuffed toys, a rabbit named Susan and a cat named Susana. Next come two pages of tiny pictures about what each girl likes about the other, presented in English and Spanish. The two toys are soon having a party—a *fiesta*—with dancing. Finally, the girls introduce their mothers to one another, and then it is time to go.

After reading the story to a small group, ask who would like to be Margaret, Margarita, Susan, and Susana. When you read the story again, ask them to repeat simple words in English or Spanish as you say them. Does anyone else want to try it? The more you repeat this story, the more words the children will remember. Be sure it is not a lesson, but simply a way to have fun. Do you have Margaret and Margarita dolls the children can play with after the story is finished? If so, listen to what the children say as they pretend with them. Do they speak any Spanish words?

This House Is Made of Mud [Esta Casa Esta Hecha de Lodo] (Buchanan, 1991) is the story of a round adobe house in the Arizona desert. The story is told in simple English and Spanish on the same page. The house resembles a Navajo *hogan* but was actually built by the author in the Sonoran Desert in southern Arizona. The colorful illustrations show desert and domestic animals, sun, cactus, and even a bit of snow. The yard around the house is the Desert—*el Desierto*; the fence is the Mountains—

las Montañas. Although no people appear in the story, it is still intriguing to children to see a round house. Can they build one in the block area? Can they remember any of the Spanish words that tell about it, such as those that follow?

mud:	*lodo* (LO doh)
round:	*redonda* (reh DON dah)
the sun:	*el sol* (el SOL)
the moon:	*la luna* (la LU nah)

Uncle Nacho's Hat [El Sombrero del Tio Nacho] (Rohmer, 1989) is a humorous Nicaraguan folktale illustrated with bright folk art on every other page. The story is presented in English at the top of a page and in Spanish at the bottom of the page. Every morning Uncle Nacho says good morning to his cat, his dog, his parrot, his monkey, and especially to his hat, which is old and full of holes. He tries to fan his fire with the hat but it is too full of holes to do any good. When his niece brings him a new hat, he can't decide what to do with the old one, so he finally throws it in the trash. His mother finds it and returns it to him. Next, Uncle Nacho takes the hat to the edge of town and hangs it on a tree, where an old gentleman finds it. But some boys take it from him and return it to Uncle Nacho. Finally Uncle Nacho's niece tells him that he must concentrate on thinking about his new hat, so he does. He takes it out to visit all his friends.

If your children like this story, bring in a straw hat for reenacting this story. Make it into a game: have one of the children pretend to be Uncle Nacho and hide the hat somewhere in the room when the others are not looking. Have the other children try to find it, and the finder be the next Uncle Nacho. Can they say the Spanish words for hat (*sombrero*), new hat (*sombrero nuevo*) or friends (*amigos*)? If they are Spanish-speaking, have them say the words in English.

Many well-known picture books have been translated into Spanish in recent years. If your children enjoy the English version, you should consider purchasing the Spanish version too, so they can see the difference. Many educational catalogs have several of these Spanish-version books:

The Doorbell Rang (Hutchins):	*Llaman a la Puerta*
Rainbow Fish (Pfister):	*El Pez Arco Iris*
Green Eggs and Ham (Seuss):	*Huevos Verdes con Jamon*
Owl Babies (Waddell):	*Las Lechucita*
A Chair for My Mother (Williams):	*Un Sillon Para Mi Mama*
Goodnight Moon (Brown):	*Buenas Noches Luna*

Cassettes with Spanish words and songs should also be used throughout the year, especially when you are reading these English/Spanish storybooks

Source for books, tapes, CD-ROM programs in Spanish:

Niños
P.O. Box 1163
Ann Arbor, MI 48106-1163

to the children and they are playing the games involved. *Sing with Me* contains original songs about numbers, names, clothing, fruit, greetings, and action words in both English and Spanish, as well as traditional children's songs from Latin America. *I Can Sing en Español!* comes with a book as well as cassette with basic Spanish vocabulary, animals, colors, numbers, and other concepts. Remember, you are not teaching the children to speak Spanish. Instead, you are introducing them to an interesting new way of saying things that some children in the class may already do.

USING MULTICULTURAL PICTURE BOOKS TO PROMOTE SPEAKING OF NATIVE AMERICAN LANGUAGES

- ◆ *My Kokum Called Today* (Loewen, 1993)
- ◆ *Seya's Song* (Hirschi, 1992)
- ◆ *Itse Selu, Cherokee Harvest Festival* (Pennington, 1994)
- ◆ *The Boy Who Dreamed of an Acorn* (Casler, 1994)
- ◆ *Ma'ii and Cousin Horned Toad* (Begay, 1992)

As mentioned in Chapter 2, an increasing number of picture books are coming on the market that depict Native Americans in a more accurate manner than was the case earlier. Nevertheless, teachers must be sensitive about using one or two of these books and expecting them to represent all Indians across the United States and Canada. As pointed out by Native American educator Winona Sample (1993):

> *Most teachers who are not Indians do not understand why it is so difficult to accurately teach about American Indians to young children or sometimes to teach Indian children. One reason is that there are over 400 federally recognized Indian tribes and about 350 Indian languages. To add to the confusion, there is a bewildering array of tribes, clans, bands, rancherias, and villages to which any Indian may belong. (p. 39)*

Sample goes on to talk about Indian children, noting:

Indian children may be intertribal—belonging to more than one tribe. They also may be more acclimated to an urban setting than to reservation life. Indian children come in all degrees of acculturation. (p. 39)

In **My Kokum Called Today** (Loewen, 1993), also described in Chapter 8, the girl narrator and her relatives are Cree Indians living in Canada. In this contemporary story, the girl lives in the city but her grandmother, her Kokum, lives on the Reserve and invites her by phone to come home for a round dance over the weekend. This simple story, with its sensitive illustrations of Indians wearing contemporary clothing but following many traditional ways, shows the girl with her grandmother, who speaks Cree to her. Although the girl does not understand much Cree, she can feel her grandmother's love and the specialness she imparts.

Very few Cree words are used in the story, but some of your children are sure to note that one of them is another way to say grandma: *kokum*. Did they remember *abuela* from the Spanish stories? Another Cree word her grandmother uses is *astum*, meaning "come here." Can your children say it? Another word is *bannock*: a type of biscuit the grandmother makes (discussed further in Chapter 9).

In **Seya's Song** (Hirschi, 1992), another Native American grandmother is remembered by her granddaughter, the narrator of this story about the S'Klallum people of Washington State. *Seya* means grandmother in the S'Klallum language. As the girl walks along the morning stream on a path down to the sea, she remembers the words her seya taught her: *kwitchin* for baby salmon, *tsshai* for cedar tree, *Skio* for beaver, *Siehu* for heron, and *Skaatl* for otter. Many other S'Klallum words are intertwined in this story, which flows like the stream that it follows and has stunning illustrations of birds, people, mountains, and sea.

As a follow-up activity, mount cutouts or figures showing the people and objects in the book and label them with signs in S'Klallum and English from the glossary at the end of the story, such as:

stars:	*tetosena* (teh TOE seenah)
sun:	*sushatsht* (sue SHOT sht)
salmon:	*kwitchin* (kweet chin)
eagle:	*kwaiegsn* (KWANGK son)
elk:	*smyets* (smye ETS)
basket:	*mohoi* (mo HOY)
father:	*tsut* (tsoot)
grandmother:	*seya* (SAE yah)
young man:	*swchewus* (shh chWAY woos)

Now take your children for a follow-the-leader walk around the room just like the girl walked with her grandmother on the path down to the sea. As you come to an object, you can point to it, to the sign, and say, "Oh, look, Seya, there is a ——!" Say the word in both S'Klallum and English. Have the children repeat what you are saying. Young children are fascinated with the sounds of language, any language.

Does this mean you are teaching them another language? Not at all. You are introducing them to the concept that another language has different words that mean the same thing as English words. Children love to say new word sounds, you will find.

In *Itse Selu, Cherokee Harvest Festival* (Pennington, 1994), a book set in long ago times, a boy, Little Wolf, tells the story about his life during Itse Selu, the Green Corn Festival. (See Chapter 8.) A Cherokee word is used on every page of text and repeated with its pronunciation at the bottom of the page. Large, beautiful illustrations depict a happy, peaceful life among the people as they prepare for the festival. Little Wolf's favorite part is his grandfather's storytelling, when he weaves his magic web of stories, this time about Rabbit, the foolish Wildcat, and the Stickyman, an Indian variant of "Brer Rabbit and the Tarbaby."

Put a number of items out on a table along with name cards showing their English and Cherokee names. To make pictures of these items which can then be colored and cut out, make a photocopy of the page of the book containing the item. Then have children go around the table and choose an item. Can they guess what the English word says? Then tell them the Cherokee word, such as:

corn:	*selu* (shay LOO)
beans:	*tuya* (TOO yah)
water:	*ama* (ah MAH)
fire:	*gotvdi* (go tuh VIH)
baby:	*usdi* (oos DIH)
mother:	*utsi* (ooh TSEE)
rabbit:	*tsistu* (jees DOO)
mountain lion or wildcat:	*tlvdatsi* (tluh dah TSIH)

The Boy Who Dreamed of an Acorn (Casler, 1994) is another old-time story about the night three Chinook boys from the Pacific Northwest go on a "vision quest" up a mountain, searching for a dream of power. They hope to dream about powerful animals, like a mountain lion, grizzly bear, or wolf. Part way up the mountain, one boy stops, builds his fire, and falls asleep. He dreams about a huge black bear. Farther up the mountainside the second boy stops, builds his fire, and falls asleep. He dreams of a white-headed eagle flying through the sky. The third boy climbs to the very top of the mountain, builds his fire, and falls asleep. He is sad to report that his dream was only of a small brown acorn lying on the ground.

When the boy reports his dream to the village wise man, he is told that in the smallest of acorns there is a thing that is mighty, and he gives him an acorn to plant. As he watches the acorn grow into an oak tree, he is sad that he does not have the strength of the boy who dreamed of a bear or the speed of the boy who dreamed of the eagle. But when he is grown, his people come to him because he is wise and gentle, and because he shares everything he has with all, for all are in his heart.

This is a beautiful story but long for preschoolers. After you have read it yourself, "read" the pictures to a small group of children at a time. Have them sit close enough to see the boys climbing the mountain by moonlight and sitting by their fires in a magical atmosphere of sparks and starlight.

Afterwards give everyone in your listening group a little animal from your toy figure box, but be sure to include an acorn. Use pictures from a toy catalog if you do not have toy figures. Ask children to hold the item in their hand, close their eyes, and try to see in their mind what that object can do. When they open their eyes, have them tell what they saw. Accept anything they say. Then give them a card to hold with the Chinook name for the item on it. You can tell them how to say it. Use the items and cards for each small group until everyone has had a chance to be the dreaming boy. Some Chinook words found in the book include:

Groups should be small enough so all can see the pictures and practice new words.

acorn:	*kahnaway* (KA na way)
black bear:	*itchwoot* (ITCH wot)
eagle:	*chakchak* (CHAK chak)
hawk:	*shakshak* (SHAHK shahk)
elk:	*moolock* (MOO luk)
fox:	*hyas opoots talapus* (hiAS O poots tala pus)
mountain lion:	*hyas pish pish* (hiAS pish pish)
mouse:	*hoolhool* (hol hol)
wolf:	*leloo* (le loo)

Ma'ii and Cousin Horned Toad (Begay, 1992) is a traditional Navajo folktale about the tricky coyote, Ma'ii, and his cousin the horned toad. The Navajo have many such stories, which they often use as teaching tales to show people the proper way to conduct themselves. This story depicts the coyote visiting his cousin, the horned toad, and eating a lot of corn from his cornfield. When Ma'ii tricks his cousin into looking for a piece of corn stuck between his teeth, he snaps up the horned toad as well. But the spiny horned toad does not rest easily in the coyote's stomach. When the coyote tries to get him to come out, he first resists all Ma'ii's tricks until he finally comes out and scares Ma'ii so badly he runs away forever.

Preschool children will not lose their attention during this long tale if you read the pictures, using the Navajo sound words, such as *shil na aash*, that the horned toad says while inside the coyote's stomach. Make paper-bag

Children can try out Native American words with their dolls.

puppets of coyote and horned toad by photocopying pictures of each from the book, having each child color one, then fastening it to the bottom of a small paper bag. Then, as you read the story again. have children be coyote or horned toad as they reenact the story with all its funny incidents. Each time they repeat the story, have them use a new Navajo word as found in the glossary:

Hello:	*ya ateeh* (YAH ah te eh)
Goodbye:	*hagoonee* (ha go NAY)
an expression of fright:	*yee yah!* (yee yah)
Thank you:	*ahehee* (A HYEH hay)
my cousin:	*shil na aash* (shellsh na ash)
my grandfather:	*shi che* (shee chay)

Whenever the Navajos find a horned toad, they place it gently over their hearts and greet it "*Ya ateeh shi che*," which means "Hello, my grandfather," because they believe it gives strength of heart and mind.

Be sure to have Native American tapes available for children to hear when you are reading or reenacting any of these stories. Some possibilities include: *American Indian Songs and Chants,* and *Walk in Beauty My Children;* also *The First Dog* (four Chippewa-Cree stories), and *How Rabbit Tricked Otter* (Cherokee legends of animals).

USING MULTICULTURAL PICTURE BOOKS TO PROMOTE THE SPEAKING OF MANY LANGUAGES

◆ *The Dancer [La Bailarina]* (Burstein, 1993)

◆ *Table—Chair—Bear: A Book in Many Languages* (Feder, 1995)

◆ *What Does the Rooster Say, Yoshio?* (Battles, 1978)

 Source for other language tapes, songs, Language Lotto games:

Claudia's Caravan
Multicultural/Multilingual Materials
P. O. Box 1582
Alameda, CA 94501

◆ *Cock-A-Doodle-Doo! What Does It Sound Like To You?* (Robinson, 1993)

◆ *The Handmade Alphabet* (Rankin, 1991)

The Dancer [La Bailarina] (Burstein, 1993) is a simple story in English, Spanish, and Japanese of a father walking through the city with his little daughter on the way to her ballet class. Opposite each full-color illustration is a page with three simple words or phrases, one under the other, in the three languages. For instance, as the father and daughter start out the door, the girl says to her mother:

Good-bye, Mommy

Hasta pronto, Mami (AH-sta PRON-to, MAH-mee)

(Japanese characters) (MA-ma, IT-te ki-MAS)

She continues on her way, smiling at people and seeing a horse, flowers, a boat on a car, fish, a street musician, and finally the ballet school.

My school

Mi academia (mee ah-kah-DAY-mee-ah)

(Japanese characters) (wa-TA-shi no gak-KO)

Once again, have the children sit close enough to see the pictures as you read the simple words in each of the three languages. Practice ahead of time so you do not have to stumble over the pronunciation yourself. Let any children who want to try to repeat the words after you. If you have a Spanish or Japanese child in the class, invite a family member to come in and read the book, too.

Write the words from the book on cards and take your small listening group with you on a walk around the class. When you come to the fish in your aquarium, stop, look at the card, and say the word for fish in the three languages. Can they find any flowers in the room? A toy horse? A boat? Those who want can try to say the names in all three languages.

Table—Chair—Bear: A Book in Many Languages (Feder, 1995) is another playful approach to languages, this time 13 of them, including English. Each page contains the picture of an item from a child's room, with the English name for the item printed at the top. On the side of the page, one under another, is the same word in 12 different languages—Korean, French, Arabic, Vietnamese, Japanese, Portuguese (Brazilian), Laotian, Spanish (Mexican), Chinese (Mandarin), Cambodian, and Navajo—along with its pronunciation.

Preschool teachers should not expect to say the name of each object in all 13 of the languages. Instead, the idea is to pique children's curiosity about languages. For instance, ask the children how they would say the word for "tricycle" if they lived in Vietnam. They would say *xe dap ba bahn*, pronounced "seh DAP ba ban." Then ask how they would say the word if they lived in the Philippines. They would say *traysikel*, pronounced "TRAI see kel." If you have a child whose particular background is from one of the countries whose language is mentioned, spend more time saying each of the objects in his or her language.

At another time, have each child in your small listening group bring one of the cultural dolls or a toy person from a different culture with them when you look at the book together. Ask each in turn who their doll or figure is. Let them choose an object from the book, and you can tell them what the word is in their doll's language. Can their doll then repeat the word?

Another fascinating way to introduce children to the concept that some people say things differently than they do is to read ***What Does the Rooster Say, Yoshio?*** (Battles, 1978), a book about animal sounds. Most people are unaware that sounds for animals are spoken differently in different countries. In this story, a Japanese boy, Yoshio, and his mother talk with an American girl, Lynn, and her mother as they walk around in the United States. Yoshio is surprised that the people he talks to do not understand him. Will animals know what he says to them?

He says "Wan, wan!" to Lynn's dog, but Lynn tells him dogs say "Bow wow!" When they see ducks swimming in a pond, Yoshio goes over to them and says "Ga, ga!" and Lynn retorts "Quack, Quack!" A sparrow hops by and Yoshio says "Choon, Choon" while Lynn says "Cheep, cheep." When they see a horse, Yoshio says "He-heen, he-heen" and Lynn corrects him by saying "Neigh, neigh." Then Yoshio tries saying "neigh." Next time, when they see a sheep, Yoshio waits until Lynn tells him what sheep say: "Baa, Baa!" He then says, "May, may." They both try each other's pig sound: "Oink, oink" and "Bu, bu." The rooster sound is even different: Yoshio says "ko-kay-ko-ko!" and Lynn says "cock-a-doodle-doo!" The rooster looks at them both in surprise. Finally the book ends on a note of agreement when they both say "moo" for the cow.

If the children enjoy this story, set up your barnyard animals on a table and ask half of your listening group to be from Japan and half from the United States. Let them make the sounds for each of the animals you point to. Can they remember? Then have them change sides.

All kinds of games can be played with animal sounds. Have each child choose a toy animal and carry it around the group until someone can say its sound in Japanese. Then it is that child's turn to carry her animal around.

A larger book with a similar theme is ***Cock-A-Doodle-Doo! What Does It Sound Like To You?*** (Robinson, 1993). Large double-page collage pictures have the rooster saying "kee-kee-ree-kee!" in Spain and "koh-keh-koh-koh!" in Japan. Dogs bark "guv guv!" in Greece, "wo wo!" in China, and "how how!" in India. Frogs croak "kroo kroo!" in Africa, "gedo gedo!" in Japan, and "kwok kwok!" in Germany. Bees buzz in England, while in Israel they "zmmm! zmmm!" and in India they "hmmm! hmmm!" Other sounds are different in other languages, too, as this story shows with its dripping faucets, pounding hammers, and chugging trains.

Play the same game here as you did with the Yoshio book, or give it a new twist as a transition-to-lunch game. Show the group various animals and let the children who can say their different sounds in another language go to lunch one by one. Then make a sound in a different language and those who can guess what animal is speaking can go to lunch next, and so on. Be sure to mount animal pictures around the classroom when you are reading these two books. Remember that preschool children may still be unsure of what the animals say in English, so make this a fun experience, not a contest where someone wins and someone loses.

Not everyone speaks a language with their voice. It is important for children to learn about hearing-impaired people who use their hands to "sign" their language. The strikingly illustrated *The Handmade Alphabet* (Rankin, 1991) shows on its cover six hands of different sizes and skin colors doing signing. Inside, large full-page pictures show each of these same hands making the manual alphabet sign for each of the letters from A to Z. For instance, a hand holding asparagus signs "A." The picture for the letter G shows a hand in a glove signing that letter, while the picture for the letter K shows a child holding toy keys.

As you show this book page by page to your small listening group, say the letter aloud and ask them to guess what object the hand sign stands for. Can they make the sign with one of their hands? It will not be easy for the youngest children. Older youngsters can place their hand next to the proper picture to check their success. Would the children like to learn how to sign the first letter of their name? If you have tissue paper or onion skin, trace over the signing hand for each child's letter and mount it on cardboard. Then have them practice. Next time you "read" this book, do it silently, with those children who can making their own name sign.

As children become aware of and interested in other languages, other language games can be used throughout the year with all of the books discussed. Language Lotto games come with picture cards of animals, nature, clothing, transportation, school and household objects, and numbers. Children can match pictures or words on the cards or play with them any way they choose. Bilingual cassettes are available in Cambodian, Cantonese, Farsi, French, German, Hmong, Japanese, Korean, Laotian, Mandarin, Russian, Spanish, Swahili, Tagalog, and Vietnamese.

For classrooms with CD-ROM computers, a series of interactive, animated software with sound in English, Spanish, and Japanese is available for children. Even young children can operate these programs easily by moving the cursor with a computer mouse and clicking on the various objects on the screen. Voices and text can be switched easily from one language to another for comparison of words in the different languages. Best of all, these programs are based on picture books of the same name which can be used with the programs. They include *Just Grandma and Me, The Tortoise and the Hare*, and *Ruff's Bone*.

Source for computer programs based on picture books:

Broderbund Software
500 Redwood Boulevard
P. O. Box 6121
Novato, CA 94948-6121

Just Grandma and Me

Ruff's Bone

The Tortoise and the Hare

USING PICTURE BOOKS TO PROMOTE THE SPEAKING OF ENGLISH BY CHILDREN WHO SPEAK ANOTHER FIRST LANGUAGE

◆ *Oh, Kojo! How Could You!* (Aardema, 1984)

◆ *Half a Moon and One Whole Star* (Dragonwagon, 1990)

◆ *Not Yet, Yvette* (Ketteman, 1992)

◆ *Hattie and the Fox* (Fox, 1992)

◆ *Nine-In-One Grr! Grr!* (Xiong, 1989)

◆ *Yo! Yes?* (Raschka, 1993)

In some classrooms, the language children need to hear and practice is English. If their first language is not English, then they will need to participate in speaking English words. You can show respect for their first language by mounting signs in English and their language on objects around the classroom. You can play cassettes having words and songs in their language. You can have books written in their language available. You can invite family members to visit the class to tell stories or read books in their language. But these children will also need to participate in speaking English words.

Some of the best picture books for this purpose are those that have repeated words or phrases which children can repeat aloud as you read the story. *Oh, Kojo! How Could You!* (Aardema, 1984), also discussed in Chapter 4, is an African trickster tale about a young man named Kojo who is sent by his mother to purchase various items but is always tricked out of his gold dust by Ananse, who sells him something worthless. Every time the boy returns his mother says: "Oh, Kojo! How could you!" and later, "It isn't one thing. It isn't two things. It's Ananse!"

As this is a long story, it is better told by you than read. Tell the story to a small group at a time while children look at the pictures. This is a wonderful phrase repetition story. For example, each time the name "River that Gurgles" is mentioned, children repeat the phrase "pon pon pon PON sa." Children love the sound of the river and can't wait to say it aloud.

Sounds of words are important to young children as they acquire a language. As they hear new words, they play around with the sounds of them, just as they play around with blocks before building with them. Children are attracted to some books simply by the sound of a certain word. For instance, young children love Margaret Wise Brown's classic *Goodnight Moon* (1947) especially because they enjoy hearing the word "mush" used in the phrase "a comb and a brush and the bowlful of mush." The river's noise of "pon pon pon PON sa" in *Oh, Kojo! How Could You!* gives them that same satisfaction.

Half a Moon and One Whole Star (Dragonwagon, 1990) is a prose poem with stunning illustrations of an African American girl going to sleep at night. The poem talks of animals, birds, and insects awake at night, but ends each verse with "Yes, yes, yes, she does, sleep, Susan, sleep." Once again, you should read this book to a small listening group and have them follow the pictures along to the end of each verse, when they all can repeat "Yes, yes, yes, she does, sleep, Susan, sleep."

In ***Not Yet, Yvette*** (Ketteman, 1992), an African American girl named Yvette and her father are preparing a surprise party for her mother when she comes home from work. At the end of each chore, Yvette asks her father, "It is time yet, Dad?" and the father answers, "Not yet, Yvette. There's more to do." Have half the group ask Yvette's question and the other half give the father's response. Point to them when it is their turn to speak. Repeating phrases like this helps keep the attention of everyone glued to the book, waiting for their cue to ask and answer the title question.

Books like this often turn out to be favorites because most children like to participate so much. The books also give non-English speakers a chance to practice unfamiliar words without fear of ridicule. If they do not participate at first, don't force the issue. Remember the stages that language learners go through; some children may still be in the preproduction stage, when they listen rather than speak.

Folktales from other countries sometimes have repetitious phrases as well. In ***Hattie and the Fox*** (Fox, 1992), an Australian tale, Hattie, the big black hen, sees parts of the fox in the bushes and tries to warn the other barnyard animals about the danger. But every time they respond:

"Good grief!" said the goose.
"Well, well!" said the pig.
"Who cares?" said the sheep.
"So what?" said the horse.
"What next?" said the cow.

Once they know the story, have your listening group repeat each phrase as you point to the picture of the animal. Later they can take turns being each of the animals and saying their part.

In *Nine-In-One, Grr! Grr!* (Xiong, 1989), a Hmong folktale from Laos, the tiger visits the sky god and asks how many cubs she will have each year. He tells her nine in one year, but that she needs to remember this number if she wants to have that many. Tiger tries to remember the number by singing a song: "Nine-in-one, grr! grr!" Your children will enjoy repeating these words. When Bird finds out what Tiger's song is about, she is appalled that there will be so many tigers in the jungle. She tricks Tiger into singing "One-in-nine, grr! grr!" and thus reduces the number of tigers the animals will have to deal with. Can your children change their words when Tiger changes hers? They will need to listen closely to the story.

A fun book that all children seem to enjoy and be able to repeat is *Yo! Yes?* (Raschka, 1993), a simple story with one huge picture of a child and one or two large words on each page. On one page is a picture of an African American boy who starts the story by saying "YO!" On the opposite page is a picture of a Caucasian boy who responds at first with a hesitant "Yes?" Their simple one- or two-word conversation finally brings them together as friends. The book ends as it started, with a loud, "YO!" and "YES!" followed on the final page with a "YOW!" as the boys jump high together.

Have half of your group be one boy and say his words and the other half be the other boy and say his words. As you turn the pages, point to each group when it is their turn to speak. If this book becomes a favorite, be prepared to have this conversation repeated in the classroom. You will know then that children not only learn to say words from another language through picture books, but also to have respect for those who speak that language.

◆ Activities To Promote Speaking Other Languages ◆

1. After reading *Abuela*, have children "fly" around the classroom like Rosalba and say a word in Spanish.

2. Invite an abuela to visit and read or tell a story.

3. After reading *Abuelita's Paradise*, bring in a shawl and have a child sit on your lap and be Marita.

4. After reading *Margaret and Margarita*, have a child take one of the parts and say a word or two in Spanish.

5. Bring in Margaret and Margarita dolls for children to play with.

6. Have a child hide Uncle Nacho's hat somewhere in the classroom and let the others try to find it.

7. Play cassettes with Spanish words or simple songs.

8. After reading *My Kokum Called Today*, pretend to be a kokum and call your granddaughter on the phone.

9. After reading *Seya's Song*, place objects labeled in the S'Klallum language around the room. Then take children on a follow-the-leader walk, point to the objects, and help children say the words like Seya.

10. Put items on a table and label them with Cherokee words and English words. Help children guess and say the words.

11. Give everyone a little animal from your toy box to dream about and tell about after hearing *The Boy Who Dreamed of an Acorn*.

12. Make horned toad and coyote paper-bag puppets with the children and reenact the story of *Ma'ii and Cousin Horned Toad*.

13. Have children find items in the classroom like those in the book *The Dancer [La Bailarina]*, and help them say the name in another language.

14. Have children bring a cultural doll to the listening group when you read *Table—Chair—Bear: A Book in Many Languages*. Identify their doll and say names of items in that language for them and their doll to repeat.

15. Put toy barnyard animals on a table and have half your children say the sound the animals make in English and the other half in Japanese.

16. Play a transition-to-lunch game, asking children to say the sound a toy animal makes in a different language.

17. Trace the hand-sign letter for each child's first name and help them practice signing it.

18. Play other games such as Language Lotto or use CD-ROM computer programs.

19. Have children repeat words from *Oh, Kojo! How Could You!*, *Half a Moon and One Whole Star*, and *Not Yet, Yvette*.

20. Have children be the animals in *Hattie and the Fox* and say the animal's words.

21. Have children repeat the tiger's chant in *Nine-In-One Grr! Grr!*

22. Have children take turns being each boy in *Yo! Yes?* and say the boys' words.

 ## LEARNING ACTIVITIES

1. Do a language assessment of the children and their families, finding out what language or languages are spoken at home or with other family members. Can you identify the stage of language acquisition each child is in?

2. Bring in blank tapes, language tapes, books like those discussed in this chapter, signs, posters, computer software, and other materials to support the use of another language in the classroom. Record how you use them and the result.

3. Read to several small groups of children one of the picture books that promote Spanish speaking, then follow up with one of the suggested activities. Record the results.

4. Invite a family member who speaks another language to visit the class and share a story, song, or activity with the children.

5. Discuss why it may be difficult to teach accurately about Native American children, and tell how you would use one or two of the picture books mentioned to promote the speaking of their languages.

 ## REFERENCES

Ramsey, P. G. (1987). *Teaching and learning in a diverse world: Multicultural education for young children.* New York: Teachers College Press.

Sample, W. (March, 1993). The American Indian child. *Day Care Exchange, 3,* 39–40.

 ## ADDITIONAL READINGS

Beaty, J. J. (1996). *Skills for preschool teachers.* Upper Saddle River, NJ: Merrill/ Prentice Hall.

King, E. W., Chipman, M., & Cruz-Janzen, M. (1994). *Educating young children in a diverse society.* Boston: Allyn and Bacon.

Little Soldier, L. (1992). Building optimum learning environments for Navajo students. *Childhood Education, 68*(3), 145–148.

Mallory, B. L., & News, R. S. (Eds.). (1994). *Diversity and developmentally appropriate practices.* New York: Teachers College Press.

Rigg, P., & Allen, V. G. (Eds.). (1989). *When they don't all speak English: Integrating the ESL student in the regular classroom.* Urbana, IL: National Council of Teachers of English.

 ## CHILDREN'S BOOKS

Aardema, V. (1984). *Oh, Kojo! How could you!* New York: Dial.

Battles, E. (1978). *What does the rooster say, Yoshio?* Morton Grove, IL: Albert Whitman.

Begay, S. (1992). *Ma'ii and Cousin Horned Toad.* New York: Scholastic Publications.

Brown, M. W. (1947). *Goodnight moon.* New York: Scholastic Publications.

Buchanan, K. (1991). *This house is made of mud [Esta casa esta hecha de lodo].* Flagstaff, AZ: Northland Publishing.

Burstein, F. (1993). *The dancer [La bailarina].* New York: Bradbury Press.

Casler, L. (1994). *The boy who dreamed of an acorn.* New York: Philomel Books.

Dorros, A. (1991). *Abuela.* New York: Dutton.

Dragonwagon, C. (1990). *Half a moon and one whole star.* New York: Aladdin/ Macmillan.

Feder, J. (1995). *Table—Chair—Bear: A book in many languages.* New York: Ticknor & Fields.

Fox, M. (1992). *Hattie and the fox.* New York: Aladdin/Macmillan.

Hirschi, R. (1992). *Seya's song.* Seattle, WA: Sasquatch Books.

Ketteman, H. (1992). *Not yet, Yvette.* Morton Grove, IL: Whitman.

Loewen, I. (1993). *My Kokum called today.* Winnipeg, Canada: Pemmican Publications.

Nodar, C. S. (1992). *Abuelita's paradise.* Morton Grove, IL: Albert Whitman.

Pennington, D. (1994). *Itse Selu, Cherokee harvest festival.* Watertown, MA: Charlesbridge.

Rankin, L. (1991). *The handmade alphabet.* New York: Dial.

Raschka, C. (1993). *Yo! Yes?* New York: Orchard Books.

Reiser, L. (1993). *Margaret and Margarita [Margaret y Margarita].* New York: Greenwillow Books.

Robinson, M. (1993). *Cock-a-doodle-do! What does it sound like to you?* New York: Stewart, Tabori & Chang.

Rohmer, H. (1989). *Uncle Nacho's hat [El sombrero del Tio Nacho].* San Francisco: Children's Book Press.

Xiong, B. (1989). *Nine-in-one Grr! Grr!* San Francisco: Children's Book Press.

Eating Fine Foods

8

I think our interest in differences is communicated when we add information such as "leche is milk in Spanish" while drinking milk with 3-year-olds or identifying Italian spaghetti. At first remembering to do this was hard. Now it's fun. (Garcia, 1984, p. 64)

BRIDGING THE CULTURAL GAP WITH EATING AND FOOD

We may not remember to talk about the cultural aspects of foods, but we don't forget to eat. Young children are fascinated with food. When they are not gobbling down their own meals or snacks, they are watching like hawks as other children eat. Early childhood educators need to take cues like this from children. Their fascination with eating and food can be used to help children grow and develop.

How? We already know that children's cooking in the classroom promotes the small-motor skills of stirring, grinding, squeezing, mashing, peeling, cutting, grating, sifting, and pouring. Their "reading" of illustrated recipe charts promotes pre-reading skills. The tasks of serving, sharing, cleaning up, and helping one another promotes social skills. Making their own snacks, setting their own tables, and pouring their own drinks help preschool children develop a positive self-image when they realize how well they are trusted by the adults around them to perform these adult-type tasks. And the eating of nutritious foods develops healthful habits that last.

Because food preparation is a real and not pretend activity, the gains children can accomplish are especially important, as Cosgrove (1991) attests:

Early experiences with food preparation may lay the foundation for a life-long habit of eating nutritious foods. . . . I can't think of a more appropriate way to involve children in accepting responsibility for their own eating habits than in the preparation of food. (p. 43)

Because all foods are cultural in that they have originated from a particular culture, foods are one of the simplest ways to focus on children's common bonds of eating while celebrating their cultural differences of eating special foods.

155

USING PICTURE BOOKS TO MOTIVATE MULTICULTURAL FOOD EXPERIENCES

◆ *Everybody Cooks Rice* (Dooley, 1991)

By now your children may recognize that when you read them a new picture book, you are planning to introduce an exciting new activity. How delighted they will be when you begin bringing in storybooks that focus on foods! (Be sure to check for food allergies before children eat any of these foods.)

Be sure to have rice ready for cooking when you read children ***Everybody Cooks Rice*** (Dooley, 1991). In this story, big sister Carry is sent out to find her little brother Anthony and bring him home for supper. She knows where to look for him because Anthony is a "moocher" who likes to visit their multicultural neighbor's houses and sample their dinners. But which neighbors? Carry begins with Mrs. D's next door, who is from Barbados, but Anthony is not there. She eats a small cup of rice and black-eyed peas while Mrs. D tells stories about Barbados people swimming even in December! Carry is soon working her way around the neighborhood, looking for Anthony but instead finding delicious rice dishes to sample. She returns home, empty-handed but full-stomached, and finds Anthony there in their own kitchen. At the end of this remarkable rice expedition are recipes you can make with your children week by week:

Mrs. D's Black-eyed Peas and Rice (Barbados)

The Diazes' Tumeric Rice with Pigeon Peas (Puerto Rico)

Tam's Nuoc Cham (Vietnam)

Mrs. Tran's Fried Rice (Vietnam)

Rajit's Biryani (India)

Mrs. Hua's Tofu with Vegetables (China)

Madame Bleu's Rice and Beans (Haiti)

Great-Grandmother's Risi e Bisi (Northern Italy)

Put each recipe on a large newsprint or posterboard for the children to follow as they add the ingredients. Make simple line drawings showing teaspoons and cups. But be sure to read first the book pages that describe what Carry experiences at the house where the particular rice dish is being prepared. It is important for the children to get a close-up view of the illustrations showing multicultural families in ordinary neighborhood kitchens preparing their native dishes. Your children should feel at ease with these folks from different cultures who cook food in such familiar surroundings.

Asian Foods

Cleversticks (Ashley, 1991)

How My Parents Learned To Eat (Friedman, 1984)

Dumpling Soup (Rattigan, 1993)

Halmoni and the Picnic (Choi, 1993)

Everyone in the Hua's house eats with chopsticks. Can your children do the same? Have they been practicing after hearing the story *Cleversticks* (Ashley, 1991), discussed in an earlier chapter? If not, better read *Cleversticks* again and let them practice first with cracker or cookie pieces before trying rice. Keep the rice sticky so they can pick it up in a clump. How well can you do it?

A book older children will enjoy is ***How My Parents Learned To Eat*** (Friedman, 1984), told in the first person by a girl who sometimes eats with chopsticks and sometimes with a knife and fork. Her father met her mother in Japan when he was a young American sailor and she was a Japanese high school girl. They both had to learn to eat with each other's utensils. This book is available in paperback in a packet that includes chopsticks and plastic rice.

Your children can pretend to be the characters in their favorite rice stories if you keep several pairs of chopsticks in the Dramatic Play Area along with the dishes and other cooking utensils. One catalog offers an entire child's Asian cooking set including a wok, tempura rack, cooking chopsticks, bamboo paddle, steamer, spoons, plates, soup bowls, and tea cups. Another catalog offers plastic food for dramatic play: an Asian food set containing egg rolls, sushi, white rice, beef and snow peas, and chicken cashew; a Japanese sushi set with three types of rolled sushi and plastic tray; a Chinese dim sum set with a spring roll, meat dumpling, fried dumpling, moon cake, shrimp dumpling, big bun, steamed bun, and birthday bun.

The Asian soup bowls and porcelain soup spoons from the first catalog set mentioned can make a big hit with children after you have read ***Dumpling Soup*** (Rattigan, 1993), mentioned in a previous chapter. This story describes Marisa's Hawaiian New Year celebration, the first time she gets to make dumplings at her Korean grandma's house. All of her aunties bring piles of beef, pork, and vegetables along with their own cutting boards, and soon are chopping up the cabbage, bean sprouts, onions—all to be mixed into the spicy filling for the dumpling dough.

 Source for "theme packet" for *How My Parents Learned to Eat*:

Lakeshore Learning Materials
2695 E. Dominguez St.
P. O. Box 6261
Carson, CA 90749

Source for Asian, Japanese, Chinese, and Hispanic plastic food sets:

Constructive Playthings
1227 East 119th Street
Grandview, Missouri 64030-1117

Such a complicated recipe may be beyond the abilities of most preschoolers, but you all can make soup together from any kind of vegetables cooked in a broth and then eat it for lunch using Asian soup bowls and spoons.

Better still, invite a member of an Asian family to your class to help prepare a recipe of his or her own. If no one is free to come during the day, perhaps the family could send a favorite recipe for you to prepare, or actually send along the dish. The importance of a family's involvement in its child's preschool program cannot be overemphasized. For children from multicultural backgrounds, their families' endorsement of their school and the school's endorsement of their families may make the difference between their own success or failure in their schooling to come. As Greenberg (1989) notes:

> *Knowing that her family and her school agree on who she is supposed to be simplifies the child's evolving self-image struggles.* (p. 63)

Halmoni and the Picnic (Choi, 1993), a New York City story for older children about a Korean grandmother, tells the tale of Yummi's grandmother, who comes to Yummi's class picnic in Central Park bringing enough of the traditional Korean food *kimbap* for everyone. Younger children can enjoy this story if you "read" the pictures.

This story not only uses the theme of food to contribute to children's multicultural perspective, it also serves to illustrate the type of family-school cooperation that you should try to achieve for your class or center. Does the teacher show that she likes a child's mother or father, just as Mrs. Nolan likes Yummi's grandmother even though she looks and acts so different? Does the family member endorse the preschool program even though it is so different from the home, as Yummi's grandmother does? Children breathe a sigh of relief when they see mutual respect and acceptance between adults at home and school.

Hispanic Foods

Too Many Tamales (Soto, 1993)

Three Stalks of Corn (Politi, 1976)

The Tortilla Factory (Paulsen, 1995)

Saturday Sancocho (Torres, 1995)

Carlos and the Squash Plant (Stevens, 1993)

Children from Hispanic backgrounds may have relatives who have come to the United States from Cuba, Puerto Rico, Mexico, or any of the Latin American countries. The children themselves may have immigrated to this country and still enjoy eating the special foods created by their people. For some children, that food may be Mexican tamales: corn flour dough with spicy meat inside, cooked in corn husk wrappers.

The picture book *Too Many Tamales* (Soto, 1993) tells the tale of Maria and her parents, who are making tamales together in preparation for a party. Maria's mother takes off her wedding ring when she and Maria are kneading the dough, but then the phone rings. Maria tries on the ring for a moment, but then forgets about it as she kneads the dough. Later, when her cousins arrive for the party, she is horrified when she remembers the ring. It must be in the tamales! So she has her cousins eat the entire platter of

Children can pretend about multicultural stories with play food.

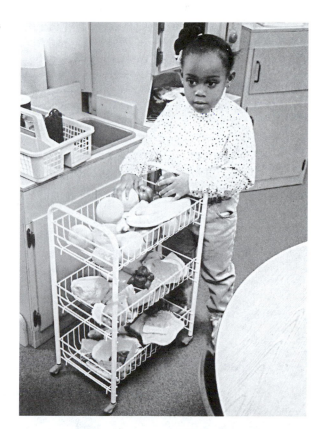

tamales, ever so carefully, but no ring appears. Unbeknownst to Maria, her mother had found the ring earlier. So everyone must remake a big batch of tamales.

The large, nearly full-page illustrations make this a book the youngest child can enjoy, although the text at the bottom may be too complex for 3-year-olds. Children at ages 4 and 5 will enjoy hearing the words and want to play the "Maria game" in your housekeeping area if you put out Hispanic food props. The picture on the front cover of this book makes a fine motivator for playing this game. Cut out the picture from the dust jacket cover of the book and mount it in the housekeeping area so children will get the idea. Dust jackets from all of the books mentioned can be mounted in the classroom and used in a similar fashion whenever you want to stimulate multicultural play and pretending.

Eventually the children will want to make real tamales, just as the book illustrates. If possible, invite a Hispanic family member who can help your class prepare tamales. Or you can purchase canned tamales and heat them in a microwave oven or covered frypan.

An easier yet somewhat similar food experience for young children is to wrap hot dogs or vienna sausages in prepared dough, such as crescent roll triangles. These "pigs-in-a-blanket" can then be baked in a toaster oven.

At some point children should experience kneading dough the way Maria does. Make play dough and have the children help knead it by hand. Be sure to use the word "kneading" as they do it. At the same time, read the *Too Many Tamales* story so the youngsters can observe someone from another culture doing the same thing they are doing. In this way children experience the common bonds all of us share in cooking food, while celebrating the differences in the types of foods we enjoy.

Hispanic food sets available from one catalog include cooking utensils such as a tortilla press, tortilla basket maker, masher, marble mortar and pestle, taco tongs, and a taco rack. The plastic food provided includes chili sauce, taco, spanish rice, corn chips, and an enchilada. If you decide to use plastic items like this in your Dramatic Play Area, you should first cook real Hispanic food, then use the plastic items to follow up the real food experience the children all have enjoyed. This is how children learn: first by expe-

 Source for Asian and Hispanic cooking sets:

Childcraft
20 Kilmer Road
P. O. Box 3081
Edison, NJ 08818-3081

riencing the real thing and then by following it up with vicarious activities such as book-reading, puppets, doll-playing, and pretend dramatic play.

If hot food preparation is not allowed in your center, plan a field trip to a fast-food taco restaurant, where its staff can show the children how Hispanic food is prepared. Back in the classroom, you can follow up the field trip by reading a book.

In *Three Stalks of Corn* (Politi, 1976), the main character, Angelica, visits her Mexican grandmother, whose vegetable garden with its three stalks of corn is in the front yard of her lovely little California-style house.

Angelica learns to make tortillas, tacos, and enchiladas from her grandmother, and at the same time listens to grandmother's wonderful stories of the Tarahumare and Toltec Indians and their use of corn. Later, Angelica's teacher invites her grandmother to class to help the children learn to make tacos and enchiladas. She teaches them a song to sing as they pat the tortillas. The recipes for tacos and enchiladas appear at the end of the story. This is a long story for young children, but they will want to spend time looking at the finely drawn illustrations, especially the double-page pictures of the neighborhood Angelica's grandmother lives in and the colorful Mexican fiesta that takes place in the story.

Your children can make tacos from prepared tortillas and taco mix—unless, of course, you are able to invite a Hispanic family member who can help them make their own tacos as Angelica's grandmother did.

Tortillas can be purchased in most supermarkets these days. Your children may be interested, though, to see where they come from and how they are made.

The Tortilla Factory (Paulsen, 1995) is a simple picture-and-prose poem of the tortilla's beginnings: from the black earth, which is worked with brown hands, which plant yellow seeds, which become green plants, to the machinery and hands that mix and push the dough into shape. When the tortillas arrive at someone's kitchen, they are wrapped around juicy refried beans with brown hands and eaten by white teeth.

This book is a fine introduction for a midmorning snack the children can make on their own. After you read this book, bring in some store-made tortillas and have your children make their own tacos with a can of refried beans, some chopped lettuce, and tomato sauce. What colors can they identify?

The book *Saturday Sancocho* (Torres, 1995) is a South American story of Maria Lili, who visits her grandparents' house every Saturday to help them make chicken stew (sancocho), until the one Saturday when they have nothing in their house to cook with except a dozen eggs. This longer story for older children is so well illustrated that preschool teachers will be able to "read" the pictures easily to their children. Have a small group of children at a time sit close enough to see the pictures.

Maria Lili's grandmother, Mama Ana, takes her to the open-air market where they are able to trade the eggs one or two at a time with the merchants for everything they need. When they return home, Papa Angelino helps them convert their plantains, cassava, corn, carrots, tomatoes, onions, cilantro, garlic, cumin, and a medium-size chicken into a delicious stew.

This story can also be acted out dramatically, or literally if you have an automatic crockpot into which the children can add the ingredients. Be sure to have this activity early in the day, so that you will have a tasty stew ready for lunch. A vegetable stew is easiest, but if children want to prepare chicken sancocho, the recipe follows the story.

You can also act out the story in a pretend mode by having children place various plastic vegetables and other food items in a play pot as you read the story.

In the story *Carlos and the Squash Plant* (Stevens, 1993), the main character is Carlos, a boy who lives in the mountains of northern New Mexico. Carlos loves to help his brother and father work in their garden, but hates to take a bath afterwards. He especially hates washing his ears, so he refuses. His mother warns him that if he doesn't wash his ears, a squash plant will grow in them. Carlos ignores her warning, and one morning he really does find a squash plant growing from one of his ears! He is so embarrassed that he hides his ears under a straw hat. As the plant grows each day, Carlos must find a larger hat to hide it. Finally he hops in the tub, scrubs his ears, and the plant disappears.

Throughout the story, illustrations show the family in the kitchen or at the breakfast or dinner table, eating hot sausage and eggs, or cornmeal cakes, or tortillas and honey, or calabacitas, Carlos' favorite dish. This book is an important one for your boys and girls to look at together because of its large, colorful illustrations of this Hispanic boy. At the end of the story, the recipe for calabacitas—a corn, squash, cheese, and green chile dish—is provided.

The text appears in English at the top of every other page and in Spanish at the bottom of the same page. Most preschoolers may not be able to pick out separate words saying the same thing, but you can read them. It is simple Spanish, some of which even non-Spanish speakers will be able to read. If not, invite a family member or language student to translate.

In addition to preparing one of the food dishes mentioned in this book, you may want your children to play the role of Carlos. Bring in several straw hats or sombreros of different sizes. Try to find a boy doll for the children to pretend with, as illustrated in the photo accompanying this text. You may even want to plant yellow squash or zucchini seeds to grow your own vegetables, depending on the length of your growing season.

Native American Foods

Dragonfly's Tale (Rodanas, 1991)

My Kokum Called Today (Loewen, 1993)

Itse Selu, The Cherokee Harvest Festival (Pennington, 1994)

Iktomi and the Berries (Goble, 1989)

Use a doll to depict Carlos and his funny problem with a squash plant.

Cooking experiences in the classroom can also include Native American foods after you have read a children's picture book as an introduction. Such experiences should be an ongoing part of the curriculum rather than a special so-called "Indian unit." For example, perhaps the children are growing corn seeds in their Science area. Then they should also be investigating corn and its properties throughout the curriculum. Dried ears of corn of different varieties can be used to decorate the classroom in the fall. For creative movement experiences, the children can sway like cornstalks in the wind to a Native American flute or drum tape. For lunch, they can eat a corn and lima bean mixture called succotash by Native Americans. In the Art area, they can make cornhusk dolls. In the Dramatic Play Area, children can pretend to be characters from books and stories that involve corn.

One such as story is ***Dragonfly's Tale*** (Rodanas, 1991), a traditional Zuni tale from the Southwest about a lesson the ancient people had to learn. When they offend the spirits who had given them bountiful harvests, the Corn Maidens withdraw their blessings. Although the tale is a long and complex one, the colorful full-page illustrations that grace every page of the book make it easy for you to tell the story orally as you show the pictures. Preschool children can understand your simpler telling of the tale as they see the two Corn Maidens blessing the corn and then withdrawing their blessing when these pueblo people display disrespect for food by throwing bread, batter, and dough at one another.

Good source for books on Native Americans and Hispanics:

Send for catalog:

Northland Publishing Co.
P. O. Box 1389
Flagstaff, AZ 86002

When the Corn Maidens come to the pueblo disguised as two ragged old women, the only people who will give them any food are a boy and his sister, who try to share their corn cakes drenched in honey. Later an army of mice, gophers, bugs, and birds swoops down on the pueblo and eats every crumb of food. The people are forced to move away, and only the boy and his sister are left behind. The boy makes his sister a butterfly toy out of a piece of cornstalk and leaves. It flies away to the Corn Maidens and they bless the children with beans, squash, and corn. When the pueblo people return, they have learned their lesson. From then on, they respect the Corn Maidens and the good Earth that provides their food. Every year when the corn is beginning to bloom, a strange corn insect also returns. It is known as Dragonfly.

Your children may want to make a cornstalk dragonfly in the Art area and then reenact this folktale. They may also want to make corn cakes, or better still, fry bread, a traditional Native American food. Hopis often use blue cornmeal ground from blue corn. This can be purchased in health food stores. Blue corn chips are also available. One recipe for Hopi Fry Bread is the following, from Allen, McNeill, and Schmidt (1992, p. 41):

2½ cups flour

⅓ cup cornmeal (or blue cornmeal)

1 tablespoon baking soda

1 teaspoon salt

2 cups water

cooking oil

A small group of children at a time can help mix the ingredients by hand. Have them wash their hands first. Place the flour in a large bowl. Have the children add the cornmeal by handfuls and then the salt and baking powder. Give each child a turn to mix the ingredients by hand. You can add the water a little at a time while the children mix. When the dough is soft, pliable but not sticky, have each child form a small ball of dough and then roll it carefully with a little rolling pin until it is about ½ inch thick. Then you (not the children) can fry the dough in hot oil in an electric fry pan until the edges are brown on both sides. The children may want to eat their fry bread with honey on it.

My Kokum Called Today (Loewen, 1993) tells the contemporary story of a modern Cree Indian girl and her mother, who live in the city, and the girl's grandmother, her Kokum, who lives on the Reserve. Her Kokum invites the girl and her mother to come home to the Reserve for the weekend for a round dance. When they arrive, her Kokum takes the girl out in the woods to gather plants for medicine and pick berries, and then has her help make *bannock*, Indian biscuits to be eaten with homemade jam.

Your children can also make biscuits from the recipe on a biscuit mix package. Can they stamp out their biscuits in the rolled-out dough with a glass like the girl in the book? These can then be baked in a toaster oven a few at a time. Be sure to work with a number of children equal to the number of biscuits that can be baked at once. Small groups can listen to the story and then make biscuits over a period of several days, until everyone has had a turn.

Itse Selu, The Cherokee Harvest Festival (Pennington, 1994) tells the story of the Cherokee Green Corn Festival as it was celebrated in the old days. Little Wolf is the main character, with his sister Skye, his baby sister Sutega, and his best friend Little Buffalo. His mother, father, grandmother, and grandfather are also involved in the action. Cherokee words are substituted for English for particular items and activities.

The story tells of a day in the life of Little Wolf, from his morning breakfast of *tuya* (beans) and *selu* (hominy), ground from last year's corn, to the Green Corn Festival of new corn which begins at sunset time. Everyone in the village is preparing for the celebration, which is also New Year's Day for the Cherokee.

Your children may want to make and eat hominy grits just like Little Wolf and his sister do. Instant grits can be prepared from a package either by boiling or in a microwave. They can make a nutritious breakfast, snack, or lunch.

Iktomi and the Berries (Goble, 1989) is a humorous story about Native American food involving the Lakota trickster Iktomi, who goes out hunting for prairie dogs but cannot find any. He then tries hunting for ducks but falls in the water and scares them away. Finally he looks for buffalo berries to make berry soup, but he cannot reach them. When he sees the berries reflected in the water he tries diving down many times to get them before realizing they are hanging from bushes at the edge of the water.

Your children can make a new kind of berry soup by using the recipe for "pretend soup" from the book of the same name (Katzen & Henderson, 1994). To make it, put two cups of orange juice in a bowl, then add ½ cup plain yogurt, one tablespoon of honey, and two teaspoons of lemon juice. Whisk all these ingredients until the mixture is all one color, then pour it over the children's dishes of berries and sliced bananas. This recipe, as well as all the others in this cookbook for preschoolers, is illustrated with drawings for each step.

African American Foods

Eat Up, Gemma (Hayes, 1988)

Feast for 10 (Falwell, 1993)

Knoxville, Tennessee (Giovanni, 1994)

Mel's Diner (Moss, 1994)

Many modern picture books featuring African Americans and foods show children involved with mainstream American food rather than ethnic food from their culture.

Eat Up, Gemma (Hayes, 1988) is a humorous story told by a little African American boy about his toddler sister who won't eat anything. At breakfast, Mom says, "Eat up, Gemma," but Gemma throws her cereal on the floor. At the market, the clerk gives Gemma a bunch of grapes. "Eat up, Gemma," says Mom, but Gemma pulls off her grapes one by one and squashes them. When Grandma makes dinner, Mom says, "Eat up, Gemma," but Gemma bangs her spoon and doesn't eat a thing. And so it goes, day after day, until Sunday at church, when Gemma is seated behind a lady with artificial grapes on her hat. Suddenly Gemma says, "Eat up, Gemma," and tries to pull a grape off the lady's hat.

That gives her brother an idea, and when they get home from church he turns a yellow bowl upside down on a yellow plate and arranges a bunch of grapes and bananas around it just like the lady's hat. Gemma says, "Eat up, Gemma," and eats every bit of the fruit, even trying to munch the banana skins!

Would your children like a snack like Gemma's? Let them help you to arrange grapes, a banana, and maybe some apple slices on yellow paper plates for everyone. Can they all eat up as well as Gemma?

Feast for 10 (Falwell, 1993) is a simple, colorful counting book in rhyme with ten African American characters who purchase, prepare, and then eat the feast for ten. They start with 1 cart in the grocery store, 2 pumpkins for pie, 3 chickens to fry, and so on until the wonderful meal is complete. Five children, their parents, and three guests sit down to enjoy it.

If you plan to have a Thanksgiving feast in your class, be sure to read this book beforehand. Children also enjoy acting out all the roles in the book as you read it. Let ten children at a time choose which characters they want to be. They can use plastic food props if you have them. Otherwise, let them pretend with blocks or their own imaginations as they purchase, take home, prepare, and then serve the meal you read about. This is wonderful practice in the pre-math skills of counting and one-to-one correspondence. Can anyone pick up 5 kinds of beans or 6 bunches of greens?

You may also want to take a small group of children at a time on a field trip to a market to purchase food. Food field trips can be done anytime if your center is located near a store. Take a few children along even if you are only buying Jell-O®. Have them point to items you name on the shelves. Have them count out different foods and fruits. Having two or three different children come along each time you go snack shopping is an excellent pre-math, pre-reading experience. You can discuss with them what kind of crackers or fruit juice you plan to buy and see if they can locate the items on the shelves.

Knoxville, Tennessee (Giovanni, 1994) is a beautifully written and illustrated prose poem about an African American girl who loves summer best and eats corn fresh from the garden, as well as okra, greens, cabbage, barbecue, buttermilk, and homemade ice cream. You and the children may want to have a picnic after reading this book. Can you make homemade ice cream with the children?

Mel's Diner (Moss, 1994) is a different kind of book altogether. This story is told in first person by Mabel, whose African American father and mother own and operate Mel's Diner. Mabel helps them by setting the breakfast tables with silverware and helping make coffee. She also greets customers when they come in and helps to serve simple items. After school she returns to the diner with her best friend Rhonda. When someone puts money in the jukebox, they dance. At last it is time to go home with her mother and wave goodbye to her father, who works late.

The foods mentioned and illustrated include pancakes, sticky buns, French fries, and Jell-O®. But even more interesting and important to your children are the detailed illustrations showing a multicultural mix of children, teens, adults, and elderly folks who visit the diner. Mabel interacts with them all. She helps them, listens to their stories, laughs at their jokes, finds lost items, and enjoys herself thoroughly.

After reading this book you may want to set up your lunch tables like a diner for one day a week. What would your children like to be—the chefs, waitresses, cashiers, or the customers? They can take turns until everyone has a chance at every role. If you have a diner-like restaurant in the neighborhood, be sure to take a field trip with the children first. Afterwards, let them play "diner" in the Dramatic Play Area.

World Food Roundup

Nothing Else But Yams for Supper! (Buchanan, 1988)

How To Make an Apple Pie and See the World (Priceman, 1994)

This Is the Way We Eat Our Lunch (Baer, 1995)

Potluck (Shelby, 1991)

Several children's picture books about food contain stories that have their characters sample a variety of different foods from around the world.

In *Nothing Else But Yams for Supper!* (Buchanan, 1988), a little Caucasian girl named Alice likes yams because they are soft and mucky and yummy. She will not eat anything else. When her family takes her on a trip to Finland, all she wants is yams, but they do not have yams. Finally the waiter brings her reindeer meatballs in thick gravy, creamed potatoes, and chestnut mousse for desert. She eats the chestnut mousse and loves it because it is soft and mucky and yummy.

In China they have no yams or chestnut mousse. After visiting various markets, Alice finally settles on bean curd in black bean sauce and loves it because it is soft and mucky and yummy. In Mexico they have no yams or chestnut mousse or bean curd, but only chiles, tortillas, avocados, bean burritos, beef tacos, and guacamole. Alice settles for guacamole and loves it because it is soft and mucky and yummy.

What about your children? Do they like foods that are soft and mucky and yummy? You may want to microwave yams for them to try. Or maybe they would like to make and try some guacamole. Mash up ripe avocadoes and mix them with Italian dressing until the mixture is creamy. This can be eaten as a dip with crackers or corn chips.

How To Make an Apple Pie and See the World (Priceman, 1994) takes another Caucasian girl in old-fashioned times on a hilarious trip around the world to find the ingredients for apple pie. She goes by ship to Italy to gather superb semolina wheat, hops a train to France to find a chicken that lays elegant eggs, visits Sri Lanka for cinnamon from the bark of the kurundu tree, hitches a ride to England to get a cow for milk, stows away on a banana boat to Jamaica to get a few stalks of sugar cane, parachutes down to Vermont for the apples, and then hurries home. Then she must grind, boil, milk, churn, slice, mix, and bake the ingredients before inviting friends in to sample her marvelous apple pie.

Your older children will be better able to understand such a story. If they want to bake their own pie, a recipe for crust and filling appears on the last page of the book. Or they can use prepared crust and canned pie filling that you buy at the store.

This Is the Way We Eat Our Lunch (Baer, 1995) takes children on another around-the-world adventure, eating lunch with youngsters from other countries. The story starts with Doug eating chowder in Massachusetts, then skips across the United States and Canada in two-line rhymes to Puerto Rico, Colombia, Ghana, Morocco, Israel, Italy, England, China, Japan, and Australia. Your children may indeed want to sample Lucinda's Florida Fruit Salad, Pete's Wild Rice Soup from Manitoba, Canada, or Mira and Jamila's hummus spread on pita bread from Israel. All of these recipes appear at the end of the story.

What about a potluck supper? In the book *Potluck* (Shelby, 1991), Alpha and Betty decide to have a potluck supper, so they clean their house and call up their friends, who represent every letter of the alphabet and every cultural or ethnic group in the neighborhood. Acton appears with asparagus soup, Ben brings bagels, and so on through an alphabet of enchanting children and delicious foods. Who would want to miss Don's dumplings or Edmund's enchiladas? Extravagant illustrations show Graham's giant garlic bread from Garbanzo's Bakery—almost ten feet long!—and Lonnie's lasagna on a tractor-size cart.

This is a good time to invite parents for an evening get-together for a potluck supper or potluck dessert. If such a feast is not feasible in your center, perhaps your children can put on their own pretend potluck in the Dramatic Play Area after hearing this story. Better still, purchase several copies of this paperback book and send them home through your lending library. Then invite a parent or grandparent to visit the class and help the children prepare one of the dishes.

Food preparation such as this can be the focus that brings home and school together gracefully. Many families are proud of the foods they prepare and may feel honored to share that food with their child's classmates. Children's picture books that feature food as part of a character's story can make this home and school sharing time possible. Obtain extra copies of any of the books mentioned here for home lending. Invite a family member to visit the class to read the book to a small group, or to tell their own food story. Could they then come back again to prepare one of their traditional dishes?

Your program's monthly newsletter may want to include a recipe from each of the families you serve, along with a listing of the picture books you are currently featuring about food. Although special foods for holidays are always welcome, it is the everyday food the children know so well at home that may make a difference in their own acceptance in the classroom.

◆ **Activities To Bridge the Cultural Gap with Food** ◆

1. Put rice recipes from *Everybody Eats Rice* on large sheets of newsprint and make one dish with the children each week.

2. Read *Cleversticks* and have children practice using chopsticks to eat cracker or cookie pieces.

3. Put plastic Asian and Hispanic foods and utensils in the Dramatic Play Area and encourage children to act out story roles.

4. Make vegetable soup together and eat from Asian soup bowls and spoons.

5. Invite a family member to help prepare a favorite recipe.

6. After reading *Too Many Tamales*, have children play a pretend "Maria game" of losing a ring while making tamales in the Dramatic Play Area.

7. Have children knead play dough like Maria does.

8. Take a field trip to a fast-food taco restaurant.

9. Have children make their own tacos.

10. Act out the story *Saturday Sancocho*.

11. Make vegetable stew in a crockpot.

12. After reading *Carlos and the Squash Plant*, have children put on straw hats and act out the role of Carlos.

13. Plant squash or zucchini seeds.

14. Decorate the classroom with dried ears of Indian corn.

15. Make a cornhusk dragonfly as in *Dragonfly's Tale*.

16. Make Hopi fry bread.

17. Make biscuits in a toaster oven.

18. Make hominy grits in a microwave oven.

19. Make berry soup using the "pretend soup" recipe given in this chapter.

20. Arrange grapes and bananas on a plate as in *Eat Up, Gemma*.

21. Reenact the story *Feast for 10* with 10 children and props.

22. Take small groups on a field trip to the store to buy snack food.

23. Have a picnic after reading *Knoxville, Tennessee*.

24. Set up a pretend diner after reading *Mel's Diner*.

25. Have yams or guacamole.

26. Make an apple pie.

27. Make hummus and spread it on pita bread.

28. Have a real or pretend potluck supper.

29. Buy several copies of *Potluck* and lend them to parents.

 ## LEARNING ACTIVITIES

1. Find out from families which cultural or ethnic foods they know about, like to eat, or could prepare.

2. Make a monthly newsletter and include in it names of children's books about food you are reading, cultural foods you are preparing, and recipes that various families have sent in.

3. Take a food field trip. For example, to a fast-food taco restaurant, a Chinese restaurant, a noodle or tortilla factory, or a farmer's market.

4. Have a family member who makes tortillas (or some other special food) come in with her equipment and demonstrate how.

5. Read one of the books mentioned in this chapter and make up a game or activity based on the story.

REFERENCES

Allen, J., McNeill, E., & Schmidt, V. (1992). *Cultural awareness for children*. Menlo Park, CA: Addison-Wesley.

Cosgrove, M. S. (1991). Cooking in the classroom: Doorway to nutrition. *Young Children, 46*(3), 43–46.

Garcia, N. In Browne, G. (1984). *Culture and children*. Austin, TX: Texas State Department of Human Resources.

Greenberg, P. (1989). Parents as partners in young children's development and education: A new American fad? Why does it matter? *Young Children, 44*(4), 61–75.

Katzen, M., & Henderson, A. (1994). *Pretend soup and other real recipes: A cookbook for preschoolers and up*. Berkeley, CA: Tricycle Press.

 ### ADDITIONAL READING

Beaty, J. J. (1994). *Picture book storytelling: Literature activities for young children*. Fort Worth, TX: Harcourt Brace.

 ### CHILDREN'S BOOKS

Ashley, B. (1991). *Cleversticks*. New York: Crown.

Baer, E. (1995). *This is the way we eat our lunch*. New York: Scholastic Publications.

Buchanan, J. (1988). *Nothing else but yams for supper!* Toronto, Canada: Black Moss Press.

Choi, S. N. (1993). *Halmoni and the picnic*. Boston: Houghton Mifflin.

Dooley, N. (1991). *Everybody cooks rice*. Minneapolis, MN: Carolrhoda.

Falwell, C. (1993). *Feast for 10*. New York: Clarion.

Friedman, I. R. (1984). *How my parents learned to eat*. Boston: Houghton Mifflin.

Giovanni, N. (1994). *Knoxville, Tennessee*. New York: Scholastic Publications.

Goble, P. (1989). *Iktomi and the berries*. New York: Orchard Books.

Hayes, S. (1988). *Eat up, Gemma*. New York: Mulberry Books.

Loewen, I. (1993). *My kokum called today*. Winnipeg, Canada: Pemmican Publications.

Moss, M. (1994). *Mel's diner*. New York: BridgeWater Books.

Paulsen, G. (1995). *The tortilla factory*. San Diego: Harcourt Brace.

Pennington, D. (1994). *Itse Selu, The Cherokee Harvest Festival*. Watertown, MA: Charlesbridge.

Politi, L. (1976). *Three stalks of corn*. New York: Scribner.

Priceman, M. (1994). *How to make an apple pie and see the world.* New York: Knopf.

Rattigan, J. K. (1993). *Dumpling soup.* Boston: Little, Brown.

Rodanas, K. (1991). *Dragonfly's tale.* New York: Clarion.

Shelby, A. (1991). *Potluck.* New York: Orchard Books.

Soto, G. (1993). *Too many tamales.* New York: Putnam.

Stevens, J. R. (1993). *Carlos and the squash plant.* Flagstaff, AZ: Northland.

Torres, L. (1995). *Saturday Sancocho.* New York: Farrar Straus & Giroux.

Creating Arts and Crafts

9

Studying children's response to picturebooks . . . has convinced me that picturebooks can and do provide children with purposeful talk, increase their literacy, deepen their response to books, and open up their awareness of art and aesthetics. (Kiefer, 1995, p. 41)

YOUNG CHILDREN'S AWARENESS OF PICTURE BOOK ART

◆ *At the Crossroads* (Isadora, 1991)

Young children approach the illustrations in picture books from an entirely different perspective than adults. First of all, everything in their world is new and unknown—and therefore exciting. Just opening a book and looking at a picture is exciting. While some children may flip through the pages quickly, many others spend time absorbing the tiniest details. Kiefer (1995), in her study of children's responses to picture books, observed:

One of the first things I noted was that children picked up the smallest details that many illustrators include in their pictures and that we adults often overlook. (p. 35)

Why is that, you may wonder? Just as infants are attracted to tiny beads, peas, or even pieces of lint they discover on the floor, preschool children often focus on the little things in the new items that come into their field of view. Because the meaning of a whole book illustration may not be as evident to them as it is to us, they seem to delight in the smaller, more familiar objects in a picture.

For example, in the South African story **At the Crossroads** (Isadora, 1991), discussed in Chapter 2, young children are excited to discover the old bicycle wheels and sticks here and there in the illustrations of the township settlement where the children are waiting for their fathers. Sticks and bicycle tires are items that they, too, would pick up and play with. Did you notice them? While looking at the picture of the worried children waiting alone in the dark, your listeners may ask, "What are all those dots of light in the dark?" When you will tell them that they are lights from the windows

175

of the houses, your children may respond that they look like stars on the ground or the eyes of the children.

Stars on the ground. Glowing eyes in the dark. What a fresh and original perspective! You may conclude that, with such originality, these children could almost be artists themselves. They almost are. Young children bring to art the same sort of freshness and creativity that adult artists do. Their tastes have not yet been forced into a stereotyped mold. Their feeling for beauty is open to any expression. They are the perfect audience to respond to the art of contemporary picture books.

When that art is multicultural in nature, they happily accept it into the artistic vocabulary they are developing. There is beauty surrounding all of us, even in a South African ghetto, if only we have eyes—like an artist's or a little child's—to see. Thus, picture books can help children learn to appreciate the beauty of artistic expression; they can be lead-ins to multicultural arts and crafts activities; and they can introduce children to multicultural characters who themselves have experiences with creating colors, drawing pictures, folding paper, or modeling clay.

USING MULTICULTURAL PICTURE BOOKS TO AWAKEN CHILDREN'S APPRECIATION OF COLOR

◆ *Moon Rope [Un Lazo a la Luna]* (Ehlert, 1992)

◆ *Raven: A Trickster Tale from the Pacific Northwest* (McDermott, 1993)

◆ *Rainbow Bird: An Aboriginal Folktale from Northern Australia* (Maddern, 1993)

◆ *Color Dance* (Jonas, 1989)

◆ *Little Blue and Little Yellow* (Lionni, 1959)

◆ *The Legend of the Indian Paintbrush* (DePaola, 1988)

◆ *Flower Garden* (Bunting, 1994)

◆ *Wild Wild Sunflower Child Anna* (Carlstrom, 1987)

Because children's first classroom experiments with art usually involve color, it is important that some of your multicultural books include lavish spreads of bright colors. As noted by child development specialist Clare Cherry (1972):

Color is the cue by which we determine the quality of a shape. Although the shape may take precedence in defining what a thing is, it is the color that touches more deeply our innermost feelings. The young child between three and five years of age, with normal perceptual development, is more concerned with the colors of objects than with their shapes. (p. 34)

Notice which books are your children's favorites. Ask them about their favorite books. The youngsters may not know why they like certain books, but they should be willing to talk about them once they realize you are interested. Young children do not differentiate between the pictures and the text of a book. To them, the picture is the story. Although some may recognize text, too, they expect it to be the caption for the picture. When you read a book to them, it is the picture you are reading that they believe at first. Not until later do they realize there is a difference between illustrations and text. (Ferreiro & Teberosky, 1979, 53–99).

Do any of the children love *Moon Rope [Un Lazo a la Luna]* (Ehlert, 1992) as one of their favorites? Brilliant colors are the trademark of all of Lois Ehlert's picture books, and this book carries its color theme to the peaks of the Andes with her clever adaptation of a Peruvian folktale. Fox wants to go to the moon but mole does not until he hears about the huge worms up there just waiting for him to eat. With a rope of grass and help from the birds, the two of them start off on their adventure, paw over paw and claw over claw. Will they make it? What do your children think?

Against stunning double-page backgrounds of blue, green, scarlet, vermillion, gold, and glistening black are large collage cutouts of the characters. The silver fox and gold mole as well as the blue, orange, and purple birds and animals are in a stylized form rather than naturalistic, from designs on Peruvian textiles, jewelry, and ceramics. This style is quite different from that of the picture book art your children are used to. Can they recognize the figures? What do they think about them? Do your youngsters discover the fox's face in the final page's huge silver moon? Did you?

Because this is a simple story with large, bright pictures, even your youngest children may be fascinated. As adults we often think that children will not understand stylized art because some of us may have difficulty with it. Try it with your children and see. Children's response to anything new and different is often one of delight rather than puzzlement or rejection.

The simple text of the story is written in a large, white typeface in English and in a silver typeface in Spanish against the colorful page background. Be sure to have the story read in both languages for children to gain the full, almost magical effect of this folktale. Read the story as many times as the children want it repeated. Repetition is a necessary part of young children's learning, you remember. Have them sit close and try to identify the animals as they appear in the story.

Afterwards, have a tableful of collage materials for children to experiment with if they are interested. Put out colored construction paper for backing, several bottles of glue, and all types and sizes of geometric shapes previously cut out of metallic paper in colors similar to those in the story. Children can glue the shapes to the backing paper in any way they want. Do not expect them to make representative pictures of the animals. For most preschool children, art is an experimental process.

Stages of Children's Learning Through Play

Rather than creating a picture or product, most preschoolers first play around with the art medium they are using, just as they first play around with blocks to see how they work before actually beginning to build with them. Early childhood specialists call this first stage of learning through play *manipulation.* In art, children at an easel first play around with the materials, trying to get control of brushes and dripping paint. You will see them splash on color after color, sometimes covering a whole sheet with a single color or with all the colors, making a splotch that turns out brown.

Once they have learned how an art medium works, children start practicing it spontaneously over and over in a second stage, called *repetition.* At the easel, they make the same colors or scribbles again and again. At the collage table, they paste the same pieces on backing paper—maybe only one or two on each sheet—and then take another backing sheet and do it again.

Finally, when children have had enough of this spontaneous practice (it may take weeks, or even months), they progress to a third stage, called *invention,* and begin to create art products that actually represent something.

Bearing in mind these three stages of learning through play, an early childhood teacher's best strategy for children's spontaneous development of art skills is as follows:

1. To set up the Art Area with many materials that children can choose from on their own.

2. To motivate children's participation in art with lead-in activities, such as reading a book like *Moon Rope.*

3. To give children as much time as necessary to accomplish their art activity.

4. To accept whatever the children do, whether or not it is a representative picture.

Tell children what you like about their work: the colors they chose, the careful way they applied the glue, the patterns they created. Just as children babble before they speak and scribble before they write, children also "mess around" with art materials before they create pictures. Keep dated samples of their art products so that you have a record of their development in art skills. Then you will know how individuals are progressing and what you can do next to help them (but not force them) along.

You have undoubtedly noted that individual children develop at different rates. It is the same with art skills. Your goal should be to promote art skill development at every level and not to stifle it by demanding that all children produce the same picture or paste on collage pieces the "right" way. Using multicultural picture books as lead-ins to art activities can help you pave the way for a burst of enthusiastic participation by everyone.

Another folktale that glows with color is the Native American story *Raven: A Trickster Tale from the Pacific Northwest* (McDermott, 1993). Beautiful Raven, in red, green, and blue on black with its huge beak, is another stylized bird, this time from the totem pole art of the Pacific Northwest. Page backgrounds at the beginning of this tale are somber and gray, for in the beginning there was no light in the world and the people lived in darkness. But Raven sees light off in the distance and flies to the brilliant house of the Sky Chief. Here he is reborn as a boy child in the same red, green, and blue on black clothing as Raven's colors. He tricks the Sky Chief into giving him a shining ball, the sun. Quickly changing back into Raven, he takes the ball in his beak, flies back to the people, and throws the sun high in the sky, where it stays.

As you go over the story of *Raven* a second time, you might ask the children in your small listening group what they notice in the house of the Sky Chief. Does anyone notice the designs on the house pillars, on the box, or on the Sky Chief himself? Where else do they see the designs? What could these patterns mean? What about the Raven-child? Can they tell that he is different from a human child? How?

Again, you may want to put out a table of collage materials as you did before. This time, have your collage pieces in the colors of Raven—red, green, blue and black—and include a number of round white balls for the sun. The backing paper can be the colors of the book's background pages: turquoise, gray, orange, and yellow.

Because you will be reading to a small group at a time, and perhaps repeating the story for several days, keep the collage table going for as long as necessary. Children may want to make more than one collage—perhaps a whole series of them! Developing an appreciation for art is like developing the art skills themselves: it takes much time and repetition. As children acquire an appreciation for this new and different art form, they will also be developing an appreciation for the people who created it.

Many cultures have folktales about animals or birds from long ago who brought light or heat to the people on Earth. One such folktale is *Rainbow Bird: An Aboriginal Folktale from Northern Australia* (Maddern, 1993), a colorful story about Crocodile Man, who has one thing nobody else has: fire. A double-page burst of orange and yellow flames erupts from his mouth. A gray and forlorn Bird Woman looks down on the orange Earth from her dark perch in the trees above. She tries to convince Crocodile Man to share his firesticks with animals and people, but he knocks her away with his tail. She keeps an eye on the crocodile until one day, when he is in the midst of a huge yawn, she swoops down, snatches up the firesticks, carries them away to the forest, and puts Fire into the heart of every tree. Now people can make fire with dry sticks from trees. Then she does a little dance and puts Fire into her own tail, becoming beautiful Rainbow Bird.

Not only are children attracted to the colorful art, but also to the huge drawings of Crocodile and Rainbow Bird, as well as the simple story about sharing. Talk with the children about the benefits of fire, such as heat, light, and cooking, but also about its dangers. The second time you read the story, have them look at the colors. Are they warm or cold? Cherry (1972) points out:

> *In general, the colors from yellow through the reds are considered to be warm. Colors from the green through the blues and violets are considered to be cold. The warm colors have a tendency to come forward; the cold colors seem to recede. All colors are affected by their tints and shades, since the darker tones seem to recede and the light tones seem to be large and closer.* (p. 36)

Put out only red and yellow tempera paint at the easels or painting table for a number of days. Let the children play around with these colors to see what happens. Do they succeed in making orange by mixing red and yellow on their papers? Let them discover this on their own. Are the colors like those in **Rainbow Bird**? Can they make different shades of orange like those shown in the book? Another time, put out the colors of red and blue and see if they can make the violet color of the night as shown in the book. And still another time, put out white with two of the colors to have the youngsters experiment with making the colors a lighter shade.

For real learning to take place, you will need to give children plenty of time—days or even weeks—to "play" with paints like this on their own. Are they painting "pictures"? Not really. They are in the process of discovering what happens when you mix one color with another.

What other colors do children notice in this book? On another day, put out yellow and blue and let children discover how these colors dramatically change into green when they are mixed. Children can mix colors in the Science Area, too. Have them put drops of red and orange food coloring (or tempera paint) into glasses of water and then carefully pour them together into an empty container. Can they make the orange darker or lighter by the amount of color they use?

Obviously, you could carry out all of these activities with paints and colored water without first reading *Rainbow Bird* or another picture book that features brilliant colors, but then you would be missing the point. Picture books make the activities of the classroom more real. They give them meaning. Otherwise, what difference does it make for children to mix colors? They can see for themselves how artists use colors when you read them picture books. Reading a picture book as a lead-in to an art activity makes the experience authentic for them. If the book features multicultural stories or characters as well, then they see that people different from themselves enjoy and appreciate colors just as they do.

An excellent book that illustrates multi-ethnic children using colors in a unique way is **Color Dance** (Jonas, 1989), the story of three girls and a boy who dance with filmy colored cloths, creating exciting new colors. The girls are dressed in leotards of red, yellow, and blue to represent the primary colors. The boy, who appears at the end of the story, wears black tights and a white top. The red-headed girl begins the dance, waving her red cloth in the air behind her. She is joined by the blond girl with a yellow cloth, and they make orange as the cloths are twirled together. The African American girl with the blue cloth watches. Then it is her turn to mix blue with yellow to make green, and blue and red to make purple. The three of them try all kinds of color mixtures until the boy finally joins them, first with his white cloth and then with his black.

You can have your own color dance using filmy scarves or even tissue paper or sheets of colored cellophane in the three primary colors. Children can choose to dance a certain color to music on the tape player as they swish their scarves around. Then put the scarves over one another two at a time and shine a flashlight through them. Can the children see a new color? On another day, have a "flashlight dance" by covering three flashlights with colored cellophane in the primary colors. How can flashlights dance? Have three children sit on chairs and shine their lights on the ceiling or wall of a darkened room.

These are exciting experiences for young children. They will all want a turn every time you read the book. Do you ask them to "predict" (guess) what color two of the flashlights will make each time? We often forget that repetition is so important in young children's learning.

With the recently reissued book *Little Blue and Little Yellow* (Lionni, 1959), your children can have a color treat at naptime as well. The story involves a blue circle and a yellow circle who want to play together but are not allowed to by their blue and yellow families. When they finally do come together a dramatic change takes place: they become green.

You can read the book to children as they lie quietly on their cots in a darkened room. Cover one flashlight with blue cellophane and another with yellow cellophane and shine them on the ceiling as the story proceeds. At the end of the story, bring the two colors together on the ceiling to make green. Then turn off the flashlights and have the children close their eyes for naptime. This is a book they really come to love and look forward to. They will want you to read it every day.

 Source for filmy colored dancing cloths:

Send for catalog:

Chime Time Movement Products
One Sportime Way
Atlanta, GA 30340

A book about painting with sunset colors is ***The Legend of the Indian Paintbrush*** (DePaola, 1988) a folktale for older children about a Plains Indian boy named Little Gopher, who is smaller than the other boys and cannot keep up with them in running, riding, and bow-and-arrow shooting. Later, in a dream-vision, he learns that he will paint pictures of the deeds the others accomplish so that people will remember them. He begins making brushes from animal's hair, paints from crushed berries and flowers, and a painting surface from animal skins stretched on wooden frames. He paints pictures of great hunts, great deeds, and dream-visions, but is never satisfied with his colors because they are not bright enough.

Then he hears a voice telling him to go back to the hilltop where he had his dream-vision and he will find his colors. There on the hill are brushes filled with paint, each one of a sunset color. When he is finally satisfied with the brilliant picture he paints, he leaves the brushes on the hilltop and takes his painting down to show the people. The next day the people find the hillside ablaze with reds, yellows, and oranges. His brushes have taken root and multiplied into masses of wildflowers, known today as Indian Paintbrush. Little Gopher himself is also given a new name: He-Who-Brought-the-Sunset-to-the-Earth.

A book like this is a good follow-up to read after a field trip to a greenhouse, supermarket garden store, a flower garden, or a meadow. What colors are the flowers the children liked the best? Can they find paints of the same colors to spread across their papers? Children at the manipulation stage of art skills will love to swish colors over their papers. Older children may be able to paint flowers.

Note that these activities are not suggested as a part of a "Unit on Native Americans." You remember that the theme of this text focuses on our common bonds of family, friends, playing, speaking, eating, and creating arts and crafts. To celebrate our differences, the idea is to read one of the multicultural picture books anytime it fits well with the topic you are pursuing with the children. If that topic happens to be "Flowers and Their Colors" and you plan to encourage children plant flowers or to paint pictures using flower colors, then *The Legend of the Indian Paintbrush* may motivate your children to do the painting.

Another book you may want to read as a motivator for this theme is ***Flower Garden*** (Bunting, 1994), a stunning story for the youngest children showing an African American city girl going shopping in the supermarket with her father to buy birthday food and flowers in pots. Each double-page spread shows a scene of the flowers—purple pansies, white daisies, daffodils, geraniums, and tulips—being carried home on the bus, up the stairs, and into the apartment, and then being planted in a window box as a surprise present for the girl's mother.

Whenever you have a child character like this in a book, be sure to let the children play her part in classroom activities. Since she is unnamed in the story, let the children name her or use their own names. Can they pretend to buy flowers for their mothers in the Dramatic Play area like this girl? Bring in some plastic flowers and let them try it. Be sure to talk about the names of the flowers and their colors. Put out flower colors on the easel and some may want to paint them. Then be sure to take a field trip to a garden center where the children can select real flowers to purchase for the classroom.

Some teachers wonder whether books like this should be read before a field trip or after one as a follow-up. Our advice is: both times. Children want and need much repetition. If we want children to love books, then they need to hear them read over and over. Then put the book in the Dramatic Play area to motivate "flower pretending." It is not necessary to require that children look at books only in the Book Area. When flower painting is going on, put this book somewhere in the Art Area—although away from dripping paints.

Another flower story involving an African American girl is ***Wild Wild Sunflower Child Anna*** (Carlstrom, 1987). This time the girl is named and the flowers are wild ones. Anna, in her yellow sunflower dress, runs, jumps, and rolls in a meadow full of yellow, purple, and white flowers and wild red raspberries. The text is a lilting poem about her actions; the illustrations are a celebration of summer for a little girl to explore.

Taking children to a meadow or wild section of a park when flowers are in bloom could be a wondrous adventure. But as a teacher in a preschool program, you may need to leave this experience to families rather than your class as a whole. The possibilities of pollen allergies and insect stings make it difficult for programs to expose children to such wild delights. They can re-create the colors that Anna experienced, if you put out yellow, purple, and white at the easel.

Berries are better eaten than used as paint. If you bring in raspberries, blackberries, or blueberries for children's snacks, put a white napkin under them, and have children comment on the colors of the berry stains left behind. Do this after the children have finished eating so you don't initiate a berry squishing episode! Can the children find crayons the same color as the berry stains on their napkins?

USING MULTICULTURAL PICTURE BOOKS TO PROMOTE CHILDREN'S DRAWING SKILLS

◆ *Young Goat's Discovery* (Tinus, 1994)
◆ *Talking Walls* (Knight, 1992)
◆ *The Shepherd Boy* (Franklin, 1994)
◆ *Cherries and Cherry Pits* (Williams, 1986)

Many cultures focus on young children's development of art skills. It seems to be a common bond among us. But we as adults must understand that most young children are not at a mature level of representational drawing during the preschool years. They must go through a rather extended period of manipulating the medium before they can begin to handle drawing tools with any skill. For example, asking children to draw a picture of themselves is a frustrating experience for a child at the scribble stage. As Seefeldt (1995) notes:

> *Preschoolers who have been deprived of a period of messing around with art materials, as too many in the United States who have been expected to produce an adult-pleasing product as toddlers, will require a great deal of time to mess around with art materials before they can use them to express ideas or feelings.* (p. 42)

Instead, we must put out a variety of materials for children to select and use on their own in the Art Area: easels and paints, colored felt-tip pens, finger paints, play dough, glue, scissors, collage materials, colored construction paper, white painting paper, and brushes of all kinds as a start. What can we expect children to do during this free-choice "messing around with art materials" period? From research and observation of young children, we know that drawing skills develop over time in a predictable pattern, provided the youngsters are given the opportunity to pursue art on their own without a great deal of adult interference.

They begin with scribbles. Two- and 3-year-old children throughout the world mainly scribble spontaneously. It gives them great pleasure to make marks of their own like this. Teachers and parents should encourage this beginning stage of art, just as they encourage infants to babble as a beginning stage of speaking. Between 2 and 4 years of age, children's scribbles take on the shapes of circles, ovals, squares, triangles, and crosses, often scribbled on top of one another. At each stage they seem to practice their markings over and over before moving on.

Between the ages of 4 and 5, children's designs often take the form of a person who seems to have evolved from a sun design they made earlier. The person is a round circle face with the rays of the sun becoming hair, arms, and legs. By age 5, children who have had this practice are beginning to make representational drawings of houses, trees, animals, and cars.

At every stage it is important for you to accept children's art work, whether scribbles or pictures. You can display it attractively on backing paper or in frames. Take photos of children painting at an easel for a personal scrapbook they are assembling. Be sure to date the work so you can follow an individual's development. When you talk with parents, share with them your knowledge about children's art development and how their own youngsters are progressing.

Young Goat's Discovery (Tinus, 1994) is a contemporary Native American story that takes place on the Hopi Reservation in Arizona. In the story, little Jeffrey follows his brother, David, as he leads a flock of sheep out to graze among the red rocks of a canyon. Young Goat trails behind every day, and David has to send Jeffrey out to bring him back. Jeffrey discovers that Young Goat has found a picture of a goat with long horns carved on the wall of the canyon. Jeffrey is intrigued and asks his father about it. His father calls it a petroglyph and sends him over to the library to find out more.

FIGURE 9.1   Stages of Art Development

1. *SCRIBBLE*
   UNCONTROLLED
   Marks made on paper for enjoyment. Child has little control of eye and hand movement. No pattern.

   CONTROLLED
   Control of eye and hand. Repeated design.

   NAMED SCRIBBLE
   Child tells you what s/he has drawn. May not be recognizable to adult.

2. *SHAPE AND DESIGN*
   Child makes shapes such as circles, squares, ovals, triangles.

   Child's muscle control is increasing and s/he is able to place shapes and designs wherever s/he wants.

3. *MANDALA*
   Child usually divides circle or square with lines.

   SUNS
   Formed from ovals, square or circle with short lines extending from the shape. The extending lines take many variations.

4. *RADIALS*
   Lines that radiate from a single point. Can be part of a mandala.

5. *HUMANS*
   Child uses SUN design and develops a face by adding human features. . . a "sun face".

   Child elongates several lines of the SUN design to create arms and legs.

6. *PICTORIALS*
   Child combines ALL stages to make recognizable design or objects.

Source: Beaty, J. (1996). *Skills for preschool teachers.* Upper Saddle River, NJ: Merrill/Prentice Hall. Reprinted with permission of B. Helm.

The Native American librarian reads a book about the petroglyphs to Jeffrey and the other children. The book tells how the Hopi people carved pictures of animals on the rocks as hunting symbols long ago, and how the Hopi clans carved their clan animal symbol on special rocks every time they made the long journey to the bottom of the Grand Canyon for salt. The story is quite long for most preschoolers, so you may want to tell it in your own words. Afterwards, the children in the story visit a petroglyph site and draw petroglyphs of their own on paper, rocks, and play dough.

The entire book reflects the earth colors of the Southwest, with page backgrounds in a rich sandy tan and illustrations of the rocks in reddish-orange. If your children are interested in making petroglyph symbols of their own, let them try out making some in orange-red finger paint or colored play dough. On another day, take a rock-collecting field trip so that your children can bring back small, flat rocks to draw on with thick tempera paint.

Accept whatever marks the youngsters make. Don't expect young children to be able to copy the petroglyphs shown in the book illustrations, although the more mature children may be able to do so. Some are sure to wonder if there are any petroglyphs in their area. You may want to bring in other books from the library showing illustrations of petroglyphs around the United States, such as the adult-level books *Petroglyphs and Pueblo Myths of the Rio Grande* (Patterson-Rudolph, 1993) or *Indian Rock Art of the Southwest* (Schaafsma, 1980).

Talking Walls (Knight, 1992) is a non-fiction book showing children looking at Australian Aborigine rock art, cave art from Lascaux cave in France, gigantic animals into cliffs near the Bay of Bengal in India, and the walls of Taos Pueblo in New Mexico, among other places. If the children show an interest in rock art, you can tell them one of the stories that goes along with each picture. The book is for older children, but the large illustrations showing pictures of children from each of the cultures is sure to attract your own youngsters.

Someone may spot the Australian Aboriginal boy pointing to handprints on one of the walls. Would your children like to make their own handprints? There are several methods. They can dip their hands into a flat pan of tempera paint and stamp them on paper backing. To make it look more like rock art, use cardboard for the backing. They can also trace around their hands and color in the outline. To make the prints look like aboriginal cave art, have the children hold their hand still against a dark backing paper while you spatter-paint white paint over it from a brush.

If the children's interest in petroglyphs continues, read them ***The Shepherd Boy*** (Franklin, 1994), a simple contemporary story set in Navajo country about a boy named Ben who cares for his father's sheep. Illustrations across double pages of this horizontal book are painted on a cloth-like texture, showing the beauty of the surroundings, such as the red cliffs soaring high above Ben's hogan (house). Ben must search for a lost lamb over the rocks, down the wash, across the mesa, and into the canyon of the Old

Ones, whose cliff dwellings and walls are covered with petroglyphs. Ben's dogs, White-Eye and No-Tail, help him track the missing lamb until he finds her in the canyon near the petroglyphs.

Talk with individual children about the petroglyphs they see in the book. Why do they think people put them there? Would they like to make their own petroglyphs on the classroom wall? Put up brown wrapping paper across one of the walls from the baseboard to the height of the children. Put newspapers on the floor for protection, and have them stamp handprints like they see in the illustrations, or draw anything they want with their fingers. Scribbles are perfectly acceptable. Thick, white tempera paint seems best to replicate the petroglyphs, but children may prefer to choose their own colors.

Some of your children may want to draw other kinds of pictures with other kinds of art tools. Felt-tip markers in a rainbow of colors are often the favorite drawing tools for preschool children. Some children take a marker and move it around the paper like a snake, making up a story as they go along. They will enjoy hearing the tale *Cherries and Cherry Pits* (Williams, 1986) about Bidemmi, the African American girl who lives in the apartment above the author and loves to draw. The author has a different colored marker ready for Bidemmi every time she comes to visit, and she starts right in, drawing another story from her incredible imagination. Her story-drawings show the big black man she sees on the elevator, the white woman on the subway, and her brother jumping on and off the stoops of the buildings.

Each of her story people carries a bag of cherries to give to someone, and each story ends with people eating cherries and spitting out the pits. Her final drawing shows herself with a huge bag of cherries, but this time she plants the pits and they grow into a forest of cherry trees, so that everyone in the neighborhood is eating cherries and spitting out pits.

Although this is a longer story for older children who can make representative drawings, young children enjoy hearing you tell the tale and show them the pictures Bidemmi creates. Eating cherries and spitting out the pits would be fun for them too, but many preschoolers may have trouble with pits, and may swallow them instead. Use your judgment before you bring in unpitted cherries. If fresh cherries are not available, bring in canned cherries for the children to try. Afterwards, put a generous array of colored markers and paper on the art table, and see what happens. Does anyone notice that some of Bidemmi's drawings are on yellow tablet paper?

USING MULTICULTURAL PICTURE BOOKS TO PROMOTE APPRECIATION OF BEAUTY IN PATTERNS AND DESIGNS

◆ *Hide and Snake* (Baker, 1991)
◆ *Baby Rattlesnake* (Ata & Moroney, 1989)
◆ *Tar Beach* (Ringgold, 1991)

◆ *My Grandmother's Patchwork Quilt* (Bolton, 1994)

◆ *Luka's Quilt* (Guback, 1994)

◆ *Abuela's Weave* (Castañeda, 1993)

Artistic patterns and designs can be recognized by young children and also created by them. Watch for the spontaneous patterns children make as they manipulate easel brushes, stack blocks, and place pegs in pegboards. Mention your appreciation of the patterns children have created and take photographs of them to be talked about later. When children recognize your interest in their endeavors, they are more likely to repeat them or find others to their liking.

A wonderfully clever and artistic book of patterns that children can respond to is *Hide and Snake* (Baker, 1991), a horizontal book that challenges children to find the "designer" snake that is sneaking through every page. To set the stage, nine rippling rows of objects are stretched across the first two pages, one above the other. A careful observer can eventually iden-

Designs can be recognized even by young children.

tify them top to bottom as: a blue sash with purple and orange diamonds; a green jump rope with orange stripes; a turquoise ribbon with yellow dots and ripples; a toy train track; a light green belt with dark green crosshatchings; a purple electric cord; a happy green snake with batik designs in orange, blue, green, yellow, and turquoise; a line of turquoise paint squeezed from an artist's tube; and a purple, green, and yellow shoelace.

Now for the fun. Only the snake needs to be identified as it weaves and winds its way through the story. As previously noted, young children are often better at seeing details in pictures than adults, so you may be surprised to find the snake hiding from you rather than from the children. Can anyone find the snake looping through the balls of yarn? That was an easy one. Designs of the same kind are everywhere, making the snake harder to find as it curls around hats, wraps around presents, and frosts the cake.

This is surely a book for one-to-one reading and then for placing on a table for others to look at. If children would like to get involved in "hide and snake" themselves, cut out some long "snake" strips from oversized colored construction paper, making one end rounded for the snake's head and the opposite end pointed for its tail. Let each child decorate his or her own snake with creative patterns from peel-off stickers of various colors and shapes. Some children may also want to use colored felt-tip markers. Be sure to identify each snake by marking it with the child's initials.

Those who want can hide their snakes when no one is looking by curling them around something in the room. They may need help with tape to make the snake stay in place. Rather than having everyone wildly scurry around looking for the snakes, have the children look for and find them secretly, and leave them in place for all to enjoy. Children can whisper to you when they have found one of the snakes and you can record their name to be reported to the others later.

Do real snakes display beautiful patterns like this? Of course they do! Real snakes are marked with diamonds, stripes, and colorful bars. Our fear of snakes has probably prevented many of us from recognizing their beauty. Children may not be prejudiced against snakes unless they have already learned it from us. This is the time to re-read **Baby Rattlesnake** (Ata & Moroney, 1989), the Chickasaw folktale discussed in Chapter 2. This time, have children pay closer attention to the colorful patterns on all of the Rattlesnake People.

Would your youngsters like to make another patterned snake to hide? Repeating a favorite art activity makes much more sense than putting out a new one every day. Children will enjoy your re-reading of favorite books when they realize it also means they get to experience the same art activity they liked previously.

Baby Rattlesnake can also be purchased commercially as a realistic puppet with markings like the snake in the book. Once again, your children can take the role of a character in the book and reenact the story.

Patterns and designs of great beauty surround us. Children often notice textile patterns in the clothes people wear, but have they ever seen a quilt

Source for puppets to use with books:

Send for catalog:
   Demco's Kids and Things
   Box 7488
   Madison, WI 53707

   Baby rattlesnake puppet

   Community Kids puppets

   Hispanic boy and girl

   Asian boy and girl

   Native American boy and girl

   African American boy and girl

   Caucasian boy and girl

pattern? Have they noticed patterns in the books you have read them? *Tar Beach* (Ringgold, 1991), another story mentioned in Chapter 2, is a book that deserves a long, careful look. Children who spot details may get a glimpse of quilt patterns. Meanwhile, everyone can enjoy Cassie, the African American/Native American narrator, who tells the tale of her nighttime adventures on the rooftop of her New York City apartment: her "tar beach." While the adults play cards, Cassie and her little brother lie on a mattress and look at the stars and the lights of the city surrounding them. But lying down does not satisfy Cassie for long. Soon she is "flying" above the George Washington Bridge, the Ice Cream Factory, and anywhere else she wants to go.

Impressive illustrations carry Cassie over tall buildings and into the real memories of the author, Faith Ringgold, who experienced this adventure as a child. The final two pages of the book show a photograph of the author and one of her "story-quilts" called "Tar Beach," which hangs in New York's Guggenheim Museum and is reproduced on the front cover of this book. Have your children go back and leaf through the pages of *Tar Beach* again. Did any of them see the patchwork quilt border around the book cover and again along the bottoms of the pages? Would they like to see more of Ms. Ringgold's creative quilts?

The picture biography *Faith Ringgold* (Turner, 1993), from the series "Portraits of Women Artists for Children," shows nine more colorful photos of other story-quilts she has created. A book for upper-grade children, this biography nevertheless is appealing to any children who are interested in the quilts. Had you heard before about quilts like this that tell a story?

Would any of your children like to pretend to be Cassie and fly around your classroom city? They can do it with the Cassie doll now available with

Cassie, the doll, can fly from her rooftop "tar beach" in the classroom.

this book. Bring in a book of wallpaper samples and several cardboard cartons for Cassie's tar beach. Cut several swatches the size of a quilt for Cassie, and put them on the tops of the upturned boxes. Now you have "beaches" for Cassie and several other dolls who may want to "picnic" on the rooftops and then go for a flying tour of your classroom. Be sure you have some boy cultural dolls in your collection, as well.

Another quilt book is ***My Grandmother's Patchwork Quilt*** (Bolton, 1994), a story about a doll quilt the author's grandmother made when she was young. Every page shows a photo of one of the patches, cleverly sewed with a farm animal: rooster, dog, cat, sheep, goat, pig, geese, horse, cow, and owl at night. Although animal duplicating patches come with the book, sewing like this is too advanced for preschool children. They can make their own patches, however, for their own doll quilt using a piece of burlap cloth and wallpaper pieces.

Bring in several pieces of colored burlap cut to the size of doll quilts. You may need to fold the borders under and sew them so they won't unravel. Children who wish to create a quilt can cut out small pieces from different wallpaper designs that interest them. Then thread a large plastic yarn needle with colored yarn and show each child how to make a big stitch through the material that will "sew" their wallpaper piece to the burlap. You can tie off the yarn when they have finished. Let each child sew one or more pieces here and there around the burlap until it is covered to their satisfaction.

Luka's Quilt (Guback, 1994) is made by her Hawaiian grandmother, her Tutu, in the traditional Hawaiian way. Luka picks out green backing material. Then she must wait patiently while Tutu covers the quilt completely with stylized flowers. Luka, who thinks the flowers will be in the colors of their garden flowers, is crushed when she sees that the quilt flowers are all white. Tutu is hurt when she realizes that Luka does not like her quilt. After that, the two of them don't have much to say to each other when Tutu takes care of Luka while her parents are at work. It is awful.

Then the two of them go on a picnic in the park where children are learning to make leis, Hawaiian flower necklaces. Luka is delighted. All of the other children string one kind of flower into a lovely lei, but Luka strings flowers of every kind in her lei. Tutu disapproves until she realizes it is Luka's necklace. Later Tutu surprises Luka with a quilted flower lei just like the one Luka made to be laid on top of her bed quilt. Best of all, the two of them are friends again.

Would your children like to make a simple lei from wallpaper flowers? Have children cut small pieces from different wallpaper samples at the art table. Then the pieces can be folded in two while you help children make a paper punch-hole through the folded pieces. When enough wallpaper flowers have collected on the table, cut a length of yarn for each child's necklace. String and tie off the first paper flower yourself, then children at the art table can string their own flowers. When there are enough flowers to complete the lei, you can tie the ends together.

A different kind of quilt altogether is described in *Abuela's Weave* (Castañeda, 1993), the Guatemalan story of Esperanza and her grandmother, Abuelita, who has taught her to weave a beautiful traditional tapestry on a backstrap loom. The story is written for older children, but yours can appreciate the lovely illustrations of the girl and her grandmother, who take their woven work to the market in the city. Because Abuelita has a birthmark on her face, some people will not buy her wares. But this time Esperanza herself sells everything because of the beauty of her elaborate weaving.

For your children's first experience with weaving, bring in plastic berry baskets (have parents or organizations save them for you) and yarn. Thread several plastic yarn needles with yarn and tie the end of a strand to each basket. Then the child weaver must pull the yarn over and under through the plastic slats of the basket. Show them how to pull up each strand tightly before starting another round. Children can make their baskets as simple or elaborate as they want with different colors of yarn. It is not necessary for them to cover the whole basket with weaving—only as much as they want.

Children at ages 3, 4, and 5 have a difficult time understanding other cultures in other countries. They are still trying to figure out their own neighborhood. Thus, is it not necessary nor appropriate to "teach" preschoolers about Guatemala. Your focus should be on the people: Abuelita, the grandmother and Esperanza, the girl who tells the story. Although she is older than they are, they too can learn to weave, not Guatemalan-style, but in their own style, thus creating a bond between children from two distant countries.

USING MULTICULTURAL PICTURE BOOKS TO PROMOTE APPRECIATION OF THREE-DIMENSIONAL ART

◆ *Galimoto* (Williams, 1990)
◆ *The Mud Family* (James, 1994)
◆ *Paper Boats* (Tagore, 1992)
◆ *Pablo's Tree* (Mora, 1994)

Many people consider art to be mainly painting and drawing, but we must remember that constructing three-dimensional objects is an important aspect of spatial art. As noted by Jenkins (1980):

> *Constructions are three-dimensional arrangements of materials, sometimes referred to as space designs. Children enjoy using some materials that offer resistance and that call for greater than usual physical effort. Here is the chance to offer children the stimulation of a variety of materials and the joy of making something from nothing.* (p. 167)

Children in different cultures have often created their own three-dimensional constructions. Can yours do the same? In the book *Galimoto* (Williams, 1990), Kondo, a clever boy from Malawi, Africa, creates his own toys. This story concerns his search for the materials to make a *galimoto*, a toy car made out of wires. Kondo's brother, Ufulu, laughs at him because he is too young to make such a toy, and anyway he doesn't have enough wire. Off goes Kondo to trade his knife for more wire, to talk his uncle into giving him packing crate wire, to trade a stick for a girl's wire, and to scrounge wire from trash piles. Soon he has enough to make his galimoto—a fine pickup truck. Tomorrow he may turn it into an ambulance or a helicopter.

How creative are your children? After hearing this story they may want to construct with wire like Kondo. Bring in plenty of colored pipe cleaners and let them get started. You will also need scissors for cutting the wire into smaller pieces, and pencils for wrapping the wires into tubes. Remember, for your children this is still a process and a time for manipulation—messing around. A few may make a representative object, but most will be trying out a new art medium to see how it works, which you should accept and acknowledge.

Mud is one medium most young children love to play with. In your classroom, playing with clay is the closest they may come to mud play, unless you bring in a pan of dirt and let children pour enough water in it to make mud. In *The Mud Family* (James, 1994), the girl Sosi is so upset with her Anasazi family she runs down to the pool of water on the canyon floor and makes a whole family of people from the red mud. This family does not scold her and there is no baby sister to bother her. Her own family is worried because there is no rain, but they will not let Sosi dance for rain because she is too young. Finally, when all the water is gone and her family must move, Sosi has her mud girl dance for rain. The mud girl's rain dance is successful—so much so that water roars down the canyon, sweeping away the mud family. Sosi's father saves her from being swept away as well by snatching her up just in time, saying, "We are your family. You are my mud girl."

Give children the experience of working with their hands in a substance other than the usual play dough you have made together. They may not be at the stage of making mud dolls, but they will enjoy the tactile experience of moving a substance like clay or mud with their fingers and shaping it into something different from what it started out to be. Pottery clay can be purchased ready-mixed, but it dries out easily. Store it in an airtight container or a plastic bag with a damp sponge to keep it moist.

Give children a piece of clay and have them work it with their hands. Because it is denser than dough and more difficult to work, keep encouraging them to squeeze and twist it, punch and poke it until it does what they want. When they are finished they can set their shapes out to dry, but it may take a week or two. The clay mud on their hands will easily come off in water, or will brush off after it dries. (Beaty, 1996)

Still another medium that may be new to the children is paper folding. Many cultures fold intricate objects from paper, but the story **Paper Boats** (Tagore, 1992) shows a boy from India making simple paper boats, writing his name on them, and floating them down the river from his village. The story is beautifully illustrated with paper cutouts of the boy, his boats, and the animals and trees in the Indian countryside. The cutouts are so three-dimensional looking you must touch them to see if they are pop-ups.

To make a simple boat with no sail, give children a square of white paper and have them fold it in two so that the opposite corners meet to form a big triangle. The folded end is the bottom of the boat. Fold up the opposite ends of this bottom to look like the boy's boats. Then fold back the open ends of the triangle onto either side. Now the children can open the boat and let it sail in the water table. Be sure the children label their boats with their names or a scribble.

Pablo's Tree (Mora, 1994) has similar cut-paper art to illustrate the story of the Hispanic boy Pablo and Lito, his grandfather. Every year on Pablo's birthday, his grandfather puts a decoration on the tree he planted for Pablo when he was adopted. Pablo's grandfather decorates the tree with colored streamers for his first birthday, balloons for his second, paper lanterns for his third, and tiny bird cages for his fourth. What will it be this time? Pablo is excited to find colored bells and wind chimes. He and his grandfather tell the story once again of Pablo's tree and how his grandfather decorated it each year. What will it be next year? That is a secret.

If you read children this story, you should plan to have a tree for them to decorate. You can use a large, bare branch with many smaller branches and stand it up in a bucket of stones. Or you can make a paper tree out of construction paper and mount it on the wall. Children can cut paper decorations of any sort to hang on the tree, perhaps changing it weekly.

Use crepe paper, metallic paper, colored construction paper, or colored file cards. Accept any shape or design the children make, but ask them to keep it small enough to fit on the tree. They may want to fold the paper and cut off corners of folded paper to make "snowflakes." What colors should they use? Some weeks the tree may look like a rainbow, but at other times children may choose to use only one color. Children can pretend to be Pablo and guess what the tree will look like when it is finished.

From these activities, prompted by the multicultural picture books discussed, you soon realize that art can also be a common-bonds experience that brings together children of different cultures in their appreciation of one another and of their arts and crafts. As Piscitelli (1988) notes:

Young children are art appreciators in their own right who, if given the opportunity, spontaneously share their joy of art appreciation with the world around them. (p. 55)

◆ Activities To Promote Creating Arts and Crafts ◆

1. After reading *Moon Rope,* put out construction backing paper and geometric shapes cut from metallic paper of different colors for children to make collages.

2. After reading *Raven,* put out backing paper and collage pieces in the colors used in the book.

3. After reading *Rainbow Bird,* put out only red and yellow tempera paint at the easels for several days to see whether children will spontaneously create orange. Later, put out red and blue paints to see whether children can create purple on their own, then yellow and blue.

4. Have children experiment with mixing colored water in the Science Area with these same colors.

5. Have a color dance with filmy scarves, tissue paper, or colored cellophane.

6. Have a flashlight dance with three flashlights covered with colored cellophane.

7. After reading *Little Blue and Little Yellow,* cover two flashlights with colored cellophane and shine them on the ceiling.

8. After reading *The Legend of the Indian Paintbrush,* take a field trip to find flowers, then have children experiment with flower colors.

9. Have children do dramatic play with plastic flowers.

10. Bring in berries for a snack and look for berry stain colors.

11. Play with orange-red fingerpaints and play dough, making symbols like petroglyphs.

12. Go on a field trip so that children can collect flat rocks and paint them.

13. Make handprints on cardboard from tempera paint, or spatter-paint white paint over a child's hand.

14. Put brown wrapping paper across a wall and do handprints on it.

15. Have many colors of felt-tip markers for children to try after reading *Cherries and Cherry Pits.*

16. Make snakes from strips of long, narrow paper and have children decorate them with peel-off stickers and markers. Then have children hide their paper snakes by secretly wrapping them around something in the room.

17. Bring in a Cassie doll and have children pretend to fly around the room from a "tar beach" on a cardboard carton.

18. Make colored burlap the size of a doll quilt and have children sew pieces of wallpaper to it with yarn.

19. Make Hawaiian leis by stringing cutout wallpaper "flowers" on yarn.

20. Weave different colors of yarn around plastic berry baskets.

21. Use colored pipe cleaners to make objects like Kondo does in *Galimoto.*

22. Have children experiment with pottery clay.

23. Help children fold a simple paper boat.

24. Bring in a tree branch and have children make paper decorations for it.

 ## LEARNING ACTIVITIES

1. Read a small group of children a book such as *At the Crossroads* and ask them to pick out things they like from the illustrations. Did any of them see items you overlooked?

2. Observe five different children in the classroom and determine which learning stage they are exhibiting in their art. How can you tell?

3. Collect several dated art products from a single child and discuss what art development stage or stages these represent and why you think so.

4. Observe the drawings of three different children and discuss which art development stage each child exhibits and how you know.

5. Read one of the books discussed in this chapter and follow up with one of the suggested art activities. Report the results.

 ## REFERENCES

Beaty, J. J. (1996). *Preschool appropriate practices.* Fort Worth, TX: Harcourt Brace.

Cherry, C. (1972). *Creative art for the developing child.* Belmont, CA: Fearon.

Ferreiro, E., & Teberosky, A. (1979). *Literacy before schooling.* Portsmouth, NH: Heinemann.

Jenkins, P. D. (1980). *Art for the fun of it.* Upper Saddle River, NJ: Merrill/Prentice Hall.

Kiefer, B. Z. (1995). *The potential of picturebooks.* Upper Saddle River, NJ: Merrill/Prentice Hall.

Patterson-Rudolph, C. (1993). *Petroglyphs and Pueblo myths of the Rio Grande.* Albuquerque, NM: Avanyu Publishing.

Piscitelli, B. (1988). Preschoolers and parents as artists and art appreciators. *Art Education, 41*(5), 48–55.

Schaafsma, P. (1980). *Indian rock art of the Southwest.* Albuquerque, NM: University of New Mexico Press.

Seefeldt, C. (1995). Art: A serious work. *Young Children, 50*(3), 39–45.

Turner, R. M. (1993). *Faith Ringgold.* Boston: Little, Brown.

 ## ADDITIONAL READINGS

Allen, J., McNeill, E., & Schmidt, V. (1992). *Cultural awareness for children.* Menlo Park, CA: Addison-Wesley.

Beaty, J. J. (1996). *Skills for preschool teachers.* Upper Saddle River, NJ: Merrill/Prentice Hall.

Clay, M. M. (1991). *Becoming literate.* Portsmouth, NH: Heinemann.

Schiller, M. (1995). An emergent art curriculum that fosters understanding. *Young Children, 50*(3), 33–45.

Warner, S. (1989). *Encouraging the artist in your child (even if you can't draw).* New York: St. Martin's.

 ## CHILDREN'S BOOKS

Ata, T., & Moroney, L. (1989). *Baby rattlesnake.* San Francisco: Children's Book Press.

Baker, K. (1991). *Hide and snake.* San Diego: Harcourt Brace.

Bolton, J. (1994). *My grandmother's patchwork quilt.* New York: Doubleday.

Bunting, E. (1994). *Flower garden.* San Diego: Harcourt Brace.

Carlstrom, N.W. (1987). *Wild wild sunflower child Anna.* New York: Macmillan.

Castañeda, C. (1993). *Abuela's weave.* New York: Lee & Low Books.

DePaola, T. (1988). *The legend of the Indian paintbrush.* New York: Putnam.

Ehlert, L. (1992). *Moon rope [Un lazo a la luna].* San Diego, CA: Harcourt Brace.

Franklin, K. L. (1994). *The shepherd boy.* New York: Atheneum.

Guback, G. (1994). *Luka's quilt.* New York: Greenwillow.

Isadora, R. (1991). *At the crossroads.* New York: Greenwillow.

James, B. (1994). *The mud family.* New York: Putnam.

Jonas, A. (1989). *Color dance.* New York: Greenwillow.

Knight, M. B. (1992). *Talking walls.* Gardiner, ME: Tilbury House.

Lionni, L. (1959). *Little Blue and Little Yellow.* Mt. Rainier, MD: Gryphon House.

Maddern, E. (1993). *Rainbow bird: An Aboriginal folktale from Northern Australia.* Boston: Little, Brown.

McDermott, G. (1993). *Raven: A trickster tale from the Pacific Northwest.* San Diego: Harcourt Brace.

Mora, P. (1994). *Pablo's tree.* New York: Macmillan.

Ringgold, F. (1991). *Tar beach.* New York: Crown.

Tagore, R. (1992). *Paper boats.* Honesdale, PA: Caroline House.

Tinus, A. W. (1994). *Young goat's discovery.* Santa Fe, NM: Red Crane Books.

Williams, K. L. (1990). *Galimoto.* New York: Mulberry Books.

Williams, V. B. (1986). *Cherries and cherry pits.* New York: Mulberry.

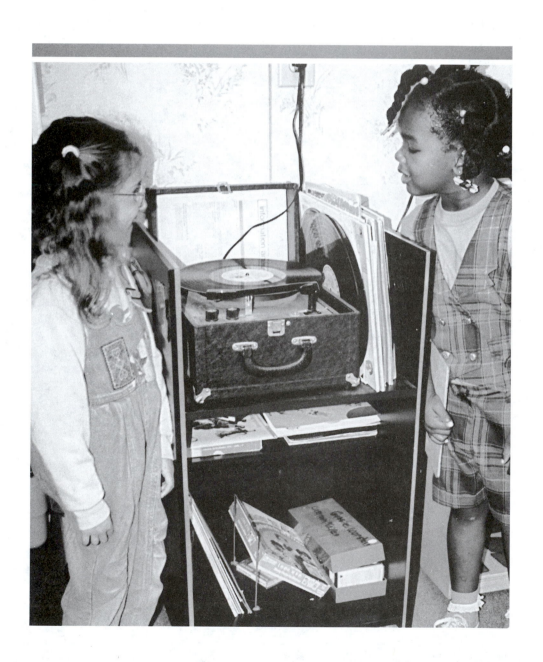

Making Music and Dance

10

Songs are an ideal way to enhance multicultural activities in child care. Share the riches of your musical heritage and the folk songs of your people. . . . (Honig, 1995, p. 78)

MUSIC AS A NATURAL LANGUAGE IN THE CLASSROOM

Music and dance are natural "languages" that cross cultural barriers for children and speak to them in tones they can quickly relate to. Sing or play a song in the classroom, and instantly you will have everyone's attention. Waltz around the room in a toe-tapping rhythm, and children will be up on their feet following you. Play a few chords on a guitar or keyboard, and everyone will crowd around to take a turn.

For children 3 to 5 years of age, music seems to be even more effective than words. Children perk up and listen when teachers sing greeting songs, give directions with music, or play musical games for a transition between activities. Are you having problems getting children to pick up the blocks during clean-up time? Sing them a challenge like this to the tune of "London Bridge":

Who can pick the blocks up now,
blocks up now, blocks up now?
Who can pick the blocks up now,
before I finish singing? [repeat]

Why do songs seem to work better than words? Perhaps it is the melody children respond to, with its happy tones that sound like fun rather than a difficult chore. Maybe it is the rhythm, which resonates with children's own internal heartbeats or breathing. Or maybe children are simply glad the teacher is cheerful enough to sing today. Whatever the reason, teachers of young children know that music makes a difference in the classroom. So, whether or not you can carry a tune, you will need to find ways to fill the room with songs.

The goal of music for preschoolers should be fun and not perfection. Some children will join in right away, others may not. If you make your musical experiences intriguing enough, eventually everyone will participate. You don't have to be a singer to have fun with musical sounds. Start with a simple chant of a few words that you make up. Chant the words in a monotone voice:

HAP-py, HAP-py, HAP-py, HAP-py,
WHO is HAP-py, WHO is HAP-py?
Re-NA-TA is HAP-py; Re-NA-TA is HAP-py.
WHO ELSE is HAP-py? [repeat with another child's name]

Invite everyone to join you in the chant. Soon you can begin to chant in a singsong voice, with the first syllable of each word at a higher pitch than the second.

Clap while you are chanting, and some of the children may follow your lead. After a few rounds of clapping, start tapping on something with your hand to carry the beat. Children may pick up this sound-making game of yours and tap with their own hands or even feet. This kind of music can occur anytime during the day, not just during a formal music period. Let's not make music formal. When children realize you are chanting and tapping because you enjoy it, they will want to participate as well.

STAGES OF LEARNING TO SING THROUGH PLAY

You may not call chanting and tapping "music," but it is. It is the beginning stage of learning through play: *manipulation.* At this stage, children are "manipulating the medium" of singing by playing around with tones. Just as children played with paints before they used them with confidence, so they also experiment with musical sounds before they put them together in a song. Children can be encouraged to experiment with mouth sounds by making it fun. For example, ask children to do the same chant with their hands held up to their mouths in an open fist like a horn. They can listen to how different it sounds. Or, ask them how long they can hold one tone before taking another breath. Let them experiment with high and low tones to find out. Which tones can they hold the longest, the high ones or the low ones, or doesn't it make any difference? What happens when they clap a hand back and forth over their mouths while they are doing the chanting? How does that sound? What other kinds of musical sounds can they make? What about humming?

Another fun way for children to experiment with sounds is to have them chant through a cardboard tissue tube. Be sure you have enough for everyone before they try it. For health's sake, mark each tube with its owner's initials and ask them to blow through only their own so they won't pass germs around. As they make a long tone through their tubes, have them clap a hand open and shut over the end of the tube to see how it sounds, just like they did over their mouths. Next, fasten a piece of clear plastic wrap over the end with tape and they will have a kazoo or "tooter" they can use as an instrument. Even shy children enjoy chanting or singing through a tube. It somehow protects them from the others because no one can see what they are doing.

Children will make all kinds of silly sounds through their tubes at first. But once they get the idea of chanting or singing a song with words, they quickly progress to the second stage of learning through play: *repetition.* Every day they will want to play the sound games you have made up—over and over. You may become bored with this activity before they are, but remember, it is an important part of the learning cycle.

Finally, the children will have experienced enough of the same thing and will progress spontaneously to the third stage: *invention.* You'll know that this has occurred when children stop repeating the original chants and begin making up their own chants or songs. Now it is time to get out the tape recorder and have them record their original creations. What a thrill not only to hear their own chants whenever they want, but also to share them with others.

By now you have probably learned from the children that singing is as natural to them as talking. In other words, it is one of the common bonds that runs through all cultures and all people. It is time to begin reading multicultural books about singing.

USING MULTICULTURAL PICTURE BOOKS TO PROMOTE SINGING

◆ *Baby-O* (Carlstrom, 1992a)
◆ *My Mama Sings* (Peterson, 1994)
◆ *The Singing Man* (Medearis, 1994)
◆ *Northern Lullaby* (Carlstrom, 1992b)
◆ *Into This Night We Are Rising* (London, 1993)

In **Baby-O** (Carlstrom, 1992), a joyous song is sung by three generations of a Caribbean family as they prepare their products for a ride to market in a jitney called Baby-O. The entire story illustrates all the verses of the song, which appears on the first page written to music. If you do not read music, make up a chant to the catchy words on every page, or use a familiar nursery song such as "Ten Little Indians." Baby tries to catch the chickens. Mama scrubs clothes in a big tin tub. Brother rolls his toy trucks down the road. Pappy gathers vegetables. Sister picks mangos. Granny weaves baskets. Papa catches fish. Finally the jitney appears and they pile their produce aboard for a ride to town.

Is "Baby-O" a Caribbean folk song? What does it matter? Remember that you are involving your children with multicultural books so that they will learn that everybody in the world enjoys singing, that singing is one of our common bonds. The songs people sing around the world may be different, but the people singing them have the same feelings as your children. Your children can identify with the book characters, which will help them to appreciate songs from different cultures.

After reading *Baby-O*, ask the children in your group to choose up character roles. Who would like to be Baby? Mama? Brother? Pappy? Sister? Granny? Papa? Then have them practice saying the sound word each character makes when it occurs in the book: *chucka chucka* for Baby, *wusha wusha* for Mama, *toma toma* for Brother, and so forth. Children love the sounds of these funny words. Which one is their favorite? Some children love to hear Grandpappy's *kongada kongada* best of all. Then, as you read the story again, point to the children when their turn comes so that they can say their words. Afterwards, you can sing the entire song as a chant or tune.

In ***My Mama Sings*** (Peterson, 1994), an African American boy who lives with Mama and their black-and-white cat, Great-Aunt Gretna, enjoys the songs his Mama makes up when winter is over and everything turns green, and in summer when it's too hot to sleep. In the fall, when they stamp through piles of leaves, Mama's songs have a clicking rhythm she makes with her tongue, which sounds like a cricket. In winter she whistles a tune. But one day when everything goes wrong, Mama stops singing. So the boy makes up his own song and sings it to Mama to help lift her spirits. When she finally sings it back to him, he knows she is feeling good again.

Can songs make people feel better? Try it with your children. If someone is grumpy, hold the child on your lap and chant or sing over and over a simple name song you make up: "Raphael, Raphael, very soon you will feel well." Another time make up a new greeting song with each child's name in it and sing it in the morning when they arrive. For example, to the tune of "Lazy Mary, Will You Get Up" sing "Rhonda Ripley, will you come in" for each child in the group. The others can join in or clap.

Can children make up their own songs? If you listen closely, you may hear some of them singing made-up songs just under their breath. Would they like to tape-record them? Once one child has put his or her song on tape, the others are sure to try it too. Then play their songs for everyone whenever it seems appropriate.

The Singing Man (Medearis, 1994) is a long but lovely West African folktale about a young man named Banzar who wants to become a musician. The village elders do not accept his choice of an occupation because he will not be growing yams to fill the belly or making crafts to fill the pocket, so they ask him to leave. Banzar takes his flute and sets off. One day he meets Sholo, a blind man with an omele drum who is a "praise singer" and goes from village to village composing songs to honor the chief and his ancestors.

Sholo takes Banzar along and shows him how to make a living as a musician. When Sholo plays his drum, *pum pum ba lum bo,* he sings or has Banzar play his flute. After Sholo passes away, Banzar carries on his tradition of singing the history of their people. One day the King of Lagos hears Banzar play and honors him by giving him a house, money, and servants. Finally Banzar returns to his own village, where he plays for the chief and then reveals himself to his family and gives them money and gifts. Now the people say: "Yams fill the belly and trade fills the pockets, but music fills the heart."

Read this long story yourself and then shorten it for your children by telling it as you turn the pages to show them the realistic illustrations in the vibrant colors of Africa. Can children visit a museum and see real African drums? The omele drum is a long cylinder with a skin top, which is held under the arm and played with a long stick. Children can make a miniature version of such a drum from a cylindrical oatmeal or salt box painted over with tempera paint and decorated with peel-off stickers. A real tone drum with a stick striker can also be purchased commercially.

Would your children like to become "praise singers" like Banzar and Sholo? Have them sing words about another child to a familiar tune like "Twinkle, Twinkle Little Star," while other children beat on their drums.

> I know Joshua. He can climb so high.
> Watch him climbing up to the sky.

There are many nursery songs and rhymes you can adapt for your praise singers:

"Here We Go Round the Mulberry Bush"

"London Bridge is Falling Down"

"This Old Man, He Played One"

"Row, Row, Row Your Boat"

"Hickory Dickory Dock"

"Three Blind Mice"

"Mary Had a Little Lamb"

"Old MacDonald Had a Farm"

Or they might sing words to the tune of "Sing a Song of Sixpence":

> Do you know Maria?
> She can count to 20.
> She knows how to whistle.
> Her best friend is Jenny.

It will be up to you to make up most of the words to the praise songs, but the children will want to help. Be sure to have a song for everyone before you begin this activity. Nobody wants to feel left out. Then, if you also want the children to hear real African music when you read this story, purchase tape cassettes such as "Africa Moves," "Chiminuka/mbira" (Zimbabwe), "Djomo/kora Music" (Senegal) and "Master Drummers of Dagbon" (Ghana).

Northern Lullaby (Carlstrom, 1992) is a large book illustrating a good-night song sung to Papa Star, Mama Moon, Grandpa Mountain, Grandma River, Great Moose Uncle, Auntie Willow, Cousins Beaver and Deer Mouse, and a host of other northern animals as they go to sleep on a winter's night. Large, stylized paintings in the colors of Northern Lights, shown against a black, snow-sprinkled sky, dwarf a little cabin in the corner of each page. In

Good source for audio cassettes and instruments:

Send for catalog:

Claudia's Caravan
Multicultural/Multilingual Materials
P. O. Box 1582
Alameda, CA 94501

Audio cassettes:

"Africa Moves"

"American Indian Songs and Chants"

"Earth Spirit"

"Walk in Beauty My Children"

"Moving within the Circle"

"Thundercord" (Native American flute)

"Chiminuka/mbira" (Zimbabwe)

"Djomo/kora Music" (Senegal)

"Master Drummers of Dagbon" (Ghana)

"Gamelan Music" (Bali)

Instruments:

Shakeree

Tone drum and striker

the cabin, a Native American baby sleeps peacefully in a deerhide basket, as shown on the last page.

Play a cassette of Native American music softly in the background as you read this lovely night song. "Earth Spirit" (flute music), "American Indian Songs and Chants," and "Walk in Beauty My Children" are available.

Can the children sing go-to-sleep songs for objects in the room when the lights are dim and they are lying on their cots ready to take a nap? Singing to the tune of "Ten Little Indians" in a soft, whispery voice, start the song with your own words:

Go to sleep, all the blocks.
Go to sleep, paints and easels.
Go to sleep, toys and puzzles.
Time to go to sleep.

When you have finished going around the room with the toys and equipment, then start with the children, naming each one. How many children will be asleep before your lullaby is finished?

Into this Night We Are Rising (London, 1993) is a dream fantasy of children lifting from their beds and flying off into the night sky from towns and villages all over Earth. Clouds are their beds, they have pillow fights with gigantic pillows, and music comes from everywhere. The stars sing while the moon sounds its gong over China, where children from every culture ride a pink dragon through the sky.

What songs would your youngsters like to sing for the night children in this story? Surely, "Twinkle, Twinkle, Little Star" is appropriate. By now they should be used to inventing a few songs of their own. Be sure to tape-record them. Then play the CD or cassette such as "The World Sings Goodnight," which contains lullabies of 33 cultures sung in native languages. Which songs do your children like best?

 Good source for multicultural music on CD and cassette:

Music for Little People
P. O. Box 1460
Redway, CA 95560-1460

"The World Sings Goodnight"

"Smilin' Island of Song"

"Reggae for Kids"

USING MULTICULTURAL BOOKS TO PROMOTE MAKING MUSIC WITH INSTRUMENTS

◆ *Max Found Two Sticks* (Pinkney, 1994)

◆ *WOOD-HOOPOE Willie* (Kroll, 1992)

◆ *Charlie Parker Played Be Bop* (Raschka, 1992)

◆ *Ben's Trumpet* (Isadora, 1979)

◆ *The Banza* (Wolkstein, 1981)

◆ *Music, Music for Everyone* (Williams, 1984)

Max Found Two Sticks (Pinkney, 1994) tells the story of an African American city boy named Max who finds two sticks which have been blown off a tree. He uses the sticks to tap out a beat on his knees as he sits on the front steps of his city apartment building. When his mother comes home from shopping, she sees Max tapping on the bottom of his grandfather's bucket. Next, he taps out his beat on the hat boxes his mother brought home. Then he uses soda bottles from the boys next store. Finally, as he taps out his beat on the garbage cans in front of the building, a marching band comes by. The last drummer in line sees Max beating his "drums" and tosses him his spare set of sticks. Max catches them without missing a beat.

As you read this book to the children, be sure to repeat the sound words several times, having the youngsters join in: *pat, pat-tat; putter-putter, pat-tat; tippy-tip, tat-tat; ding, dong, ding.* Children love to play with sound words just as they do with the special sounds themselves. The art in this book is special, too. The large illustrations spread across each double page are done in "scratch-board" style, in which the artist scratches through the paint with a fine point, making swirly lines.

Do you have any children like Max in your group? Ask the children who are interested whether they can find two sticks in the room to use as drumsticks. Then have children one at a time beat out one of Max's drum beats on something. Have your next "Max" find something different to beat on. You can tape record the sounds and then play them back when everyone is finished. Which sounds do the children like best?

WOOD-HOOPOE Willie (Kroll, 1992) is a story about another African American boy, Willie, who loves to drum, rapping with his knuckles, tapping with a fork on a glass, and even clicking together two pepper shakers at a restaurant. Grandpa says there must be a wood-hoopoe trapped inside Willie—one of those colorful African birds with a curved bill that's always pecking at trees or making a rhythmic cackling. He also tells Willie about the drums and shakers made by their African ancestors that he saw on his trip to Africa.

When they go to the African American Center for the Kwanzaa celebration, Willie is surprised not to hear any music. Then he learns that the

Do you have any children like Max in your group? Have them look at Max Found Two Sticks.

drummer has had a car accident. Willie looks at the "do-nothing" drums in the corner, and his grandfather tells him it's time to set that wood-hoopoe free. Willie steps up to the African drums, and his hands begin to beat out a rhythm. Soon the other musicians join in with their tambourines and gourd shakers. Then everyone joins in the dancing.

Tone drums, stick drums, sisal shakers and shakerees (African gourd rattles) can be purchased from multicultural supply houses. Better still, have the children make their own. Shakers can be made from paper-towel tubes by placing a few beans or pebbles inside and taping the ends securely. Children can have fun painting their shakers with the colors they see in Willie's story. Drums can be inverted plastic waste baskets. Have parents save cardboard tubes of every kind for your instrument-making.

Charlie Parker Played Be Bop (Raschka, 1992) is a story for everyone, whether or not they've ever heard of Charlie Parker, the great jazz saxophone player. And it's especially for young children, with its simple one-sentence lines on a single white page opposite wonderful drawings of Charlie "swinging and spinning" all over the pages until, at the center of the

Good source for musical instruments:

Lakeshore Learning Materials
2695 E. Dominguez St.
P. O. Box 6261
Carson, CA 90749

Hand bongo (arm drum)

Hand tom-tom

Plastic maracas

Handle castanets

Native American dance bells

book, the be bop takes over. Then birds and shoes and lollipops and bus stops take over, to *ZZnnzznn* and *boppitty, bibbity, bop* through page after page. Young children are caught up in zany sounds and pictures. They will especially enjoy this book if you play a tape of jazz saxophone music.

Children can play along with the music if they make their own saxophones from long wrapping-paper tubes painted yellow. Once again, for health's sake, be sure to mark the tubes with children's initials so that they blow through only their own. If children do not want to be Charlie and play be bop, maybe they would like to be Charlie's cat. Challenge them to sit or curl up as a cat would while waiting for Charlie to finish playing.

Ben's Trumpet (Isadora, 1979), with its stunning white-on-black illustrations, shows young Ben sitting on his apartment steps in the Harlem of the 1920s, listening to music from the Zig Zag Jazz Club across the street. The music zigs and zags in white lightning streaks and curlicue patterns across the black pages. Ben thinks the trumpeter is the cat's meow. Ben makes his own trumpet sounds by blowing through his fists until the neighborhood boys tease him about not having a real trumpet. Then one day during a practice break, the trumpeter from the band comes outside, sees Ben, and invites him over to the club to try out a real trumpet.

Can your children play a trumpet through their fists? Put on a tape of jazz trumpet music and have them try, or invite a trumpet player to the class to demonstrate. Then have the children make their own "tooter" trumpets with paper-towel tubes painted yellow. Next, tape-record their trumpet playing, first separately and then as a group.

The Banza (Wolkstein, 1981) is a folktale from Haiti about a little goat named Cabree and a little tiger named Teegra who become best friends and romp together in a wonderful jungle of feather-like palm trees and pink and blue vegetation. When Teegra leaves to go home to his family, he returns briefly to give Cabree a banza, a magic banjo that will protect him if he plays it with his heart. Later, when ten tigers have the little goat cornered, Cabree begins playing the banza and out comes a ferocious song about eating ten fat tigers. The frightened tigers disappear into the jungle two by two, until only the chief tiger is left. Cabree promises to let him go if he takes a message to Teegra to say that today Cabree's heart and the banza are one.

Play Caribbean island music such as "Smilin' Island of Song" or "Reggae for Kids" after reading this story. Would your youngsters like to make their own banzas? Have everyone save shoe boxes for your class, and when you have enough, the children can paint them in Caribbean colors. You should be the one to cut a hole in the cover, tape the cover on tightly, cut notches at both ends, and string two or three rubber bands around the box lengthwise for the banjo strings. Purchase rubber bands the right length in an office supply store. Would the children like to have a heart on their banza like Cabree does? Help them to fold a paper in two, cut half a heart shape (like a candy cane), and open it into a whole heart. Then they can paint the heart red and paste it to their banza. Now the children can strum along with the music, just like Cabree.

Music, Music for Everyone (Williams, 1984) is a long story for preschoolers that you should read to yourself first and then tell to the children. It is important to share a book like this when the other books about instrument-playing feature boys. This one shows four multicultural girls making music with bongos, a violin, accordion, and flute. The girls decide to start a band with the help of their music teachers, and Leora's mother invites the band to play for a special anniversary party in their back yard. Many people from the neighborhood attend. The girls are scared at first, but soon they get into the swing of things, and everyone enjoys dancing to their music.

Take time every day to let the children play the instruments they have made, with taped music from various cultures playing softly in the background.

USING MULTICULTURAL PICTURE BOOKS TO PROMOTE DANCING

◆ *My Best Shoes* (Burton, 1994)

◆ *Can't Sit Still* (Lotz, 1993)

◆ *Dancing with the Indians* (Medearis, 1991)

◆ *Ayu and the Perfect Moon* (Cox, 1983)

◆ *Aunt Elaine Does the Dance from Spain* (Komaiko, 1992)

Dancing and creative movement are other ways for children to express themselves. Many youngsters have a natural or intuitive talent for moving their bodies to music. Others need help in loosening up and letting themselves go. We cannot expect 3-, 4-, and 5-year-old children to imitate a dance

Dancing and creative movement are other ways for children to express themselves.

an adult shows them, but teachers can move to particular rhythms to motivate children's own movements. As Andress notes (1991):

> *When a loved and respected adult models an action, the child seems to accept the activity with blind faith. An adult can model movement to music by freely expressing his or her own ideas about what is heard. An appropriate goal for this activity is for children to become aware that people enjoy moving to music, both alone and with others. It is not assumed that the child will imitate the actions of the adult model.* (p. 26)

My Best Shoes (Burton, 1994) shows a different multicultural child on every page for each day of the week using a pair of shoes to motivate her or his movements. On Monday, an African American girl steps into high-laced shoes and twists back and forth without moving her feet. On Tuesday, an Asian girl wears tap shoes to twirl and prance. On Wednesday, a Caucasian boy wears tennis shoes to race, skip, and hop in a meadow. What are your children's favorite shoes? In this book, on Sunday a little girl goes barefoot—and those are her best feeling shoes of all.

Children love to dress up and pretend. Which child would they like to be in this book? Bring in several pairs of shoes for them to dress up with. Then they can pretend to be each of the different children in the story whirling, prancing, and twirling in a different pair of shoes . . . or they can be barefoot. Use a special musical tape for each shoe dance. Record the children's dancing with a camcorder if you have one, and share the dances with everyone another day.

In *Can't Sit Still* (Lotz, 1993), an African American city girl twirls through the four seasons with creative movements. In autumn, she sways like the little tree in front of her apartment or stretches and bends to the sidewalk like the falling red leaves. In winter, she dances through a snow storm, skipping, tumbling, and finally lying on her back in the snow with her legs in motion. Inside her apartment, she hops, skiddles, and glides on the cold floor. In spring, she dances down the sidewalk with a green umbrella, climbs up to the roof, and bounces back down the steps dragging a bag of garbage behind her. But summer in the city is the best time of all. In her red swimsuit, she splashes through the water coming from the hydrant and performs her water dance. Then she hops down the sidewalk on one foot at a time, avoiding every crack.

In this first-person story, the girl calls herself "I." This means your children can give her a name—their own name if they want. Put on a tape of music to represent fall and have children bend and sway like trees in the wind. You take the lead. Can they be a red leaf falling from the tree, whirling and twirling until they end up flopping on the floor? Shy or awkward children may join in if they have something to hide behind as they move. Provide a basketful of colored scarves, and have each child choose a scarf and make it whirl in the wind. For winter, give the children knit winter scarves they can twirl through "snow." For spring, can they dance with balloons on a string? What about summer? Have them choose their own object to dance with as they bond with this lively African American girl.

Dancing with the Indians (Medearis, 1991) is based on the true experience of the author's great-grandfather and his family. In four-line verses that accompany each page illustration, the long-ago story unfolds. An African American family packs up the children in their wagon and rides off to visit the Seminole Indians for their annual Pow Wow. The grandfather was rescued from slavery by the Indians, so every year the family honors them by joining in the dancing at the Pow Wow.

Realistic pictures capture the tom-tom beat and sway of the women in the Ribbon Dance. Shells and bells on wrists and ankles tinkle in the night. Next comes the men in their powerful Rattlesnake Dance, and finally the Indian Stomp Dance, where everyone joins in a circle to dip and stomp to the drummer's beat.

Would your children like to join in a dance like this? Tie-on dance bells, tom-toms, and Native American recordings can be purchased from educational supply houses. "Authentic Indian Dances and Folklore" and "Songs About Native Americans" are good examples. Long streamers made from crepe paper or satin ribbons can be twirled by the children as they move to the music. Don't expect preschoolers to learn certain steps. Let them follow their own beat and experience the enjoyment of moving their bodies to Native American music as the children did in *Dancing with the Indians*.

Good source for Native American music on cassette:

Send for catalog:

Kimbo Educational
P. O. Box 477
Long Branch, NJ 07740-0477

"Authentic Indian Dances and
    Folklore

"Songs About Native Americans"

Ayu and the Perfect Moon (Cox, 1983) is a story from the island of Bali, where the dancing of traditional dances to tinkling gamelan music is still enjoyed. Children still perform the Legong dance for which the Balinese are famous. Old Ayu, a dance teacher, tells three little village girls about her first Legong dance when she was a girl. Exotic illustrations set the stage, with a great procession of giant puppets, gongs, and dancers in masks. Ayu practices her dance movements diligently in the thatched village pavilion. One day, the prince of the village tells Ayu she must dance for the people when the moon is full. When that night comes, Ayu's mother dresses her in dancer's clothes of red and gold and places a golden crown on her head, decked with frangipani flowers. Musicians begin to play on hand drums, gongs, a bamboo flute, and the tinkling keys of the gamelan, and Ayu dances in the light of the full moon. She dances with her feet, her hands, and her eyes under the perfect moon.

If your children would like to be a Balinese dancer like Ayu, a cassette called "Gamelan Music" is available. They can make fans to carry in each hand, just as Ayu did, from colored construction paper that you help them fold back and forth in strips and then fan open. Golden crowns can be a wide strip of yellow construction paper fastened around their heads. Can they dance with their hands, their feet, and their eyes? Have them look at the pictures in the book to see how Ayu did it.

Aunt Elaine Does the Dance from Spain (Komaiko, 1992) is a light, upbeat story told in rhyme about a Caucasian girl named Katy and her Aunt Elaine, who thinks she's from Spain but was born in Maine. Elaine takes Katy backstage one night to see her perform her Spanish dance, when she is transformed into the exciting dancer, Elena. Katy meets all the multicultural people who dance with Elena: Paco, Pablo, Pedro, Puchita, Lupe, Lola, and Libocita. When the dancers go on stage, Katy ends up in the costume closet by mistake and soon finds herself in a gorgeous Spanish dancer's dress. She misses the whole program, but when her aunt sees how lovely

Katy looks, she asks her to come back on stage with her for the encore as Catalina. And Katy says, "Si."

With maracas and a cassette of Spanish music, your children can also do the Dance from Spain, just like Katy and her aunt.

Once children are at ease with moving their bodies to music, they will be free to express themselves and communicate their feelings in a bond with youngsters from other cultures all over our country and around the world. You yourself will have come to understand that multicultural music and movement experiences in preschool are not for the purpose of teaching children how Spanish people dance or that African Americans play jazz, but that people everywhere have music and movement experiences that they enjoy and want to share. As Benzwie notes (1987):

> *Movement helps to bridge the differences that are sometimes associated with age, size, sex, or abilities. These individual differences can then be celebrated, affirmed, and developed. Through movement, our bodies connect with the world of abstraction and our dreams to the world of possible reality. As the world changes, the arts, of which creative movement is one, persist and fulfill our lives.* (p. iv)

◆ Activities To Promote Music and Dance ◆

1. If you can't sing, chant in a monotone and clap.
2. Have children try to hold a tone as long as they can.
3. Make kazoos with tissue tubes and have children make sounds through them.
4. Have children choose roles from *Baby-O* and make the sound words that each character makes.
5. Sing a song/chant to a child to make him or her feel better.
6. Make up a new greeting song to a familiar nursery song tune.
7. Have children make tone drums from oatmeal boxes and praise songs to familiar tunes.
8. Have children sing go-to-sleep songs to various objects in the room after hearing *Northern Lullaby.*
9. Have youngsters invent their own night songs for the children in *Into this Night We Are Rising.*
10. Have children find two sticks and beat out a rhythm like Max does in *Max Found Two Sticks.*
11. Help children make their own shakerees from paper-towel tubes and pebbles or beans.
12. Make play saxophones from wrapping paper tubes painted yellow.
13. Have children play a trumpet through their fists, then make a play trumpet with a paper-towel tube.

14. Make a banza from a shoe box with rubber bands strung across a hole cut out of the cover.

15. Have the children play their homemade instruments every day to the sounds of music cassettes from different cultures.

16. Have children bend and sway like trees to autumn music or use winter scarves to whirl in the winter wind.

17. Children can whirl crepe paper or satin streamers to Native American music in a Ribbon Dance.

18. Children can dance with homemade fans like Ayu did.

19. Bring in maracas and Spanish music for your children to do the Dance from Spain any way they want.

 LEARNING ACTIVITIES

1. Find out for yourself why young children respond more delightedly to music and dance than to words. What did you do and what were the results?

2. Sing a new song or chant with the children until they know it. Then have fun with it by clapping or tapping or some other creative expression the children may invent.

3. Find out how many of the children are at the "invention" stage of learning music through play. How can you tell?

4. Read one of the multicultural books listed to promote instrument-making, and have children make a play instrument afterward.

5. Read one of the multicultural books to promote dancing, then play a tape of music from the culture and encourage the children to move to the music. Record the results.

 REFERENCES

Andress, B. (1991). From research to practice: Preschool children and their movement responses to music. *Young Children, 47*(1), 22–27.

Benzwie, T. (1987). *A moving experience: Dance for lovers of children and the child within.* Tucson, AZ: Zephyr Press.

Honig, A. S. (1995). Singing with infants and toddlers. *Young Children, 50*(5), 72–78.

 ADDITIONAL READINGS

Allen, J., McNeill, E., & Schmidt, V. (1992). *Cultural awareness for children.* Menlo Park, CA: Addison-Wesley.

Beaty, J. J. (1996). *Skills for preschool teachers.* Upper Saddle River, NJ: Merrill/ Prentice Hall.

Buchoff, R. (1994). Joyful voices: Facilitating language growth through the rhythmic response to chants. *Young Children, 49*(4), 26–30.

Wolf, J. (1994). Singing with children is a cinch! *Young Children, 49*(4), 20–25.

 ## CHILDREN'S BOOKS

Burton, M. R. (1994). *My best shoes.* New York: Tambourine Books.

Carlstrom, N. W. (1992a). *Baby-O.* Boston: Little, Brown.

Carlstrom, N. W. (1992b). *Northern lullaby.* New York: Philomel.

Cox, D. (1983). *Ayu and the perfect moon.* London: The Bodley Head.

Isadora, R. (1979). *Ben's trumpet.* New York: Mulberry Books.

Komaiko, L. (1992). *Aunt Elaine does the dance from Spain.* New York: Dell.

Kroll, V. (1992). *WOOD-HOOPOE Willie.* Watertown, MA: Charlesbridge.

London, J. (1993). *Into this night we are rising.* New York: Viking.

Lotz, K. E. (1993). *Can't sit still.* New York: Dutton.

Medearis, A. S. (1991). *Dancing with Indians.* New York: Holiday House.

Medearis, A. S. (1994). *The singing man.* New York: Holiday House.

Peterson, J. W. (1994). *My mama sings.* New York: HarperCollins.

Pinkney, B. (1994). *Max found two sticks.* New York: Simon & Schuster.

Raschka, C. (1992). *Charlie Parker played be bop.* New York: Orchard Books.

Williams, V. B. (1984). *Music, music for everyone.* New York: Mulberry Books.

Wolkstein, D. (1981). *The banza.* New York: Dial.

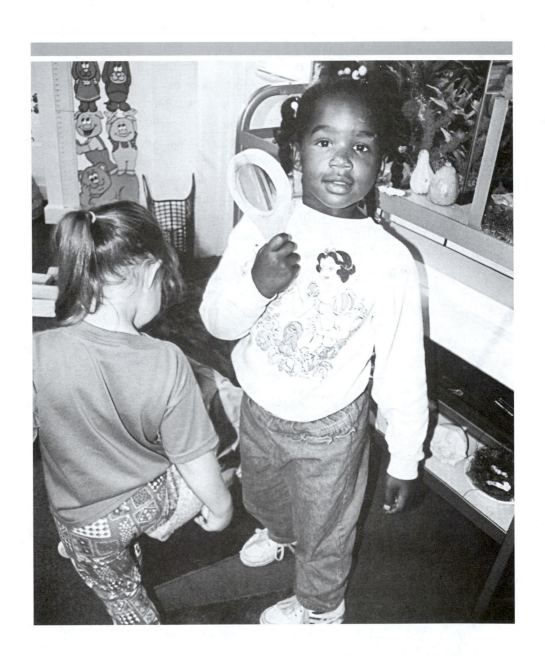

Caring About the Earth

11

Children learn to love and to care about our environment by observing adults. When adults handle tree buds, flowers, or insects gently and with respect, children begin to comprehend the value of nature. (Galvin, 1994, p. 5)

PRESCHOOL SCIENCE ACTIVITIES THAT HELP CHILDREN THINK ABOUT, LEARN ABOUT, AND CARE ABOUT THE EARTH

Most preschool classrooms have a Science Center where children's collections are displayed, aquariums and terrariums are full of life, and seed experiments are going on. Some have a Discovery Center where the tools for finding out are displayed: magnifying glasses, scales, magnets, and binoculars, along with items for children to interact with. These areas in the classroom make a significant statement to children, telling them how important it is for them to find out about the natural environment around them: the air they breathe, the water they drink, the earth they walk on, the plants and animals living nearby.

Providing such curriculum areas is the first step in engaging young children's interest in their environment. The second step is displaying your own interest in these activities by showing your own curiosity about the natural world around you. Look at the world at your feet. This is what young children see first of all because they are so much closer to the ground. Take a focused look yourself to see what children see when they step outside.

Dandelions! Maybe not your own favorite flower, but for the sake of the children, take a closer look. What is a dandelion really all about? Why does it grow so low to the ground in lawns and sidewalks and so high in meadows? Why are there so many of them? How does the sight of its yellow blossoms make you feel? Do the children feel the same? These are questions the curious nature explorer needs to consider. They are questions your own curious youngsters may ask, especially if you yourself model such curiosity. If you serve as such a model, then you and the children will be on your way to an exciting adventure of discovery together.

GOALS FOR PRESCHOOL SCIENCE ACTIVITIES

Sort out your goals for your children and your preschool science program, and then begin the exhilarating quest of getting to know about and care about the world around you. Many teachers consider the following goals to be uppermost in their programs:

1. Help children awaken and keep alive their sense of wonder and curiosity about their world.
2. Help children use their senses for thinking about, asking about, and finding out about their world.
3. Help children learn to care for the world around them.

Rachel Carson, the famous naturalist who wrote *Silent Spring* to warn us about the danger of using insecticides such as DDT, believes that a sense of wonder is the most important gift anyone can possess. She tells us:

> *If a child is to keep alive his inborn sense of wonder . . . he needs the companionship of at least one adult who can share it, rediscovering with him the joy, excitement, and mystery of the world we live in. . . . It is not half so important to know as to feel.* (Carson, 1956, p. 42)

You can be that adult. You can model for children the excitement you feel when you see a bird, a flower, or the first green leaves of spring. You can help children to think about the natural life around them, to ask questions about it, and find out about it by using their senses. All children are born with these five senses, these wonderful tools for exploring:

The sense of seeing

The sense of hearing

The sense of touching

The sense of smelling

The sense of tasting

But there is a sixth sense they were born with that some may have lost along the way: the sense of wonder. It is up to you to help awaken this sense of wonder in your youngsters and help them to keep it alive. You do this by displaying your own sense of wonder.

All children everywhere use their senses to find out about their world. It is a common bond they all share. Thus, you can use picture books about children from different cultures to motivate your own children to wonder, explore, and find out about the natural world around them, and at the same time to bond with their brothers and sisters from every culture as they learn to care about the Earth together.

USING MULTICULTURAL PICTURE BOOKS TO PROMOTE PRESCHOOL SCIENCE GOALS

Sensory Exploration

◆ *Where Does the Trail Lead?* (Albert, 1991)

◆ *Looking for Crabs* (Whatley, 1992)

◆ *The Listening Walk* (Showers, 1991)

◆ *My Night Forest* (Owen, 1994)

◆ *Wild Wild Sunflower Child Anna* (Carlstrom, 1987)

◆ *Where Butterflies Grow* (Ryder, 1989)

◆ *The Butterfly Hunt* (Yoshi, 1990)

Where Does the Trail Lead? (Albert, 1991) is a question wondered about by an African American boy who goes out on his own to explore the beach at sunset. Using his senses, he examines buttercups and snapdragons, tide pools with periwinkles, and families of pheasants and rabbits. He hears the roar of waves and the crackle of the campfire, where the smell of fresh-caught fish brings him back to his family. Jerry Pinkney's double-page scratchboard drawings in the sunset colors of the beach make the story a real adventure for the boy and for your listeners, who should sit close to see it themselves.

After reading this story, take a small group of youngsters at a time on a "trail hike" of their own around the playground or building if you have grass, trees, or bushes they can see, smell, and touch. Before you set out, ask the children what they think they will see on their own hike. Give them paper sacks to collect things in. Have them each carry a tissue tube to look through for a different one-eyed view of things. Carry a tape recorder to record the sounds you hear or the comments the children make.

Afterwards, bring the group together again to talk about their hike. What did they collect? Leaves? Seeds? Twigs? Pebbles? Trash? Would they like to make a collage of their collections and glue them to a cardboard backing? Talk about what they saw through their tube viewers and play the tape of sounds and comments. Can they tell what the sounds are and who made the comments? The next day, read the book to another small group and take them on a playground hike. Children need to learn about the environment close at hand before they venture farther away in their explorations. This hike can be repeated several times during the year as the vegetation changes with the seasons.

Looking for Crabs (Whatley, 1992) takes a Caucasian boy, his sister, and their mother and father on a humorous beach adventure to find crabs. Large, double-page illustrations look down from a child's-eye perspective and up from a crab's-eye view as the children search fruitlessly for their elusive prey. The boy narrator tells how carefully you must look and how quiet you must be not to scare the crabs. Goggle-eyed crabs are everywhere in tide pools, under rocks, and inside shells, peering at the children, but just out of their sight. Finally the family gives up and leaves.

What do your listeners think about the crabs on this beach? What would the children have done if they had been there? Talk about what should happen if they found crabs. Should they take them home? Should they keep the hermit crabs in shells? What would happen if they did? Talk to them about the respect we owe to the wildlife around us. If possible, take your group on a field trip to a beach or aquarium. Or bring in some shells and display them on the sand table.

Another sensory exploration by foot is described in *The Listening Walk* (Showers, 1991). A Caucasian girl, her father, and their dog go for a walk through the neighborhood, the city streets, and the park while the little girl narrator listens for sounds. She hears the dog's toenails clicking, a lawnmower zoooooming, sprinklers whith, whith, whithing, new cars hmmmmm-mmmming, a baby waaaing, and so on.

Take your children on their own listening walk and use a tape recorder to record sounds as you did before. This time, go to a different location so that the children will hear new sounds—perhaps to a park, a river, the desert, or a forest trail.

My Night Forest (Owen, 1994) tells the tale of a girl's sensory imaginings at night before she goes to sleep. In this prose poem to the Earth, the girl tries to imagine what the owl can see, what the wolf hears, what the bear smells, what the deer tastes, and what the mouse touches. The dark-skinned girl and her mother wonder together as she closes her eyes in sleep. Large, rich, but simple illustrations show each animal framed by colorful animal tracks, leaves, and flowers drawn by artist Amy Cordova that "strongly reflect her belief in the dignity of human experience as it relates to Mother Earth, and often offer a bridge between cultures" (dust jacket).

Since this is a bedtime sensory adventure, read the story during the children's rest time or naptime. Dim the lights and ask them to close their eyes and imagine what the girl is seeing. After naptime, read the book again to small groups to see if their imaginings looked anything like the girl's.

Read again the book described in Chapter 9, *Wild Wild Sunflower Child Anna* (Carlstrom, 1987), to see what African American Anna experiences in her romp through a meadow. She not only sees but feels dandelion fluff, soil, burr babies, trickles of water, and prickles of grass. Anna also tastes the tang of wild raspberries, hears bees buzzing in purple clover, and watches beetles scurry away when she picks up a stone. What about flowers? Can your listeners pick out colors of the flowers she sees? What would they do if they saw a spider like Anna did? What do they think she did?

In *Where Butterflies Grow* (Ryder, 1989), a Caucasian boy and girl also explore a meadow, but this time they get down close to the grasses and weeds to find a tiny egg on the under side of a leaf. They pretend to be a caterpillar creeping through the vegetation balancing on stems, eating leaves and flowers, and finally bursting out of its old skin wearing a new, striped skin. Then they pretend to find a bare branch where they cast off their striped skin and become a pupa. Intricate, accurate drawings fill the pages with colorful details of the metamorphosis of a caterpillar into a black swallowtail butterfly.

You and your children can search for a pupa, perhaps on milkweed stalks; or you can purchase one from a museum gift shop or educational supply house. Months may pass before one of your sharp-eyed children spots the change in the pupa just before the butterfly emerges. Hopefully school will be in session when this miraculous transformation occurs. What do the children think will happen when the butterfly emerges? What do they think it will look like?

The questions you ask set the tone for questions from the children. If you are always asking questions about the things all of you see and hear, children will join in. Where will you find the answers? First of all, have the children guess what some of the factual answers might be. You can write them down on a newsprint sheet. Then all of you can look together in an large illustrated book such as *My First Nature Book* (Wilkes, 1990), which tells how to set up a caterpillar house and prepare for the hatching of the butterfly. Were any of the children's answers correct? Be sure to plan ahead of time, letting the children know that the butterfly will be let go on a sunny day after everyone has had a good look at it.

The simple text and realistic illustrations in **The Butterfly Hunt** (Yoshi, 1990) portray the dramatic chase of a net-wielding Caucasian boy who hopes to catch a certain yellow butterfly. He catches blue butterflies, orange butterflies, and even brown moths, but the yellow one somehow eludes him. He tears his net in a tree and finally falls on his face in the mud before finally capturing his prey. But as he sits down to look at the bottles and bags and boxes of butterflies he has caught, he changes his mind about the butterfly, and sets them all free.

Talk with the children about this story. Why did the boy want the butterfly in the first place? Why do they think he set the butterflies free at the end? What would they have done? Take children for a walk among flowers in the spring or summer. Do they spy any butterflies? What are the butterflies doing? Do they see them sipping nectar from the flowers?

Back in the classroom, some children may want to paint butterfly colors on easel paper. Can anyone draw a butterfly in fingerpaint? Others may want to make paper butterflies with squares of colored tissue paper squeezed together in the middle and clipped to a clothespin for a body. You can make a mobile with these paper butterflies by hanging them from strings. Aren't they beautiful? Be sure to talk about the beauty of nature. After all, it is the beauty of the flitting butterflies that attracts our attention in the first place.

Children learn about the beauty of nature by exploring it inside and outside the classroom.

Air and Water Exploration

◆ *Gilberto and the Wind* (Ets, 1963)

◆ *Blow Away Soon* (James, 1995)

◆ *It Rained on the Desert Today* (Buchanan, 1994)

◆ *Bringing the Rain to Kapiti Plain* (Aardema, 1981)

We so often take for granted these most precious gifts of the air we breathe and the water we drink until something happens to them like a smog alert or the pollution of our water supply. Then we realize how vulnerable we are and how respectfully we should be treating these treasures. Children can learn firsthand about air and water through multicultural picture-book characters and their interaction with these elements. Here is another common bond children have with youngsters from every culture.

Gilberto and the Wind (Ets, 1963), mentioned in Chapter 6, is the classic story of the a little Hispanic boy named Gilberto and his adventures with the wind. He floats his balloon in the breeze until the wind suddenly jerks it away and up into a tree. He carries an umbrella in a storm until the wind turns it inside out. He tries to fly his kite but the wind just drops it. Finally he succeeds in sailing his sailboat in a puddle, whirling his pinwheel, and blowing bubbles in the wind.

Can your children be Gilberto on a windy day? Save the reading of this book for such a day and then take the children outside to experience the wind in their faces and ruffling up their hair. Would they like to make pinwheels? You can help them. Cut four straight lines in a square of paper from the corner to the center but not all the way through. Then bend the paper from each corner over to the center and run a pin through all four corners. The pinwheel can then be pinned to a straight stick or even a drinking straw. Be sure to bend the end of the pin so the children aren't pricked by it. On other days, help children make kites, sail sailboats, or blow bubbles.

In the contemporary story ***Blow Away Soon*** (James, 1995), Native American Sophie lives with her grandmother Nana in the last house in the village at the edge of the desert. She, like Gilberto, has her own adventures with the wind. It blows her cowboy hat away, blows her winter jacket off the line, and rolls her wagon out into the street. Her grandmother tells her the wind is a tough old lady that is just doing her work, and that tomorrow they can build her a "blow-away-soon."

Off they go the next day, through the wild grass where the wind is shaking off seeds for next year's grass. Sophie picks a long stem as they climb to the top of the canyon. Up among the rocks she finds a blue feather for Nana and a wonderful shell for herself where a long-ago ocean once rolled. At the very top they build their blow-away-soon: two stones at the bottom, one large flat stone on top of them, three stones on top of the flat stone, then another flat stone, then three small stones together on top of it.

Next comes the hard part, says Nana. They must give the wind something she can blow away. Sophie sticks her blade of grass into the top stones like a flag. Then she pours sandy "footprints" from her shoe onto the flat stone. Nana adds the blue feather. But something else is still needed. Is it Sophie's shell? She wants to keep it more than almost anything. But then she thinks of something she'd rather keep more than the shell: Nana. So she adds the shell to her stone tower.

This tender story of love is a science adventure as well, in demonstrating how the wind helps scatter seeds and how an ocean once covered the land until shells turned into stone fossils, which the wind later carved from the rocks. Can you take your children for a nature walk on a windy day so they can feel the power of the wind? Can they see the chores that the wind performs? Do they mention that it blows leaves off the trees in the fall, keeps mosquitoes from biting on summer evenings, keeps us cool on hot days, or fills sails on boats to make them go? Of course, children's answers will depend upon the season and their location.

Bring in a fan so that the youngsters can experiment with their own classroom wind. Have them hold paper streamers in front of a fan or blow bubbles near it. Can the wind dry up water, too? Have them wash the doll clothes and hang them up where the fan can blow on them. How long do they take to dry? Compare them to wet clothes that have been left to dry without the fan. Is there any difference? Simple experiments like this help young children understand science concepts, as well as gain an appreciation for nature.

Another contemporary desert story from Arizona is ***It Rained on the Desert Today*** (Buchanan, 1994), mentioned in Chapter 2. The story begins with a Native American girl looking out the window and coming out into her desert yard to watch the arrival of a thunderstorm, which is far in the distance but coming closer. The rain is so thick that the desert turns "fuzzy gray and disappears." The older children sing to the rain, the giver of life, while the younger ones slip and slide in mud puddles in the yard. Then the rain is gone, and a brilliant rainbow arches across the sky. At night, the insects and frogs come out to sing their own songs to the first rain.

What do your children think about rain? Ask them how it helps all of us. Is it a "giver of life" for us like it is to the dry desert? Make a picture collage of things that need rain. From old magazines, have children cut out pictures of people, animals, and objects that use rain, then paste their pictures on a large posterboard. When the collage is finished, tape-record their stories about why their objects need rain.

Bringing the Rain to Kapiti Plain (Aardema, 1981) is a cumulative tale from Africa in the rhyming and rhythmic style of "This is the House that Jack Built." It tells the story of Ki-Pat, a young man who makes an arrow from an eagle's feather and shoots it into a black rain cloud to make the rain fall for his thirsty cows. Your children may laugh and even clap at the repeated rhymes each time something new happens: first the cloud, then the dead grass, then the mooing cows, then Ki-Pat, the eagle feather, the arrow, the bow, the shot, and finally the thunder and the rain.

The children who sit closest to the illustrations will have fun finding the different animals across the plain. Do they know the names of these African animals? Bring in a set of toy African animals for the children to play with at the sand table when this book is being enjoyed. Be sure to add some cows to the animal group. Ask the children what will happen to the animals if it doesn't rain. They can learn a new word: "migration." Even the African herders must move with their animals to find water.

Endangered Animals

◆ *The Hunter* (Geraghty, 1994)

◆ *Mcheshi Goes to the Game Park* (Jacaranda Designs, 1992)

◆ *Hey! Get Off Our Train* (Burningham, 1989)

◆ *Three at Sea* (Bush, 1994)

◆ *The Whales' Song* (Sheldon, 1990)

Some of your children may have heard about "endangered animals" from their families or from watching television. They may even have helped to rescue an injured bird or animal. While you are reading books such as *Bringing the Rain to Kapiti Plain*, consider following up with a book or two on Africa's endangered animals. Once more, be sure to read stories that have characters like the children themselves, to make the experience more meaningful and to help them form a bond with children from other cultures.

The Hunter (Geraghty, 1994) tells the story of the African girl named Jamina, who rescues a baby elephant. Jamina goes with her grandfather into the bush to collect honey by following a honey bird. But Jamina wants to see elephants. Her grandfather tells her there are not many elephants around any more since the hunters came. Jamina decides she wants to be a hunter. Off she goes, pretending to be a hunter, until she wanders so far into the bush that she loses her way. Then in the distance she hears a sad cry. It is a baby elephant trying to wake its dead mother, which has been shot by hunters.

Jamina talks to the baby, calming it down and finally getting it to follow her. Maybe she can find the elephant herd. Her grandfather once told her to follow the animal herds to the river if she ever became lost. Now Jamina and the baby elephant walk beside a herd of zebras. At the river they do not find other elephants, but see hunters in the distance. At night she sleeps beside the baby elephant in fear of being hunted herself, and dreams of great herds of elephants. When she awakens in the moonlight, the elephants are there. She returns the baby to their care. In the morning, Jamina's own mother finds her, and they cling together all the way home. Jamina decides she will never be a hunter.

Dramatic illustrations of the birds, insects, and plant life of Africa frame Jamina's adventure. Can your children find her with the baby elephant as they follow the zebra herd? What would the children have done if they had found the baby elephant? Have any of them been out all night like Jamina? Have any of them ever rescued a baby animal or bird? Did they return it to its family?

Put out on a table your groups of toy zoo animals, farm animals, and African animals, and mix them up. Have children try to sort them out, putting families of animals or the same kinds of animals together.

Mcheshi Goes to the Game Park (Jacaranda Designs, 1992) tells another story about Mcheshi, the same little girl character from the book *Mcheshi Goes to the Market* discussed in Chapter 2. This time, Mcheshi and her brother ride in a Land Rover through a Kenyan game preserve to see the animals. They see a hippo, crocodiles, a leopard, water bucks, elephants, buffaloes, giraffes, lions with their cubs, a rhino, and many more animals. A Game Ranger with a gun guards the rhino day and night so no one tries to "poach" its horn. Monkeys try to get Mcheshi's banana and she must close the window. The text is written in English on one page and Swahili on the opposite page as a conversation between Mcheshi and her uncle, a Game Ranger.

Have one of your African dolls or a puppet pretend to be Mcheshi and do the talking for her throughout the book. Children closest to the book can count the different animals Mcheshi sees. Are they close to her or far away? Can they find any birds or insects? Mcheshi uses binoculars to see the animals in the distance. Can your children use small binoculars or opera glasses to see toy African animals you have placed on a table across the room? Which ones can they identify? The address of the Wildlife Clubs of Kenya is given for any teachers who would like more information.

Can preschool children and kindergartners understand the concept of "endangered animals"? The book ***Hey! Get Off Our Train*** (Burningham, 1989) may help them see the point in terms they can understand. In the story, a boy dreams that he is the engineer of a steam railroad train and that his dog is the fireman. As the train moves through the countryside, various endangered animals try to climb aboard. First is an elephant. The boy and dog shout "Hey, get off our train!" But the elephant persuades them to let him come along because people are cutting his tusks off and soon there will be no elephants left. Next comes a seal, who tells about people making the water very dirty and catching all the fish, and that soon no seals will be left. Next, a crane flies aboard to tell them that people are draining the marshes where he lives and soon there will be no cranes left. Then a tiger comes aboard and tells them that people are cutting down his forests. Finally a polar bear hops on and tells how people want to make a coat out of his fur. Meanwhile, all of them enjoy swimming together, flying kites, carrying umbrellas in the rain, and throwing snowballs whenever the train stops.

You can have your own wildlife train in the classroom with children taking the part of the animals. Cut out pictures of similar animals or photocopy the pictures in the book, mount them on cardboard, and hang each picture sign around the neck of the child who wants to be that animal. Make a picture sign for the boy and his dog, too. Then have the children start up their pretend train and chug around the classroom. Stop it each time an animal wants to climb on board. You can read their lines at first, but after you have played this game several times, children can say in their own words why they want to climb aboard.

A humorous adventure about endangered animals is ***Three at Sea*** (Bush, 1994), in which three boys, Alex, Joel, and Zachariah Jr., start out tube-floating on a river with a large innertube, but end up out at sea. Their

Source of information on endangered animals of Africa:

Wildlife Clubs of Kenya
Post Office Box 40658
Nairobi, Kenya

adventure becomes real scary as they drift farther away, and the animals they meet are no help at all. The giant sea turtles say that they never go near the shore because they are endangered. A pair of dolphins laughs at the boys. Zachariah Jr., the African American boy who knows all the answers, says dolphins are becoming endangered too. Then an enormous crocodile appears and decides to endanger *them*. Zachariah Jr. keeps the crocodile engaged in a conversation about alligators long enough to tie Joel's red bandanna around his snout, making him helpless. The crocodile is forced to tow them back to shore, where they set his jaws free since he is endangered, too.

Read the story several times if the children like it. Then have three boy dolls or puppets represent Joel, Alex, and Zachariah Jr. If you have a plastic or stuffed toy crocodile, tie his jaws shut with a small piece of red cloth. Have children choose roles for the next reading of the book. When it is their turn to speak, they can make up their own words or say the words they remember from the story.

The Whales' Song (Sheldon, 1990) tells the story of Lilly, who visits her grandmother by the sea and listens to her grandmother's wonderful story about waiting at the end of the pier to see whales when she was a girl. Sometimes, she says, if you gave them something special, they would take your gift and give you something in return. Lilly wants to know what the whales would give, and her grandmother whispers that once or twice she heard them sing. Lilly's great-uncle Frederick stomps into the room to pooh-pooh that silly old tale.

But Lilly remembers the story. She dreams about whales, and in the morning goes down to the ocean and walks to the end of an old pier. She drops a yellow flower in the water and calls out, "This is for you, whales."

 Sources of audio tapes of nature sounds:

Holborne Distributing Co.
P. O. Box 309S
Mt. Albert, Ontario, Canada

"Beneath the Waves: Vocals by the Humpback Whales"

Studio Horizon Productions
P. O. Box 419
Nambour, Queensland, Australia

"Rain Forest Magic"

She waits all day but nothing happens. That night, Lilly awakens in the moonlight and hears something from her window. She rushes down to the shore, and there they are: whales leaping in the moonlight and singing. After a long time a breeze stirs her awake. Was she dreaming? Far off in the distance she hears sounds. It is the whales calling her name.

Is there a nature museum or sea wildlife park in your community where the children can go for a field trip to see a whale? If not, bring in pictures of whales and a tape cassette of whales' songs. The audio tape "Beneath the Waves" has vocals by humpback whales. Also available from school supply catalogs and toy stores are sets of Whales of the World, as well as a 13" plush toy orca (killer whale) along with a tape of its song. Play a tape of whales singing after you read *The Whales' Song*.

Discovering Trees

◆ *The Great Kapok Tree* (Cherry, 1990)

◆ *Rain Forest* (Cowcher, 1988)

◆ *Jen and the Great One* (Eyvindson, 1990)

◆ *Brother Eagle, Sister Sky* (Seattle & Jeffers, 1991)

Of all the plant forms on Earth, trees are the largest and most stately. They are so common that we often take them for granted. They have always been around and probably always will be, we assume. But will they? More and more we are coming to realize that when trees are cut down, we lose much more than a beautiful plant, we lose an important part of the environment. A tree's roots absorb water and help prevent flooding. They also hold soil together and help prevent it from washing away. Its leaves make oxygen for us to breathe and enrich the soil when they fall. Its branches and trunks provide nesting sites for birds. And forests of trees help the rain to fall. Early settlers who cleared the trees from tropical Caribbean islands found, to their great dismay, that the rain ceased to fall as it had before the trees were destroyed. Trees all over the world are important to the people and wildlife around them.

To motivate your children's interest in trees, read them a book like ***The Great Kapok Tree*** (Cherry, 1990), so that they can hear what the rain-forest creatures have to say when a Brazilian woodcutter tries to cut down their home. The man begins to chop with his ax at the trunk of a huge kapok tree, but it is so hot that when he sits down to rest he falls asleep. One by one, animals come out of its leaves and branches to whisper in the man's ear while he sleeps, telling him why he should not cut down the tree.

A boa constrictor tells him that generations of his ancestors have lived there. A bee buzzes in his ear that his hive is in the tree and he must polli-nate the trees and flowers because all living things depend on one another. A troupe of monkeys tells the man that when the roots of such trees die, there will be nothing left to hold the soil in place when the heavy rains come. A toucan and macaw tell him that when trees are cut down, people come and burn away all of the underbrush, leaving nothing but black ruins. A tiny tree frog squeaks that killing the tree will leave many of them homeless. A jaguar leaps down to say that if the tree is cut down, where will he find his dinner? Tree porcupines tell him trees give us oxygen. Anteaters say his children may have to live in a world without trees. A three-toed sloth complains that cutting down the tree will destroy the beauty of the forest. And finally a child from a rain forest tribe tells him to wake up and look around him with new eyes.

The man awakens and is surprised to find all of the wondrous animals of the rain forest silently staring at him. He looks around and sees strange and beautiful flowers hanging from the giant trunk. He picks up his ax but then drops it and turns and walks away.

To help your children's imaginations, take them to this wondrous world so different from theirs. Start by playing a cassette recording of sounds of the rain forest, such as "Rain Forest Magic." They can also pretend to be the woodcutter who falls asleep at the foot of a cardboard tree you erect in a corner. Then each child who represents a rain forest animal can whisper in his ear why he shouldn't cut down the tree.

Rain Forest (Cowcher, 1988), with its simple text and full-page illustrations of the green forest and the exotic birds and animals that live there, tells the story of a great rumbling in the jungle as the trees begin to fall down. Toucan and macaw birds lose their perches. The giant sloth is alarmed. Anteaters stop eating and creep into the jungle. Tapirs troop away. Howler monkeys screech warnings. A jaguar bounds off. Machines have come to push down the trees and clear the land. But then the rains come and wash away the machines and men, the broken trees, and the land. The animals look down from trees on the high ground and wonder how much longer the trees can protect them.

Children can take the part of these animals by using stuffed animals and puppets available through children's book stores and school supply catalogs. Large plush animals include: a 7-foot emerald tree boa, 7-inch toucan, 10-inch macaw, 31-inch hanging macaw, 24-inch monkey puppet, anteater, and 7-inch tree frog. Read the story frequently if youngsters like it, and let them say the words from the book when it is their turn. Then have them make up their own story about what happens next, which you can tape-record and play back the next time.

In ***Jen and the Great One*** (Eyvindson, 1990), Jen is a Native American girl who loves the large spruce tree that stands all alone at the edge of the valley. Jen loves to hug the old tree she calls the Great One, but her arms cannot wrap all the way around him because of his huge size. Sometimes when Jen is very still, she can hear the Great One speak. He tells her the story of his birth from a seed and how the valley was once covered by a for-

Source for plush animals and puppets:

Send for catalog:

Demco's Kids & Things
Box 7488
Madison, WI 53707

Orca whale and tape	Plush macaw
Red-eyed tree frog	Anteater
Hanging macaw	Monkey puppet
Emerald tree boa snake	Plush toucan
Plush sea turtle	Plush dolphin
Hermit crab	Crab
Molded hand puppets (whale, dolphin)	

est of Great Ones until Businessman came to the valley bringing Road-builder with him. They bulldozed all the trees but the Great One. Now the air is polluted and the rain is full of poison.

Jen is so touched by his story that she brings her friends to gather pine cones, plant seeds, and restore the valley. They all hold hands and circle around the Great One and promise to look after him. He tells them it is the children of the world that give him hope.

Your children can also gather seeds from the trees they know, and sprout seedlings. Maple seeds with their "wings" are good tree sprouters. Also gather acorns from oak trees and horse chestnuts from horse chestnut trees. Put pebbles at the bottom of small flowerpots and fill them with seed compost. Plant a different tree seed in each pot, pushing it one-half inch into the soil. Then water it, label it, and put it outside to grow. Be sure to keep the compost moist by watering it regularly. If planted in the fall, some of the trees will have started to grow by spring. Transplant these seedlings to a safe place in the ground when they have reached 4 to 5 inches. Children will be learning that seeds need soil, water, air, and sunlight to grow, and that we need to care for the plants we are growing by providing these essentials.

Brother Eagle, Sister Sky (Seattle & Jeffers, 1991) is the large, beautifully illustrated message Chief Seattle delivered to the Commissioner of Indian Affairs in Washington, D.C., in the 1850s during treaty negotiations to purchase his land. The Chief asks: "How can you buy the sky? How can you own the rain and wind?" Susan Jeffers' stunning double-page illustrations show Native American families with their children riding horses through birch woods, pine woods, and daisy fields. Then they show the dead timberlands after they have been clear-cut. Finally a Caucasian family is shown among the tree stumps, planting new trees. The Chief calls all of nature the web of life, and says: "Whatever we do to the web, we do to ourselves."

Hidden among the trees, water, and rocks of two of Jeffers' illustrations are large faces of Indians. Did you see them? Can the sharp eyes of your children pick them out? How many faces can they find? Why do they think the artist put them there?

The best way for young children to come to appreciate nature is through a hands-on experience with a live object like a tree, after hearing a story such as *Brother Eagle, Sister Sky*. Take a field trip to a tree near your building or in a nearby park with small groups of children at least once a month. Let them choose a tree of their own and get to know it. They can make picture rubbings of its bark by taping a sheet of thin but tough paper to the bark and rubbing the side of a crayon up and down on the paper until marks appear in the pattern of the bark underneath.

They can collect leaves, pieces of bark, and seeds that fall. Leaves can be pressed between two sheets of waxed paper and then ironed by you with a hot iron. Children can take a photo of their tree every time they visit it to keep in a tree scrapbook. You can help them identify their tree from a tree guide. Do they see any birds in their tree? Any insects? A good book to help young children understand trees and their seasonal changes is *The Tree* (Jeunesse & de Bourgoing, 1989). They can see a horse chestnut tree with its buds, blossoms, leaves, and nuts changing through the seasons by turning transparent overleafs on every other page.

One of the important concepts that your multicultural books should show children is the interdependence of all things on Earth. As noted by Holt (1992):

> *Each child's interactions with the world affect not only the child but the world. . . . Concepts of balance, harmony, cooperation, and interdependence can be found in any nature study. Teachers should make certain that these ideas are emphasized. These are ways in which all forms of life coexist and support each other naturally. It is an emphasis long overdue.* (pp. 132–133)

As children come to understand that trees, flowers, butterflies, birds, animals, air, and water are dependent on one another for their continued existence, be sure that the human element is also included. The books you are reading have child characters from different cultures interacting with nature. Your children can pretend to be these characters through the activities you provide. They also witness you interacting with each of them and with the natural environment with respect. Thus, they learn firsthand that people too, no matter what their culture, can live together and support one another helpfully and happily.

◆ **Activities To Promote Caring About the Earth** ◆

1. Take a small group of children on a trail hike around the building to see what they can see, smell, and touch. Give children a bag to collect things and a tissue tube to view things up close. Carry a tape recorder to record sounds and comments.

2. Have the children make a collage of the things they have collected on the trail hike.

3. Take children on a field trip to a beach or aquarium, or bring in shells for the sand table.

4. Take the children on a listening walk to a new location and tape record the sounds you hear.

5. Read *My Night Forest* at naptime and have children close their eyes and try to imagine what the girl character is seeing.

6. Have children pick out the colors of the flowers *Wild Wild Sunflower Child Anna* saw. What would they do about a spider like Anna's?

7. Look for a butterfly pupa or order one from an educational supply house and keep it until it turns into a butterfly.

8. Take children on a butterfly walk and then have them paint with butterfly colors or make paper butterflies.

9. After reading *Gilberto and the Wind*, do one of Gilberto's wind activities with the children with balloons, kites, bubbles, or pinwheels.

10. After reading *Blow Away Soon*, bring in a fan and have children experiment with blowing air on wet doll clothes.

11. Have children use pictures cut out of magazines to make a collage of items that need rain to live, and then tell why each item needs rain.

12. After reading *Bringing the Rain to Kapiti Plain*, put a set of African animals and cows on the sand table.

13. Put all of your toy animals together on a table and have the children try to put the proper ones together: zoo animals, African animals, farm animals, forest animals, or animal families.

14. Have your children use binoculars or opera glasses to see the toy African animals you have placed around the room.

15. Hang pictures of endangered animals around the children's necks and have each child try to join the train of children chugging around the room.

16. Have children speak through dolls or puppets for the three boys in *Three at Sea*.

17. After reading *The Whales' Song*, bring in a recording of whales' songs and a set of plastic whales.

18. Play a recording of sounds of the rain forest and have children pretend to be the woodcutter and animals from *The Great Kapok Tree*.

19. Using stuffed animals or puppets, have children pretend to be the animals depicted in *Rain Forest*, speaking the words from the book or making up their own words.

20. Have children gather tree seeds and nuts and plant trees in flower pots.

21. Have children choose a tree to visit once a month to make bark rubbings, take photos, collect leaves, seeds, and bark that has dropped, and keep a scrapbook of their tree.

 ## LEARNING ACTIVITIES

1. Set up a Science Center or Discovery Center in your classroom and have the children help to establish an aquarium or terrarium. Be sure to include tools for exploration: magnifying glasses, scales, magnets, binoculars, and so forth.

2. Model for your children your own interest in the natural things around them by wondering, asking questions, making comments, and trying to find answers through sensory explorations. Record what you do and the results.

3. Take small groups of children around the building to see, hear, smell, and touch what interests them. Tape-record their comments and your own. What do they discover that you missed? Which children are most curious? How can you awaken the curiosity of children who show little interest?

4. Work on a tree scrapbook with a small group of children after each field trip they take to the tree. Transcribe any recorded comments the children make and write them in the scrapbook.

5. From the books mentioned in this chapter, read to the children one that seems appropriate for your own circumstances and carry out the activity suggested. Record the results.

 ## REFERENCES

Carson, R. (1956). *The sense of wonder.* New York: Harper & Row.

Galvin, E. S. (1994). The joy of seasons: With the children, discover the joys of nature. *Young Children, 49*(4), 4–9.

Holt, B. G. (1992). In M. Rivin (Ed.). Science is a way of life. *Young Children 47*(4), 4–8.

Wilkes, A. (1990). *My first nature book.* New York: Knopf.

 ## ADDITIONAL READINGS

Beaty, J. J. (1996). *Skills for preschool teachers.* Upper Saddle River, NJ: Merrill/ Prentice Hall.

Dighe, J. (1993). Children and the earth. *Young Children, 48*(3), 58–63.

Haiman, P. E. (1991). Developing a sense of wonder in young children: There is more to early childhood education than cognitive development. *Young Children, 46*(6), 52–53.

Hofschield, K. A. (1991). The gift of a butterfly. *Young Children, 46*(3), 3–6.

Rockwell, R. E., Sherwood, E. A., & Williams, R. A. (1986). *Hug a tree: And other things to do outdoors with young children.* Mt. Rainier, MD: Gryphon House.

Taylor, B. I. (1993). *Science everywhere: Opportunities for very young children.* Fort Worth, TX: Harcourt Brace.

Wilkes, A. (1991). *My first green book.* New York: Knopf.

 ## CHILDREN'S BOOKS

Aardema, V. (1981). *Bringing the rain to Kapiti Plain.* New York: Dial.

Albert, B. (1991). *Where does the trail lead?* New York: Simon & Schuster.

Buchanan, K., & Buchanan, D. (1994). *It rained on the desert today.* Flagstaff, AZ: Northland.

Burningham, J. (1989). *Hey! Get off our train.* New York: Crown.

Bush, T. (1994). *Three at sea.* New York: Crown.

Carlstrom, N. W. (1987). *Wild wild sunflower child Anna.* New York: Macmillan.

Cherry, L. (1990). *The great kapok tree.* San Diego, CA: Harcourt Brace.

Cowcher, H. (1988). *Rain forest.* New York: Farrar, Straus & Giroux.

Ets, M. H. (1963). *Gilberto and the wind.* New York: Viking.

Eyvindson, P. (1990). *Jen and the Great One.* Winnipeg, Canada. Pemmican Publications.

Geraghty, P. (1994). *The hunter.* New York: Crown.

Jacaranda Designs (1992). *Mcheshi goes to the game park.* Nairobi, Kenya, Africa: Author.

James, B. (1995). *Blow away soon.* New York: Putnam.

Jeunesse, G., & de Bourgoing, P. (1989). *The tree.* New York: Scholastic.

Owen, R. (1994). *My night forest.* New York: Four Winds Press.

Ryder, J. (1989). *Where butterflies grow.* New York: Dutton.

Seattle & Jeffers, S. (1991). *Brother Eagle, Sister Sky.* New York: Dial.

Sheldon, D. (1990). *The whales' song.* New York: Dial.

Showers, P. (1991). *The listening walk.* New York: HarperCollins.

Whatley, B. (1992). *Looking for crabs.* New York: HarperCollins.

Yoshi. (1990). *The butterfly hunt.* Saxonville, MA: Picture Book Studio.

Creating a Multicultural Curriculum

12

Apparently we had unwittingly told our students to emphasize differences rather than similarities between cultures; therefore, our students' first intuition in creating what we called a "multicultural classroom" resulted in a culturally assaultive classroom. (Clark, DeWolf, & Clark, 1992, p. 5)

CREATING A MULTICULTURAL CURRICULUM BASED ON CHILDREN

Teachers who focus on differences between cultures in their curriculum can expect to create uneasiness among their youngsters. What will children think of their Native American classmate Simon when we tell them he comes from a culture of people who live in teepees, wear headdresses, and carry tomahawks? What will they think of Maria when we tell them that people of her Hispanic culture wear sombreros and ride on donkeys? What will they think of Gah-ning when we tell them that Chinese people wear pajamas and parade a dragon through the streets?

These messages are, of course, cultural stereotypes. When we design a multicultural curriculum featuring separate units on Native Americans, African Americans, Asian Americans, and Hispanic peoples, we may unwittingly be perpetuating these very stereotypes we are trying to eliminate. When we portray different cultures in our curriculum only through their special holidays or special foods, we do the same. We are exposing children to the culture's "different-ness." We are inviting our children to view Simon and Maria and Gah-ning as somehow different from themselves. And, in our society, all too often "different" means "not as good."

By now you may have decided that using multicultural children's books as discussed in this text is a better method. You learned in Chapter 1 how such books can focus on the common bonds among children rather than their differences. You understand how these books can help youngsters learn that all children everywhere need to feel good about themselves, to relate to families, to get along with one another, to enjoy physical activities, to speak a language, to eat good food, to create art, to make music, and to care about the Earth. But is this a curriculum? you may wonder.

What is it that makes up a curriculum in preschool and kindergarten in the first place? Jones and Nimmo (1994) tell us:

> *In early childhood education, curriculum isn't the focus, children are. It's easy for teachers to get hooked on curriculum because it's so much more manageable than children. But curriculum is what happens in an educational environment—not what is rationally planned to happen, but what actually takes place.* (p. 12)

If curriculum is "what happens," then the next question we must ask ourselves is: What do we want to happen in our multicultural curriculum? If we want our children to grow and develop in harmony with one another, then we will focus on children as the springboard into our curriculum: the multicultural children our own youngsters can meet in the books we read to them.

The physical framework for such a curriculum is delineated by curriculum areas or learning centers in the classroom. If set up properly, these areas can do the teaching for you, as children choose the areas and interact independently with the activities and materials you provide, thus freeing you to work with individual children and small groups. This chapter, then, will demonstrate how to set up these areas so that you can use multicultural picture book characters to integrate the areas of:

Blocks	Music
Books	Art
Dramatic Play	Writing
Manipulative/Math	Science

What book characters should you choose? Look at the main characters of the multicultural books you have available, and decide which area of the classroom they most closely relate to. For example, Cassie, the African American/Native American girl from *Tar Beach* (see Chapter 9) lies on the rooftop of a tall building in New York City. Then, in her imagination, she flies over buildings and the George Washington Bridge. In considering how to build a curriculum based on this story, you quickly note that buildings and bridges are found in the Block Area. So Cassie can be used to invite children into this area. How will she do that? Following are examples of ways to integrate multicultural education into your curriculum areas on a daily basis.

Block Area

Multicultural Character: Cassie, the African American girl from *Tar Beach* (Ringgold, 1991).

Setup: The Block Area should be set up in a corner or at one side of the classroom, out of the main traffic lane. Because children will be sitting on the floor to play with the blocks, a flat carpet is recommended for floor covering. Place shelves of blocks and block-play accessories so as to divide this area from other areas nearby, making it easier for children to choose and use it independently. Pull block shelves away from the wall and use them as dividers. Store blocks lengthwise on the shelves with cutout labels outlining block shapes mounted on each shelf, making it easier for children to see what is available and return blocks to their proper shelves.

Block accessories can be stored on adjacent shelves, also with labels marking their space on the shelves. The accessories can include small cars, trucks, trains, planes, construction and other vehicles, and figures of people, including multicultural families and community helpers. Entire sets of block play people that include Caucasian, Native American, Asian, African American, and Hispanic figures are available from educational supply houses. Dollhouse furniture is also useful in children's buildings. Store these small items in plastic bins with their picture label on the outside.

Other accessories can include traffic signs, plastic tubing, small boxes, and all kinds of animals: jungle, farm, forest, sea, zoo animals, and dinosaurs. Plastic animals from particular habitats—polar, mountain, desert, ocean, and grasslands—are also available. These are especially helpful to allow children to create habitats that go along with those found in multicultural storybooks.

On the walls of the Block Area, place colorful posters showing buildings, bridges, farms, zoos, airports, vehicles, construction sites, and so forth, depending on topics you may be pursuing or field trips you may have taken. Posters are available from educational supply houses and children's bookstores, or you can cut pictures out of magazines. Leave room for displaying photos of children with their block buildings or on field trips. When you are reading particular books whose characters can stimulate your children to do block building, mount the dust jacket from the book or a photocopy of the character on the wall of the Block Area.

Now you are ready to have your book character invite children to participate in block building. Starting with Cassie from *Tar Beach* (Ringgold, 1991), you will need a figure to represent Cassie. A Cassie doll is available from catalogs and stores that sell this book, or you can use a cloth Culture Doll from the set mentioned in Chapter 3. Also available are hand puppets in family groups of four: African American, Hispanic, Asian, and Caucasian mother, father, sister, and brother. If you prefer to make your own Cassie figure, make a photocopy of her from the book, enlarge it to the size you want, color it, and laminate it on a cardboard cutout.

Bring your Cassie figure and the book *Tar Beach* over to the Block Area to read the book to the small group who have chosen to play with blocks during this free-choice period. Have a box of props with you to leave in the area after you have finished reading. Have Cassie read the story, since it is in the first person. If the children would like to build Cassie's building and rooftop, tell them you will take their photo with their completed building later. Your props can include:

A square of black construction paper for the rooftop

A rectangle of wallpaper for Cassie's quilt

Dollhouse furniture for the table and chairs

Figures of people representing family and friends

Pretend to be Cassie, showing children the props and asking them how they would use them. Maybe they have better ideas on how to represent Cassie's tar beach. If some children prefer to build the George Washington Bridge, Cassie can agree to that by helping them cut out a blue river for their bridge to cross. Some children may even prefer to build The Union Building or The Ice Cream Factory.

Not all children are at the "invention" stage of block building, you realize. But this is a story to stimulate them to try. That is the point of engaging Cassie, an African American book character, to tell them her tale about buildings and bridges, and to motivate them to try building on their own. Listen to your children's reactions. If they are enthused about constructing buildings, be prepared to follow up, perhaps by going on a field trip to a construction site and reading several other books about building, such as:

Building a Bridge (Begaye, 1993)

> Anna, a Caucasian girl, and Juanita, a Navajo girl, build a block bridge together.

This Is My House (Dorros, 1992)

> Children around the world show off their houses.

Road Builders (Hennessy, 1994)

> A multicultural crew shows how road-building vehicles work.

You may have an entire block city in your block area before the children run out of ideas. On the other hand, if there is no interest in building after Cassie tells her story, leave the props, the book, and a doll for them to play with in any way they choose. The next day, have Cassie invite a new small group to hear her story. In this manner you can keep the block-building emphasis going for many days, as well as make children aware that people from every culture build all kinds of buildings to live and work in. In this manner, a multicultural curriculum can emerge from your classroom's physical arrangement and the book characters you use as motivators, and can go in whatever direction the children's interest takes it. As Jones and Nimmo (1994) point out:

> *Still, regardless of what the teacher does, Danny's, Paco's, and Marguerite's actions will be part of what actually happens—the curriculum. Traditional*

school-type lesson plans, the kind that go in a straight line from objectives to activities to evaluation, oversimplify the teaching-learning process. (p. 12)

Traditional linear curriculum planning seldom takes into consideration the children's on-the-spot interests. The curriculum ideas leading from Cassie's tale may sprout out in every direction, causing the teaching staff to jot them down on a curriculum web instead of a lesson plan. An example is shown in Figure 12.1.

How long you and your youngsters spend on implementing these free-flowing plans depends on everyone's interests and enthusiasm. Involve as many classroom curriculum areas as appropriate as children pursue their ideas derived from Cassie's adventures. At the same time, keep a record on cards of each child's accomplishments in each of the classroom areas.

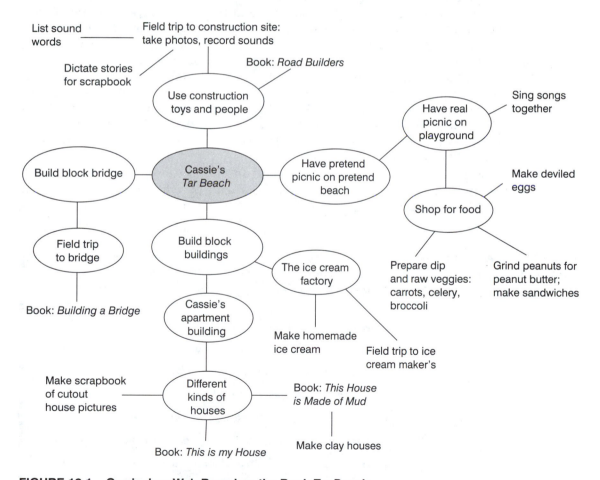

FIGURE 12.1   Curriculum Web Based on the Book *Tar Beach*

EVALUATING A MULTICULTURAL CURRICULUM BASED ON CHILDREN

In any curriculum based on children and their accomplishments, evaluations should also be child-based. Since a curriculum like this is ongoing and ever-changing, the evaluation should also be ongoing. Informal child observation has become the method of choice in early childhood programs. Any of the staff members can contribute to such an assessment. After they read stories to the children, listening to their comments and watching how they become involved in the activities, they can jot down their own comments about individual children's accomplishments on separate cards. Make a master Accomplishment Card and run off as many photocopies as you need. For example, after being involved in with Cassie's activities for a week, Ramon's Accomplishment Card might read as shown in Figure 12.2.

Be sure that staff members observe and record accomplishments of individual children week by week. Individual children's cards can be kept in a pocket holder in some convenient location so that any staff member can add to them or start a new card whenever they observe an accomplishment. In this way you maintain an ongoing record not only of children's personal development, but also an evaluation of how your curriculum is working. Many programs use such cards in their weekly planning sessions to determine how things are progressing for the children and the curriculum. Changes in the plans for the following weeks make more sense when based on child observations like this.

Filled-out cards are eventually kept in children's folders. The accumulated cards can be used for conferences with parents, to share what their child is accomplishing. The dated cards also form the basis for developing

FIGURE 12.2   Accomplishment Card

> **Curriculum Web in Use:** *Cassie's Tar Beach*
> **Name:** Ramon G.   **Date:** 10/13
>
> ---
>
> Built tall block tower every day.
>
> Put toy figures of boys on his tower.
>
> Made sign with his name for his buildings.
>
> Asked to have photo taken of his tower.
>
> Dictated story about his tower to student teacher.
>
> Looked at book *This is My House* several times.
>
> Built cooperatively with Joel for first time.

an individual profile for every child in each area of child development: physical, cognitive, language, social, emotional, and creative. The dated curriculum webs, on the other hand, are placed in a ring binder for next year's staff to consider. Comments can be written in colored ink across the parts of the web that were especially effective or least effective.

Looking at such webs makes it evident that one thing leads to another in dynamic early childhood programs. The teaching staff thus needs to keep eyes and ears open for ideas, both the children's and their own. This is not a predetermined, carved-in-stone curriculum, but an "emergent curriculum." According to Jones and Nimmo (1994):

> *An emergent curriculum is a continuous revision process, an honest response to what is actually happening. Good teachers plan and let go. If you're paying attention to children, an accurate lesson plan can be written only after the fact.* (p. 12)

When interest in a topic lags, it may be time to introduce a new multicultural book character to lead children to a different topic in a different curriculum area.

Book Area

Multicultural Character: Gah-ning, the Chinese girl from *Where Is Gah-ning?* (Munsch, 1994)

Setup: The Book Area should be tucked away in a cozy corner, away from the traffic and bustle of noisier areas. This area needs softer carpeting than the Block Area: perhaps a shag rug with puffy pillows or beanbag chairs for snuggling up with a book. In one program, an old clawfoot bathtub, painted pink and filled with colorful pillows, served as a snug reading corner. Low shelves, built for displaying books cover-out, can be pulled away from the wall and used as room dividers, as you did with the block shelves. Keep twenty or so of the favorite books on the shelves at all times, but add new ones and retire some of the older ones as the children's interests change. Having too many books makes it difficult for young children to choose one.

Book accessories in this very important curriculum area can include character dolls to accompany the multicultural books you are reading; people and animal puppets; a clothes tree for the puppets, hats, or costumes of book characters; and a tape recorder with a few blank tapes and many recorded tapes of music or sounds to accompany the books you are using. Wall space should be filled with book posters available from children's book stores or purchased from The Children's Book Council, Inc. (350 Scotland Road, Orange, NJ 07050). To make your own posters, use book jackets from your own books, mounted attractively on colored backing paper.

Some programs keep a small puppet theater in the Book Area. You should be aware that children below kindergarten age often use puppets differently from older children. They seem to view the puppets as a part of themselves rather than a separate doll that can act on a stage. Puppet theaters are fine, but you can expect that the youngest children will pay more attention to what is going on behind the scenes than the puppet play in front! Preschool teachers often prefer to use one puppet at a time on their own hand to tell a story.

The Book Area should be large enough to accommodate a small group of children who will listen to the books you will be reading. Some programs also provide a small couch with pillows where children can read together or the teacher can read to individuals. If there is a rocking chair, be sure it is in a corner so that it will not rock on the hands and feet of youngsters on the floor.

If your Book Area is designed attractively, it will be filled with children every day. Have colored streamers framing the book posters and a standing inflatable from a party store in the corner. Mr. Banana, pink flamingos, and cartoon characters are available. Bring in paper lanterns, a Hmong wall hanging of "The Peaceable Kingdom," a fish net with shells entwined, or a Navajo rug at appropriate times. Use your own and the children's imaginations to change the Book Area accessories every time a new multicultural book character visits the class.

Are you ready to meet Gah-ning, the main character from the book *Where Is Gah-ning?* (Munsch, 1994)? Gah-ning is a little Chinese girl who lives with her family in contemporary Canada. She dresses like all the other kids in town, except maybe a little brighter, in her red track suit with its orange and yellow dots. She is always on the go, and in this humorous story she is on the go to Kapuskasing. Her father tries to nip Gah-ning's plan in the bud, saying when people go to Kapuskasing they shop and shop and spend all their money, but she starts off anyway. First she rides away on her bicycle with a green bike helmet on her head, but her father jumps in the car and catches up with her. The next day, she takes off on rollerblades, but her father jumps in the car and catches her. Finally she gives up her plan and goes downtown to the library instead.

What a library! A clown happens to be visiting and giving out balloons to the huge crowd of children. Most of them want one or two balloons, but Gah-ning takes 300! Soon she is floating out the door and on her way to . . . Kapuskasing! When her father finds out, he jumps in his car and drives all the way to a shopping mall in Kapuskasing, where Gah-ning comes floating down right on top of the car. She is happy that he has come to take her shopping!

Since this story, as you note, has a wonderful library scene with swarms of colorful kids reading books amid the balloons, it makes sense to feature Gah-ning as an invitation to your Book Area. Be sure to decorate it with plenty of balloons that you can give to every child in each small group after Gah-ning has told her story. Use an Asian puppet or doll to speak for Gah-ning or make your own colorful cutout character from a photocopy of Gah-ning from the book. Keep the Gah-ning story going until all of the children have experienced meeting her.

Most children will want you to repeat this happy tale another day. Remember that repetition plays an important part in young children's learning through play. To give the story a different twist, have Gah-ning change it a bit and get paper streamers or little kites instead of balloons, which you can give to the children on other days. What other colorful items can Gah-ning be involved with? How about colored scarves?

What have children learned from Gah-ning? They have learned that Chinese kids, just like the rest of us, are often determined to have their own way, no matter what their parents want. And they have learned that libraries are exciting places to visit! What other curriculum ideas emerge from this story? One that you might consider is safety. Gah-ning's father is frantic because she might be killed on the highway by trucks, buses, cars, or motorcycles, first when she rides her bicycle and then when she goes by rollerblades. Your Gah-ning puppet or doll can ask the children what they think. If your children want to pretend to be Gah-ning "riding" or "rollerblading" around your own classroom, have someone be the father who is so concerned about his daughter's safety. Next time you go on a walking field trip, be sure to take Gah-ning along to have her talk about safety.

Dramatic Play Area

Multicultural Character: Hugo, the Hispanic boy from *Going Home* (Wild, 1993)

Setup: The Dramatic Play Area, an important learning center in every early childhood classroom, should be large enough to contain furniture and props for all kinds of pretending to take place. You recall that children learn best through exploratory play. At the preschool age, much of this play takes place through pretending to be someone else in some other place. The place most often set up is a kitchen, with a child-size sink, refrigerator, stove, cupboards, and a table and chairs. Some programs set up a store, with empty food boxes from home on shelves and a cash register on a table. Other possibilities have included a shoe store, a restaurant, a beauty/barber shop, or a doctor's clinic because children enjoy playing the roles of doctor and nurse. Youngsters are often frightened to visit the doctor and get a shot, so role play like this can be therapeutic.

Working through uncomfortable situations in play helps children reduce anxiety. The Hispanic boy Hugo from **Going Home** (Wild, 1993) is just the child to help children overcome their fear of hospitals. Hugo is in a small children's hospital overlooking a zoo. Two other children, Simon and Nirmala, share Hugo's hospital room. His female doctor and male nurse tell him that he'll be going home soon.

Set up part of your Dramatic Play area as a hospital room like Hugo's, and have a Hugo character doll invite a small group at a time to hear his story. Put three cots in a row with pairs of slippers under each cot. Hang animal posters on the wall. Put out doctor and nurse props such as toy stethoscopes and white shirts for doctors' and nurses' jackets. Use the book illustrations to set up your area like Hugo's hospital room.

In the story, Hugo hears animal noises from the zoo next door and looks out the window. He knows that the elephant is calling for him, so he puts on his "magic" slippers and slips away in his imagination on an exciting trip on the elephant's back across the African plains. The next time his family comes to visit, Hugo tells his little sister, Cathy, about his trip to Africa and gives her a paper elephant he has made.

In his next imaginary trip, Hugo follows a howler monkey through the Amazon jungle, and afterwards makes a monkey finger puppet for his sister. After his final trip, to the Himalaya Mountains on the back of a snow leopard, Hugo makes Cathy a leopard mask. Before he goes home, Hugo tells Simon and Nirmala the secret of the magic slippers so they, too, can journey to far places while waiting for their parents to take them home.

Have children from your reading group lie on each cot with their eyes closed while you play a tape of animal sounds from the *Tropical Rain Forest* or *Jungle* tape cassettes. Can they imagine going on a romp through the jungle with one of the animals they hear? Ask each one where they went on their pretend trip, and tape-record their answers. In the days to come, have everyone in class pretend to be Hugo and record the stories of their adventures. In the meantime, leave Hugo's book in the Dramatic Play area for children to look at and pretend with on their own.

Hugo's adventures in *Going Home* provide especially good lead-ins to activities in several other curriculum areas. As you brainstorm together you may come out with an open-ended curriculum web something like that shown in Figure 12.3.

 Source for animal sounds cassettes:

Send for catalog:

Claudia's Caravan
Multicultural/Multilingual Materials
P. O. Box 1582
Alameda, CA 94501

"Tropical Rain Forest"

"Jungle"

"Africa Moves"

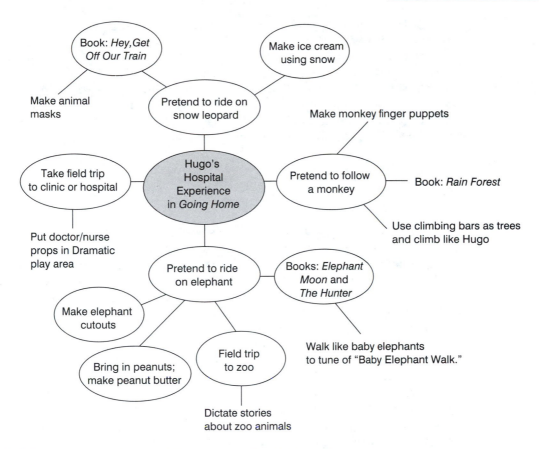

FIGURE 12.3   Curriculum Web Based on the Book *Going Home*

CREATING A MULTICULTURAL CURRICULUM BASED ON THEMES

Early childhood programs frequently use themes to tie together the activities in their curriculum areas. While the program's focus is still on children and their interests and needs, themes are used as a framework for classroom activities. Such themes as the family, the neighborhood, the community, and the seasons can lead the youngsters through an entire year of activities. As Wortham (1994) notes:

> *When themes can be used to design the total curriculum for a preschool program, they become the framework, or scaffold, for the program. The teacher studies the educational goals or objectives for the program and correlates them with the units or themes that are developed during the course of the year.* (p. 197)

When the program's principal goal is for children to grow and develop in harmony with one another, then one theme may focus on "the neighborhood," with activities in each curriculum area to show children how the people in the neighborhood live and get along with each other. Multicultural book characters fit in well with such a theme and can lead children into many of the other curriculum areas. Starting this time with the Manipulative/Math Area, you can introduce the African American girl Sister to a small group of children at a time by inviting them to this area to hear her story.

Manipulative/Math Area

Multicultural Character: Sister, the African American girl from *One of Three* (Johnson, 1991)

Setup: The Manipulative/Math Area should have a table and shelf space where children can play with table games, puzzles, magnetic shapes, interlocking blocks, stringing beads, threading spools, lacing shapes, pegboards, button boards, sorting trays, lotto games, number boards, a large abacus, giant dominoes, plastic animal counters, a toy cash register, plastic numerals, and more. Some classrooms include a computer along with simple manipulation and number computer programs for children to use on their own. Children will be developing eye-hand coordination and learning early math correspondence and counting skills.

First of all, they learn about numbers. All kinds of number chants and counting games help children learn number names. Most can rattle off the numbers one through ten even before they enter your program. Learning one-to-one correspondence is the next step, involving them in using the right number to identify that same number of objects. They must learn what "one" of anything is, what "two" is, what "three" is, and so forth. Just because preschool children can say the numbers does not mean they understand how to count out objects.

Teachers realize that the most effective way for young children to learn one-to-one correspondence is to involve them with counting themselves and other children. Can Ramon tell how many children are in his group in the Math Area today? Four? Did he forget to count himself? The African American doll "Sister" would like to invite Ramon and his four companions to listen to her story *One of Three* (Johnson, 1991).

Sister tells the story about being one of three sisters: Eva, Nikki, and herself. They play dressup together, walk to school together, and play sidewalk hopscotch together. When they squeeze into a taxi with Mama, Aunt Sara, and Grandma, then she is one of six. The sisters look like triplets—almost, except that they are "stairstep" in size. They ride on the subway with their Mama, live in Apartment No. 2 above Mr. Lowen's flower shop, and sit outside the bakery looking and smelling. Sometimes two of them go to the park without Sister. Then she becomes one of one—until Mama and Daddy come, and then she is one of three again.

Sister tells the story about being one of three sisters: Eva, Nikki, and herself.

Can your children identify with these cheerful city girls? Have them play some "one of" games among themselves. Can they make themselves one of two? One of three? One of four? What if Sister wants to join them—then how many will each child be one of? Children also learn new number words such as "twins" and "triplets" from this story.

Before you introduce Sister to small groups of children in the Math Area, be sure to brainstorm with your staff about follow-up activities in other curriculum areas of the classroom to support your themes of "the neighborhood" and "one-to-one correspondence." Listen to what the children say, too. Jot down ideas on an area curriculum web. An example is shown in Figure 12.4.

Music Area

Multicultural Character: Minho, the Asian city boy from *One Afternoon* (Heo, 1994)

Setup: The Music Area is often a small one in the classroom, with a record or tape player with audio tapes and headsets, rhythm instruments hanging from a labeled pegboard, and a shelf with a keyboard, strumming instruments, and perhaps a xylophone. Its size should not belie its importance for young children's growth and development. Just as the youngsters strive

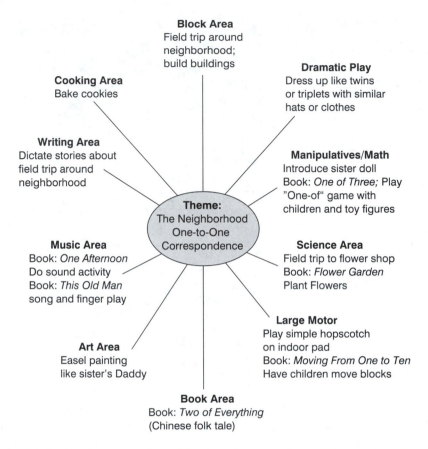

FIGURE 12.4   Curriculum Web for "The Neighborhood" and "One-to-One Correspondence" Themes

to communicate in speaking, so they also need the freedom and support to express themselves in chanting, singing, sound-making, and music-making.

Have Minho, the Asian boy, invite a small group of children at a time to the Music Area to hear his story **One Afternoon** (Heo, 1994). It should fit well with your previous theme, the neighborhood, for Minho and his mother walk from their city apartment building to stores and shops nearby on a series of errands. Minho seems fascinated by the sounds in every store they visit: washing machines going *tump thud* in the laundromat; a milkshake maker going *eeeeee* in the ice cream store; puppies and kittens woofing and meowing in the pet store window; the shoe repair man's sewing machine going *whurra, whurra*; the supermarket cash register going *clink, clink, ka-ching*; the traffic going *honk honk* and *vroom*, and the subway train going *clickety clack*. Minho is happy to get home and flop on the couch for a snooze until he hears a sound from the bathroom sink: *plunk.*

Children are intrigued by noises and sound words. They will want the story repeated, especially if you have sounded out the wonderful clamor. Can they make their own sounds for the various noise-makers? Pass the tape recorder around the group and have everyone try to make the sounds for each of the illustrations. Now play the tape back to them. Can they make a song from these noises? Have everyone clap out a rhythm as you play the tape of Minho's adventures a second time. Now have everyone hum a familiar tune as you play the tape. What about "Ten Little Indians"? Children can make their own hummers from tissue tubes with paper covering one end. If they hum through the open end, their sounds will vibrate.

Some children will surely suggest going on a walking field trip like Minho did, and tape-recording the sounds they hear. Make plans to take a small group at a time on a short walk through the neighborhood searching for sounds and recording them. Once back in the classroom they can listen to the tape and add their own rhythm and melody. Perhaps they will want to stamp their feet, tap a drumstick, or strum a rubber banjo like the banza they made in Chapter 10.

DECIDING WHETHER TO USE AN OPEN-ENDED WEB OR AN AREA WEB FOR PLANNING

Both the open-ended curriculum web, like the one illustrated in Figure 12.3, and the area web, like the one shown in Figure 12.4, work well for planning an emergent curriculum based on characters from multicultural picture books. But which kind of web works best? You can often tell by reading ahead of time the book you plan to use, and trying to spin off ideas into your different areas. If this does not seem to work well, then make an open-ended web.

Art Area

Multicultural Character: Isabela, the island girl from *Isabela's Ribbons* (Ichikawa, 1995)

Setup: The Art Area needs a prominent position in any early childhood classroom. Its setup is based on your goals for children. If you want children to develop creativity, then you must arrange the area so that children can choose and use art materials on their own. Most classrooms have one or two easels with paper and paint already set up and ready to go when the children arrive. Other materials, such as white paper, colored paper, crayons, markers, brushes, squeeze tubes of paint, sponges, watercolors, glue, scissors, and collage materials, are located on low shelves near art tables with shelf picture labels designating their places for easy selection and return by the children. Teachers' art supplies are stored in cupboards for their use only.

Chapter 9 has described several art activities involving identifying colors and mixing paints to make new colors. There are many picture books that can help children become involved with color activities. One such book is *Isabela's Ribbons* (Ichikawa, 1995). Have an Isabela doll or puppet invite your children to have fun hiding with colors—in other words, using color for camouflage. Many natural creatures use their own colors for camouflage, so you can use Isabela to lead the children into certain other curriculum areas as well.

Isabela, a Caucasian girl from Puerto Rico, loves ribbons. She always wears a big bow in her hair, and keeps a big basket of ribbons in her room. Her favorite game is playing hide-and-seek among the flowering shrubs and trees with her dog, Samantha, her neighbor, Patria, and her Grandma. Everyone calls her Ribbon Lady. She is very difficult to see among the flowering bushes and trees when she wears a bow of the flower's color. Can your children find her among the pink hibiscus, the yellow bananas, or the red flamboyant tree?

One day when there is no one to play with, Isabela takes a basket full of ribbons and climbs up in the mango tree to play by herself. Then she sees a green parrot and decides to play her hiding game with it. She ties her ribbons all over the tree, but the parrot flies away and doesn't return. Isabela falls asleep in the tree and dreams she is underwater and that her ribbons have turned into fish of every color. They swim together until they reach the sunlight, where multicultural children are playing. When the children look up, they see ribbons of every color flying out of the mango tree. Then they discover Isabela, and soon she has as many playmates as she does ribbons. And Patria still cannot find her!

You may decide after reading this book that planning curriculum activities with a lead-in like *Isabela's Ribbons* seems to work better with an open-ended curriculum web rather than one based on all the classroom areas. Trying to fit activity spin-offs into the other areas may be too restricting. Instead, you may want to plan an activity to follow up reading Isabela's story, and then brainstorm other possibilities for an open-ended web.

An art activity that some children enjoy is cutting out simple fish shapes you have drawn on colored construction paper. Give each child a different color sheet to cut out a five-inch long fish drawn with two curved lines. Youngsters can practice cutting along a line in this activity. You need to accept anything they produce, whether or not it looks like a fish. Some children will want to make more than one. Children can then take a piece of tape and tape their fish somewhere in the room where its color will blend in with a similar color, so that the fish will be camouflaged.

Preschoolers love to learn big words like "camouflage," so be sure to use it over and over. After the paper fish are all hidden, have them ask other children, one at a time, to try to find a particular colored fish. Keep this activity going for as many days as your small listening groups desire. Then decide what happens next based on your curriculum web. A curriculum web based on *Isabela's Ribbons* is shown in Figure 12.5.

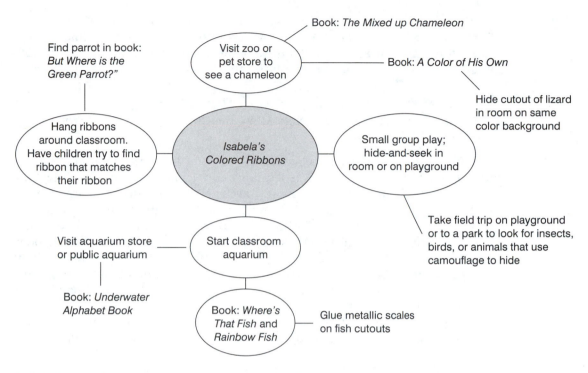

FIGURE 12.5 **Curriculum Web Based on the Book *Isabela's Ribbons***

DEVELOPING AN APPROPRIATE CURRICULUM FOR INDIVIDUALS AND FOR THE GROUP

Teachers of young children soon realize that not every youngster is interested in pursuing an activity they have planned for the group. Forcing a child to participate is neither productive nor appropriate for the child or for the other children. If your classroom is set up so that children can choose and use curriculum areas independently, then children who are not ready to make music with the others, for example, can pursue a different activity.

Reading picture books like this to small groups helps you to determine who is interested in a topic and who may not be ready to pursue it at the moment. Your curriculum plans need to take account of individual children's interests, but also provide for children who are ready to progress in new directions. As noted by Jones and Nimmo (1994):

> *A thoughtful emergent curriculum does not require teachers to actively pursue all of the interests shown by children. . . . In deciding what interests to plan for and actively support, teachers need to assess the potential of any interest for in-depth learning by both the individual child and other members of the adult-child classroom community.* (p. 33)

Writing is a case in point. Some children can already print their names. Others are still at the scribble stage. Nevertheless, it is important for teachers to read books that show multicultural characters that children can identify with involved with writing. Then all the children can try it at their own level.

Writing Area

Multicultural Character: Xiao Ming, the Chinese boy from *At the Beach* (Lee, 1994)

Setup: Many preschool classrooms and pre-kindergartens now have a learning center for writing. This is an area for children to explore playfully just as they do the other curriculum areas. It takes time and practice for children to hold and manipulate a marker and then make marks on a page the way they want them to look. This area allows them to try it on their own. Fill the area with all kinds of writing tools: markers, crayons, pens and pencils, chalk and a chalkboard, stamp pads and alphabet letter stampers, peel-off letters, a typewriter, typing paper, pads, notebooks, stationery, envelopes, stamps, and post cards. A child's desk or small table and chair make it more personal.

Accept whatever scribbles or writing the children produce and display it on a bulletin board in the area if the children agree. Encourage children to

Accept whatever scribbles or writing the children produce.

write/scribble notes to one another by providing individual mailboxes made from half-gallon milk or juice cartons by you and the children.

Invite a small group into the Writing Area to hear Xiao Ming's story *At the Beach* (Lee, 1994). He goes to the beach with his mother, who is teaching him to write Chinese in the sand. She tells him how many of the characters are like pictures. He remembers the first character she draws, "person," because it looks like someone walking. The word "big" looks like a person stretching out his arms and legs. Xiao Ming draws the character meaning "small" in the sand with a stick. Then his mother shows him how to draw "sky" by writing "person" and putting a line above it. They also draw "water," "mountain," "sand," and "woman," which looks like a mother holding a baby. Then they make a word by putting "woman" and "child" together: the word is "good." And it has been a good day for Xiao Ming at the beach.

The pictures, characters, their meanings, and their pronunciations appear on the end papers at the front and back of the book. Are you teaching the children to write in Chinese when you use this book? Not at all. You are helping them become aware that all people write words, but some people write differently from others. Can your children write a letter or a word? The first letter of their names is often one many children attempt to make. Others may want to try a Chinese letter.

They can practice in the sand table with their fingers or a stick. If you do not have a sand table, bring in some sand and spread it across small trays for the children to write and scribble in with their fingers. Salt can also be used. Another day let them "write" on trays with fingerpaints. To save their writing, have them press a paper on the paint, rub over the paper, and peel it off carefully.

Be sure to keep records of the children's writing and pre-writing scribbles on Accomplishment Cards. For children who have no interest in writing at this point, there are other activities they can do in sand.

Science Area

Multicultural Character: Simon, the Native American boy from *A Salmon for Simon* (Waterton, 1980)

Setup: Be sure your Science Area is set up like the center discussed in Chapter 11. Then bring in a Native American doll, puppet, or boy figure to speak as Simon, the Inuit boy who has been fishing for a salmon all summer long without success. But Simon is very good at digging for clams. He helps his sisters dig a bucketful of clams, which they carry home. Then he digs up some clams for the seagulls flying around. They carry his clams high over the rocks and drop them to break them open. Then Simon sees an eagle with a fish in its talons. He gets so excited he jumps up and down, flapping his arms like the eagle flying. This excites the gulls and they fly up, flapping their wings. In all the commotion the eagle drops its fish, and it falls down, down, down—right into Simon's water-filled clam hole.

Simon can hardly believe his eyes to discover that the fish is a salmon, a beautiful coho or silver salmon, and it is still alive. He knows that it has come from the deep Pacific Ocean to find the river where it was born so it can lay its eggs. Now that he has caught a salmon, Simon suddenly wants to save it so that it can swim home and lay its eggs. But how can he do it? The fish is too big and slippery for him to carry across the beach to the sea. Then he remembers what he is good at doing: digging for clams. So he begins digging a watery ditch from his clam hole to the ocean, and soon the salmon is swimming back to its home. The big fish gives a great leap, flicks its tail in thanks, and is gone.

Your children who prefer to dig in sand rather than write in it can have fun helping Simon save his fish in the sand table. Can they dig a ditch with sand shovels to help a plastic fish find its way to a dish of water you have set in the sand at the other end of the table? If you have an outside sand box, bring your plastic fish, sand shovels, and a bucket of water outside for the children to pretend to be Simon.

USING ONE MULTICULTURAL BOOK TO CROSS OVER AMONG CURRICULUM TOPICS

Many of the multicultural picture books discussed in this text can be used in several different classroom areas as well as for introducing different topics. As you read these books yourself before introducing them to the children, look for a strong story line with a number of exciting but different episodes that will catch the children's interest. A brief text is more effective for the youngest children, and a strong character is essential for children to identify with. Jot down information from the episodes as they occur before planning how to use the book.

For example, the book *Mama, Do You Love Me?* (Joose, 1991), discussed in Chapter 4 is a favorite among preschool teachers and children alike. The Inuit child narrator of the story, called Dear One, can be purchased with the book as a cloth doll in a colorful blue dress holding her own little doll. In planning to use this book as a lead-in to curriculum topics, first jot down the characters, objects and events as they happen:

Mother, daughter	Ermine in mittens
Mother sewing doll	Lemmings in mukluks
Braiding girl's hair	Mama's anger
Brightly colored dresses	Mama weaving basket
Mama kissing daughter	Oil lamp
Raven and treasure	Dog sled and Dogs
Whale spouting	Girl running away

Umiak boat on ocean	Northern lights
Snow, moon	Musk ox
Puffin	Walrus
Girl's accident	Polar bear
Dropping ptarmigan eggs	Tent
Girl's mischief	Mother crying
Salmon in parka	Mama's unconditional love

The story itself is a simple one with minimal text and large illustrations of mother and daughter on each page as Dear One questions Mama about "How much to you love me?" One reason preschoolers find the book so delightful is its "what if" nature. The girl pretends about the various episodes, just as all young children delight in doing, and the illustrations depict her pretending humorously.

A reason early childhood teachers like the book is its extensive presentation of life in the cold North country through striking illustrations and simple words. Topics that this book and its character, Dear One, could introduce include:

The Inuit people of the North

Family relationships: mother, daughter

Love can overcome problems

Humor and its use for child's understanding

Emotions of anger, sadness, surprise, fear

Difference between accidents and mischief

Animals of the North

Birds of the North

Winter season

Snow and cold weather

Clothing for cold weather

Transportation by boat, dog sled

Shelter: house, cave, tent

Light, heat: oil lamp

As you consider which of these multicultural books to purchase or borrow from the library, be sure to keep in mind the classroom curriculum areas. How many different areas can the book relate to? Here are a few possibilities:

Dramatic Play	Pretending to be Dear One
	Props: parkas, boots, doll

Manipulative	Simple weaving with yarn
	Simple sewing with yarn on burlap
Art	Making Inuit masks (cutting out simple fish, circle faces)
Language	Using simple Inuit words: parka, mukluk, umiak in a game of "Who can find the mukluk?"
Science	Animal camouflage (polar bear, ermine, ptarmigan)
Cooking	Making ice cream with snow
Large Motor	Outside: Using wagon as dog sled

Once again, we must emphasize not using *Mama, Do You Love Me?* as an introduction to a unit or project on people of the North, as has been done in years past, as this contributes to unfortunate stereotypes. Instead, the character of Dear One is an excellent one to introduce to the children when they are learning about words in different languages, or when they are sewing with yarn on burlap, or when they are finding out about how animals protect themselves through camouflage. In other words, the curriculum areas listed above, should serve merely as an activity data base. When one of the above activities is being done, then you can bring in Dear One and her Mama to portray how they also carry out the activity.

MULTICULTURAL PICTURE BOOKS THAT CROSS OVER CURRICULUM TOPICS

Not all of the books discussed in this text lend themselves so well to so many different curriculum areas, but many do. The following books and their characters are ones that can lead children into a great many activities if teachers will list characters, objects, and events as they did with *Mama, Do You Love Me?* (For additional ideas, see the Topical Children's Book Index at the end of this book.)

Not So Fast Songololo (Chapter 2)
>   Songololo, South African boy

Cleversticks (Chapter 3)
>   Ling Sung, Chinese boy

Abuela (Chapter 4)
>   Rosalba, Hispanic girl

On a Hot, Hot Day (Chapter 4)
>   Angel, Hispanic boy

Hue Boy (Chapter 6)
>   Hue Boy, Caribbean boy

Dumpling Soup (Chapter 8)

     Marisa, Hawaiian girl

Gilberto and the Wind (Chapter 11)

     Gilberto, Hispanic boy

Blow Away Soon (Chapter 11)

     Sophie, Native American girl

It Rained on the Desert Today (Chapter 11)

     Native American girl

Tar Beach (Chapters 9, 12)

     Cassie, African American girl

One of Three (Chapter 12)

     Sister, African American girl

Your children will relish meeting the exuberant multicultural characters from these books. Their stories will remain with the youngsters for years to come because the characters will become real to the children. Not only will

Help make your program multicultural by introducing children to characters from multicultural books.

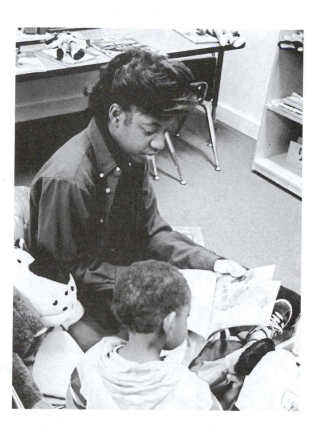

the topics they represent help children in their growth and development, but the backgrounds they represent will become a natural part of the children's own experience. You as a teacher, student teacher, or staff member of an early childhood program can be assured that your program is becoming multicultural every time you pick up one of these books and introduce its main character to the children. It is as simple as that: picking up and reading a book, and following up with activities based on the character. It is something you will want to do every day. As Patricia Ramsey (1987) points out:

> *A multicultural perspective does not entail developing a whole new curriculum; rather, it is a perspective that becomes part of teachers' day-to-day planning and long-range goals. Each activity, theme, area of the room, and educational material is viewed in terms of its potential for conveying the goals of this perspective. While this approach requires imagination and effort, it generates a lot of excitement and enriches the curriculum.* (p. 190)

 ## LEARNING ACTIVITIES

1. Discuss how you would create a curriculum based on children and multicultural books.

2. How can you determine which books and book characters to choose? Give an example in some detail.

3. Observe three children and fill out Accomplishment Cards for them showing their accomplishments in a multicultural activity from one of the books discussed.

4. Design a curriculum web showing activities in each area of the classroom based on the theme "the family" and using one or more of the multicultural books discussed in this text.

5. Make a list of topics that the main character from one of the following books could introduce in your classroom. Then list the curriculum areas in the room and the activities pertinent to each area that the book suggests: *Cleversticks; Abuela; On a Hot, Hot Day; Hue Boy; Dumpling Soup; Gilberto and the Wind;* or *It Rained on the Desert Today.*

 ## REFERENCES

Clark, L., DeWolf, S., & Clark, C. (1992). Teaching teachers to avoid having culturally assaultive classrooms. *Young Children, 47*(5), 4–9.

Jones, E., & Nimmo, J. (1994). *Emergent curriculum.* Washington, DC: National Association for the Education of Young Children.

Ramsey, P. G. (1987). *Teaching and learning in a diverse world: Multicultural education for young children.* New York: Teachers College Press.

Wortham, S. C. (1994). *Early childhood curriculum: Developmental bases for learning and teaching.* Upper Saddle River, NJ: Merrill/Prentice Hall.

 ## ADDITIONAL READINGS

Beaty, J. J. (1996). *Skills for preschool teachers.* Upper Saddle River, NJ: Merrill/Prentice Hall.

Billman, J. (1992). The Native American curriculum: Attempting alternatives to tepees and headbands. *Young Children, 47*(6), 22–25.

Ramsey, P. G., & Derman-Sparks, L. (1992). Multicultural education reaffirmed. *Young Children, 47*(2), 10–11.

Workman, S., & Anziano, M. C. (1993). Curriculum webs: Weaving connections from children to teachers. *Young Children, 48*(2), 4–9.

 ## CHILDREN'S BOOKS

Ashley, B. (1991). *Cleversticks.* New York: Crown.

Begaye, L. S. (1993). *Building a bridge.* Flagstaff, AZ: Northland Publishing.

Brenner, B., & Chardiet, B. (1994). *Where's that fish?* New York: Scholastic.

Buchanan, K. (1994). *It rained on the desert today.* Flagstaff, AZ: Northland Publishing.

Bunting, E. (1994). *Flower garden.* San Diego: Harcourt Brace.

Carle, E. (1984). *The mixed up chameleon.* New York: Harper & Row.

Crews, D. (1991). *Bigmamma's.* New York: Greenwillow Books.

Dorros, A. (1991). *Abuela.* New York: Dutton.

Dorros, A. (1992). *This is my house.* New York: Scholastic.

Ets, M. H. (1963). *Gilberto and the wind.* New York: Viking.

Heo, Y. (1994). *One afternoon.* New York: Orchard.

Hennessy, B. G. (1994). *Road builders.* New York: Viking.

Hong, L. T. (1993). *Two of everything.* Morton Grove, IL: Whitman.

Ichikawa, S. (1995). *Isabela's ribbons.* New York: Philomel.

James, B. (1995). *Blow away soon.* New York: Putnam.

Johnson, A. (1991). *One of three.* New York: Orchard.

Jones, C. (1990). *This old man.* Boston: Houghton Mifflin.

Joose, B. M. (1991). *Mama, do you love me?* San Francisco: Chronicle Books.

Le Tord, B. (1993). *Elephant moon.* New York: Doubleday.

Lee, H. V. (1994). *At the beach.* New York: Henry Holt.

Lionni, L. (1975). *A color of his own.* New York: Knopf.

Munsch, R. (1994). *Where is Gah-ning?* Toronto, Canada: Annick.

Pallotta, J. (1991). *The underwater alphabet book.* Watertown, MA: Charlesbridge.

Rattigan, J. K. (1993). *Dumpling soup.* Boston: Little, Brown.

Ringgold, F. (1991). *Tar beach.* New York: Crown.

Waterton, B. (1980). *A salmon for Simon.* Toronto, Canada: Douglas & McIntyre.

Wild, M. (1993). *Going home.* New York: Scholastic Publications.

Weiss, N. (1992). *On a hot, hot day.* New York: Putnam.

Zacharias, T., & Zacharias, W. (1965). *But where is the green parrot?* New York: Delacourt.

Topical Children's Book List

Adoption

If I Ran the Family (multicultural)
Through Moon and Stars and Night Skies (Caucasian, Asian)
We Adopted You, Benjamin Koo (Caucasian, Korean)

Animals

Baby Rattlesnake (Native American)
Cock-a-Doodle-Doo, What Does It Sound Like to You? (multicultural)
A Color of His Own (chameleon)
Coyote (animals)
Daniel's Dog (African American)
Do You Want To Be My Friend? (animals)
Elephant Moon (elephants)
Fish Is Fish (fish and frog)
Going Home (Hispanic, zoo animals)
The Grouchy Ladybug (animals)
Hattie and the Fox (Australian)
Herman the Helper (octopus)
Hey! Get Off Our Train! (Caucasian, endangered animals)
Hi, Cat! (African American)
The Hunter (African animals)
I Like Me! (pig)
I Wish I Could Fly (turtle, animals)
Looking for Crabs (Caucasian)
Mai'i and Cousin Horned Toad (Navajo)
Me First (pig)
The Mixed Up Chameleon (chameleon)
Moon Rope (animals)
My Name is ALICE (animals)
My Night Forest (animals)
The Mystery of the Navajo Moon (Native American)
Nine-in-One Grr! Grr! (Hmong/Laotian)
Northern Lullaby (Native American)

A Porcupine Named Fluffy (animals)
Rain Forest (Amazon animals)
Rainbow Bird (Australian)
Raven (Native American)
A Salmon for Simon (Native Alaskan)
Seya's Song (Native American)
The Shepherd Boy (Native American, Navajo)
Storm in the Night (African American, cat)
Three at Sea (multicultural)
The Underwater Alphabet Book (fish)
Way Out West Lives a Coyote Named Frank (animals)
What Does the Rooster Say, Yoshio? (Japanese)
Where's that Fish? (fish)
White Dynamite and Curly Kidd (Caucasian)
Whistle for Willie (African American, dog)
Who Is the Beast? (animals)
Young Goat's Discovery (Native American, Hopi)

Arts and Crafts

Abuela's Weave (Hispanic)
Annie and the Old One (Navajo)
Cherries and Cherry Pits (African American)
Galimoto (African)
Hide and Snake (designs)
Luka's Quilt (Hawaiian)
Moon Rope (Hispanic)
The Mud Family (Pueblo)
My Grandmother's Patchwork Quilt (Caucasian)
Pablo's Tree (Hispanic)
Paper Boats (India)
Tar Beach (African American)
Vejigante Masquerader (Puerto Rican)

Baby

Baby-O (Caribbean)
She Come Bringing Me That Little Baby Girl (African American)

265

Balloon

Rachel's Splendifilous Adventure (Caucasian)
Where Is Gah-ning? (Chinese Canadian)

Ball-Playing

Harry and Willy and Carrothead (Caucasian)
Jamaica Tag-Along (African American, multicultural)
Northern Lights, Soccer Trails (Native Alaskan)

Blocks

Building a Bridge (Navajo, Caucasian)
Road Builders (multicultural)
This Is My House (multicultural)

Bridge

Building a Bridge (Navajo, Caucasian)
Tar Beach (African American)

Brothers and Sisters

Bet You Can't (African American)
Do Like Kyla (African American)
I Need a Lunch Box (African American)
Jamaica Tag-Along (African American)
One of Three (African American)

City Life

Abuela (Hispanic)
The Day of Ahmed's Secret (Cairo)
The Day of the Rainbow (South African)
Goggles (African American)
Hi, Cat! (African American)
Halmoni and the Picnic (Korean)
The Leaving Morning (African American)
A Letter to Amy (African American)
Louie (Hispanic, multicultural)
Not So Fast Songololo (South African)
On a Hot, Hot Day (Hispanic)
One Afternoon (Asian American)
One of Three (African American)
The Snowy Day (African American)
Tar Beach (African American)
The Trip (Hispanic, multicultural)
Whistle for Willie (African American)

Clothing

Aunt Elaine Does the Dance from Spain (Caucasian, multicultural)
Aunt Flossie's Hats and Crab Cakes Later (African American)
Ayu and the Perfect Moon (Balinese)
Goggles (African American)
My Best Shoes (African American)
Red Dancing Shoes (African American)
Two Pairs of Shoes (Native American)
Uncle Nacho's Hat (Hispanic)

Color

But Where Is the Green Parrot? (designs)
Color Dance (multicultural)
A Color of His Own (chameleon)
Isabela's Ribbons (Puerto Rican)
Little Blue and Little Yellow (colors)
The Mixed Up Chameleon (chameleon)
Rainbow Bird (Australian)
Raven (Native American)

Desert

Blow Away Soon (Native American)
Dragonfly's Tale (Pueblo)
It Rained on the Desert Today (Native American, multicultural)
The Mud Family (Native American)
The Mystery of the Navajo Moon (Navajo)
The Shepherd Boy (Native American)
Young Goat's Discovery (Native American, Hopi)

Dreams

Hey! Get Off Our Train! (Caucasian, endangered animals)
Into this Night We Are Rising (multicultural)
Isabela's Ribbons (Caucasian, multicultural)
My Night Forest (Native American)
The Mystery of the Navajo Moon (Native American)

Ecology

Bringing the Rain to Kapiti Plain (African)
Brother Eagle, Sister Sky (Native American)

The Butterfly Hunt (Caucasian)
The Great Kapok Tree (Hispanic)
Hey! Get Off Our Train! (Caucasian, animals)
The Hunter (African)
It Rained on the Desert Today (Native American, multicultural)
Jen and the Great One (Native American)
Looking for Crabs (Caucasian)
Mcheshi Goes to the Game Park (African)
My Night Forest (Native American)
Rain Forest (Amazon animals)
A Salmon for Simon (Native Alaskan)
Three at Sea (animals, multicultural)
The Whales' Song (Caucasian)
Where Butterflies Grow (Caucasian)
Where Does the Trail Lead? (African American)

Emotions

Angel Child, Dragon Child (Vietnamese)
Daniel's Dog (African American)
Double-Dip Feelings (African American, Caucasian)
Feelings (multicultural)
The Hating Book (Caucasian)
I Hate English! (Chinese)
If I Ran the Family (multicultural)
Jamaica's Find (African American)
Just Not the Same (Caucasian)
Kinda Blue (African American)
Let's Be Enemies (Caucasian)
The Lost Children (Native American)
Maggie and the Pirate (multicultural)
When Emily Woke Up Angry (Caucasian)

Family

Aunt Flossie's Hats and Crab Cakes Later (African American)
Baby-O (Caribbean)
Black Is Brown Is Tan (Caucasian, African American)
Black, White, Just Right (African American, Caucasian)
Carlos and the Squash Plant (Hispanic)
Dumpling Soup (Hawaiian, Asian)
Eat Up, Gemma (African American)
Feast for 10 (African American)
Flower Garden (African American)

Friday Night Is Papa Night (Hispanic)
Grandmother and I (African American)
Gregory Cool (Caribbean)
Hue Boy (Caribbean)
If I Ran the Family (multicultural)
Kelly in the Mirror (African American)
Kinda Blue (African American)
Knoxville, Tennessee (African American)
Mud Family (Pueblo)
Rise and Shine, Mariko-Chan! (Japanese)
Too Many Tamales (Hispanic)
Uncle Nacho's Hat (Hispanic)

Father

At the Crossroads (South African)
The Best Time of Day (African American)
Carousel (African American)
Cleversticks (Chinese, multicultural)
Daddy (African American)
Dumpling Soup (Hawaian, Asian)
Father and Son (African American)
First Pink Light (African American)
Flower Garden (African American)
Friday Night Is Papa Night (Hispanic)
How Many Stars in the Sky? (African American)
Hue Boy (Caribbean)
Not Yet, Yvette (African American)
Our People (African American)
Tar Beach (African American)
Where Is Gah-ning? (Chinese Canadian)
White Dynamite and Curly Kidd (Caucasian)
Your Dad Was Just Like You (African American)

Flowers

Flower Garden (African American)
The Legend of the Bluebonnet (Native American)
The Legend of the Indian Paintbrush (Native American)
Where Butterflies Grow (Caucasian)
Wild Wild Sunflower Child Anna (African American)

Folktales

Arrow to the Sun (Pueblo)
Baby Rattlesnake (Native American)

The Badger and the Magic Fan (Japanese)
The Banza (Haitian)
Coyote (Native American)
Dragonfly's Tale (Pueblo)
The Eye of the Needle (Native Alaskan)
The Five Chinese Brothers (Chinese)
The Funny Little Woman (Japanese)
Iktomi and the Berries (Native American)
Iktomi and the Boulder (Native American)
Iktomi and the Buzzard (Native American)
Iktomi and the Ducks (Native American)
Jack and the Beanstalk (Caucasian)
The Legend of the Bluebonnet (Native American)
The Legend of the Indian Paintbrush (Native American)
The Lost Children (Native American)
Moon Rope (Peruvian)
Nanabosho: How the Turtle Got Its Shell (Native American)
Nine-In-One, Grr! Grr! (Laotian/Hmong)
Oh, Kojo! How Could You! (African)
Pedro and the Padre (Mexican)
Rabbit Makes a Monkey of Lion (African)
Rainbow Bird (Australian)
Raven (Native American)
The Seven Chinese Brothers (Chinese)
Tikki Tikki Tembo (Chinese)
Two of Everything (Chinese)
What's So Funny, Ketu? (African)
Why Ducks Sleep on One Leg (Vietnamese)
Why Mosquitoes Buzz in People's Ears (African)

Food

Aunt Flossie's Hats and Crab Cakes Later (African American)
Carlos and the Squash Plant (Hispanic)
Cleversticks (Chinese, multicultural)
Dragonfly's Tale (Native American)
Dumpling Soup (Hawaiian, Asian)
Eat Up, Gemma (African American)
Everybody Cooks Rice (multicultural)
Feast for 10 (African American)
The Funny Little Woman (Japanese)
Halmoni and the Picnic (Korean)
How My Parents Learned To Eat (Japanese American)

How To Make an Apple Pie and See the World (multicultural)
Iktomi and the Berries (Native American)
Itse Selu (Cherokee)
Knoxville, Tennessee (African American)
Mcheshi Goes to the Market (African)
Mel's Diner (African American, multicultural)
Nothing Else But Yams for Supper (Caucasian, multicultural)
Potluck (multicultural)
Saturday Sancocho (Hispanic)
This Is the Way We Eat Our Lunch (multicultural)
Three Stalks of Corn (Hispanic)
Too Many Tamales (Hispanic)
The Tortilla Factory (Hispanic)

Friends

All the Colors of the Earth (multicultural)
Best Friends (multicultural)
Best Friends for Frances (animals)
Jamaica and Brianna (African American, Asian)
Jessica (Caucasian)
Into this Night We Are Rising (multicultural)
Isabela's Ribbons (multicultural)
Let's Be Enemies (Caucasian)
Little Critter's This Is My Friend (animals)
Margaret and Margarita (Caucasian, Hispanic)
Will I Have a Friend? (multicultural)
The Yesterday Stone (Native American)

Garden, Farm

Baby-O (Caribbean)
Bigmama's (African American)
Carlos and the Squash Plant (Hispanic)
Dragonfly's Tale (Pueblo)
Flower Garden (African American)
Kinda Blue (African American)
Knoxville, Tennessee (African American)
Three Stalks of Corn (Hispanic)
The Tortilla Factory (Hispanic)

Grandfather

Grandpa's Face (African American)
Grandpa's Town (Japanese)

Knots on a Counting Rope (Native American)
Little Eagle Lots of Owls (Native American)
My Grandpa and the Sea (Caribbean)
Pablo's Tree (Hispanic)
Storm in the Night (African American)
When I Am Old With You (African American)

Grandmother

Abuela (Hispanic)
Abuelita's Paradise (Puerto Rican)
Annie and the Old One (Navajo)
Bigmama's (African American)
A Christmas Surprise for Chabelita (Hispanic)
Dumpling Soup (Hawiian, Asian)
Grandmother and I (African American)
Halmoni and the Picnic (Korean)
Knoxville, Tennessee (African American)
My Kokum Called Yesterday (Cree)
Not So Fast Songololo (South African)
Red Dancing Shoes (African American)
Saturday Sancocho (Hispanic)
Two Pairs of Shoes (Native American)

House

Annie and the Old One (Navajo)
Bigmama's (African American)
The Day of Ahmed's Secret (Arab)
Dragonfly's Tale (Pueblo)
Flower Garden (African American)
Grandpa's Town (Japanese)
The Leaving Morning (African American)
One Afternoon (Chinese)
Tar Beach (African American)
This House Is Made of Mud (Hispanic, multicultural)
This Is My House (multicultural)
The Village of Round and Square Houses (African)

Language

Abuela (English, Spanish)
Abuelita's Paradise (English, Spanish)
Angel Child, Dragon Child (English, Vietnamese)
Aunt Elaine Does the Dance from Spain (English, Spanish)

The Boy Who Dreamed of an Acorn (English, Chinook)
Carlos and the Squash Plant (English, Spanish)
Chatterbox Jamie (English)
Cock-A-Doodle Doo, What Does It Sound Like to You? (multicultural)
A Christmas Surprise for Chabelita (English, Spanish)
The Dancer [La Bailarina] (English, Spanish, Japanese)
The Day of Ahmed's Secret (English, Arabic)
Grandpa's Town (English, Japanese)
Halmoni and the Picnic (English, Korean)
The Handmade Alphabet (Sign)
I Hate English! (English, Chinese)
Itse Selu (English, Cherokee)
Jambo Means Hello (English, Swahili)
Louie (English)
Luka's Quilt (English, Hawaiian, multicultural)
Mcheshi Goes to the Game Park (English, Kiswahili)
Mcheshi Goes to the Market (English, Kiswahili)
Mai'i and Cousin Horned Toad (English, Navajo)
Margaret and Marguerita (English, Spanish)
My Kokum Called Today (English, Cree)
Nine-in-One Grr! Grr! (English, Hmong/Laotian)
Pablo's Tree (English, Spanish)
The Park Bench (English, Japanese)
Pedro and the Padre (English, Spanish)
Seya's Song (English, S'klallum)
Table—Chair—Bear (English, multilingual)
This House Is Made of Mud (English, Spanish)
This Is My House (English, multilingual)
Three Stalks of Corn (English, Spanish)
Too Many Tamales (English, Spanish)
Uncle Nacho's Hat (English, Spanish)
Vejigante Masquerader (English, Spanish)
What Does the Rooster Say, Yoshio? (English, Japanese)

Mother

A Christmas Surprise for Chabelita (Hispanic)
Jonathan and His Mommy (African American)
Laney's Lost Momma (African American)
Mama, Do You Love Me? (Native Alaskan)
Mcheshi Goes to the Market (African)

My Mom Is So Unusual (Native American)
On a Hot, Hot Day (Hispanic)
On Mother's Lap (Native Alaskan)
She Come Bringing Me That Little Baby Girl (African American)
Tucking Mommy In (Asian American)
Will You Come Back for Me? (Asian, multicultural)

Moving

The Leaving Morning (African American)

Music and Dance

Aunt Elaine Does the Dance From Spain (Caucasian, multicultural)
Ayu and the Perfect Moon (Balinese)
Baby-O (Caribbean)
The Banza (Haitian)
Ben's Trumpet (African American)
Can't Sit Still (African American)
Charlie Parker Played Be Bop (African American)
Color Dance (multicultural)
Dancing With the Indians (African American, Native American)
Into this Night We Are Rising (multicultural)
Max Found Two Sticks (African American)
Music Music for Everyone (multicultural)
My Best Shoes (African American)
My Mama Sings (African American)
Northern Lullaby (Inuit)
The Singing Man (African)
This Old Man (Caucasian)
Whistle for Willie (African American)
WOOD-HOOPOE Willie (African American)

Names

Angel Child, Dragon Child (Vietnamese)
Aunt Elaine Does the Dance from Spain (Caucasian, Spanish)
Cleversticks (Chinese, multicultural)
Emily Umily (Caucasian)
Harry and Willy and Carrothead (Caucasian)
Little Eagle Lots of Owls (Native American)
Margaret and Marguerita (Caucasian, Spanish)
My Name Is ALICE (animals)
A Porcupine Named Fluffy (animals)

Sabrina (Caucasian, multicultural)
Tikki Tikki Tembo (Chinese)
Way Out West Lives a Coyote Named Frank (animals)
White Dynamite and Curly Kidd (Caucasian)

Petroglyphs

The Shepherd Boy (Native American)
Talking Walls (multicultural)
Young Goat's Discovery (Native American)

Physical Activities

Bein' With You this Way (African American, multicultural)
Bet You Can't (African American)
A Bicycle for Rosura (Hispanic)
The Bicycle Man (Japanese)
Bigmama's (African American)
Can't Sit Still (African American)
Coconut Kind of Day (Caribbean)
Color Dance (multicultural)
Darlene (African American)
The Day of Ahmed's Secret (Arab)
Gregory Cool (Caribbean)
Father and Son (African American)
Harry and Willy and Carrothead (Caucasian)
Hopscotch Around the World (multicultural)
Hue Boy (Caribbean)
I Wish I Could Fly (animals)
Jack and the Beanstalk (Caucasian)
Jafta (African)
Jamaica Tag-Along (African American)
Knoxville, Tennessee (African American)
Mermaid Janine (African American)
Moon Jump (East Indian)
No Jumping on the Bed (Caucasian)
Northern Lights, Soccer Trails (Native Alaskan)
Pretend You're a Cat (multicultural)
A Salmon for Simon (Native Alaskan)
So What? (multicultural)
Swinging on a Rainbow (African American)
Trouble with Trolls (Scandinavian)
Wait Skates! (African American)

Plants, Trees

Brother Eagle, Sister Sky (Native American)
Cherries and Cherry Pits (African American)

Flower Garden (African American)
The Great Kapok Tree (Hispanic)
Gregory Cool (Caribbean)
Jen and the Great One (Native American)
Kinda Blue (African American)
The Legend of the Bluebonnet (Native American)
The Legend of the Indian Paintbrush (Native American)
Pablo's Tree (Hispanic)
Rain Forest (African)
The Tree (horse chestnut tree)
Where the Butterflies Grow (Caucasian)
Wild Wild Sunflower Child Anna (African American)

Play-Acting

Amazing Grace (African American)
The Best Bug To Be (African American)

Pretending

Abuela (Hispanic)
All the Colors of the Earth (multicultural)
Amazing Grace (African American)
Aunt Flossie's Hats and Crab Cakes Later (African American)
Going Home (Hispanic, multicultural)
The Mud Family (Native American)
Our People (African American)
Pretend You're a Cat (multicultural)
Tar Beach (African American)
The Wing Shop (Caucasian)

Race

All the Colors of the Earth (multicultural)
Black Is Brown Is Tan (Caucasian, African American)
Black, White, Just Right (African American, Caucasian)
Our People (African American)
You Be Me, I'll Be You (Caucasian, African American)

Rainbow

Arrow to the Sun (Native American)
The Day of the Rainbow (South African)
Swinging on a Rainbow (African American)

Russia

Rachel's Splendifilous Adventure (Caucasian)

School

Amazing Grace (African American, multicultural)
Angel Child, Dragon Child (Vietnamese, multicultural)
Best Friends (Caucasian, multicultural)
Building a Bridge (Caucasian, Navajo)
Chatterbox Jamie (Caucasian)
Cleversticks (Chinese, multicultural)
Emily Umily (Caucasian)
Halmoni and the Picnic (Korean)
Harry and Willie and Carrothead (Caucasian)
Hue Boy (Caribbean)
I Hate English! (Chinese)
Jessica (Caucasian)
Sabrina (Caucasian, multicultural)
So What! (multicultural)
Where Are You Going Manyoni? (African)
Will I Have a Friend? (Caucasian, multicultural)
Will You Come Back for Me? (Asian, multicultural)

Self-Esteem

Am I Beautiful? (animal)
Angel Child, Dragon Child (Vietnamese)
Aunt Elaine Does the Dance from Spain (Caucasian, multicultural)
Bein' with You this Way (African American, multicultural)
Building a Bridge (Caucasian, Navajo)
Chatterbox Jamie (Caucasian)
Crow Boy (Japanese)
Emily Umily (Caucasian)
Gregory Cool (African American, Caribbean)
Hue Boy (Caribbean)
I Can Do It By Myself (African American)
I'll Do It Myself (Caucasian)
I Want To Be (African American)
Jessica (Caucasian)
Kelly in the Mirror (African American)
Maggie and the Pirate (multicultural)
So What? (multicultural)
Something Special for Me (Hispanic)

Will I Have a Friend? (Caucasian, multicultural)
Will You Come Back for Me? (Asian, multicultural)

Shopping

Feast for 10 (African American)
Flower Garden (African American)
It Takes a Village (African)
Mcheshi Goes to the Market (African)
Not So Fast Songololo (South African)
On a Hot, Hot Day (Hispanic)
One Afternoon (Chinese)
One of Three (African American)
Saturday Sancocho (Hispanic)
Where Is Gah-ning? (Chinese Canadian)

Stars

How Many Stars in the Sky? (African American)

Toys

At the Crossroads (South African)
Chester Bear, Where Are You? (Native American)
Galimoto (African)
Goggles (African American)
Going Home (Hispanic)
Jamaica's Find (African American)
The Legend of the Bluebonnet (Native American)
Louie (Hispanic)
Mama, Do You Love Me? (Native Alaskan)

The Mud Family (Pueblo)
On Mother's Lap (Native Alaskan)

Walking

The Day of the Rainbow (South African)
Jonathan and His Mommy (African American)
The Listening Walk (Caucasian)
Mirandy and Brother Wind (African American)
Not So Fast Songololo (South African)
Seya's Song (Native American)
The Shepherd Boy (Navajo)
Where Are You Going Manyoni? (African)

Weather

A Letter to Amy (African American)
Blow Away Soon (Native American)
Bringing the Rain to Kapiti Plain (African)
Dragonfly's Tale (Pueblo)
Gilberto and the Wind (Hispanic)
It Rained on the Desert Today (Native American, multicultural)
The Mud Family (Native American)
The Snowy Day (African American)
Storm in the Night (African American)

Writing

A Day at the Beach (Chinese)
The Day of Ahmed's Secret (Arab)
A Letter to Amy (African American)
The Shepherd Boy (Native American)
Talking Walls (multicultural)
Young Goat's Discovery (Native American)

Index